C. Faulhaber

VII 73

Proto-Indo-European Trees

PAUL FRIEDRICH

Proto-Indo-European Trees

The Arboreal System of a Prehistoric People

The University of Chicago Press
Chicago and London

International Standard Book Number: 226-26480-7
Library of Congress Catalog Card Number: 70-104332

The University of Chicago Press, Chicago 60637
The University of Chicago Press, Ltd., London

To the scholars, past and present, who have
contributed to the understanding of the problems
with which this book is concerned

Contents

Illustrations

MAPS

CHARTS

Tables

Preface

This monograph, an outgrowth of my working paper at the Third International Conference of Indo-Europeanists, is the first major study of the arboreal system of the Proto-Indo-Europeans (PIE) since that of Hoops in 1905.

I have sought to test two hypotheses—one taxonomic and the other methodological. The taxonomic hypothesis is that the PIE speakers differentiated at least eighteen major categories of trees ("arboreal units") by the application of between twenty and thirty tree names. My methodological hypothesis is that the rich scholarship on tree names within Indo-Europeanist philology can be significantly correlated with the results of paleobotanical analysis to yield a more realistic and interesting inference of the PIE arboreal system.

The monograph falls into four chapters. In the first are stated certain essential questions and assumptions of method and conceptualization, particularly as regards the so-called conjunctive approach and the use of the comparative method in semantic reconstruction (the subtopics are "over- and underdifferentiation," "denotation and connotation," and the "protomorpheme"). The second chapter contains a brief discussion of the biological concept of succession, and of the inferred succession of trees of central and eastern Europe from the Pre- to the Subboreal; particular attention is given to the crucial new palynological evidence from the Atlantic period (about 5500 to 3000 B.C.), the last part of which corresponds roughly to the last millennium of PIE unity. In the third chapter, I analyze in some detail the philological evidence on eighteen categories of trees (and thirty tree names): birch, conifers, juniper-cedar, aspen-poplar, willow, apple, maple, alder, hazel, nut tree, elm, linden, ash, hornbeam, beech, cherry, yew, and oak. For each, the results of a primary concern with comparative linguistics have been related to the evidence of botany and paleobotany.

My final chapter summarizes what appear to be the positive results of the historical-comparative test of the two basic hypotheses. The inferred arboreal inventory is stated in detail and discussed in relation to the question of tree names as semantic primitives. The second set of conclusions in this final chapter is a by-product of my original goal, and consists of broader cultural and linguistic points: the uses and functions of the trees in PIE culture and the significance of the preceding analysis for relating the early speech communities to each other and to their natural habitats. Several patterns have emerged here, including: a high number of shifts in denotation between PIE and Greek and a high number of semantic innovations shared by Greek and Albanian; a high attrition of the posited PIE arboreal terms in six relatively peripheral stocks—Indic, Iranian, Albanian, Armenian, Anatolian, and Tocharian; the cohesion between the three western stocks and between the four stocks which seem to be basic in terms of the arboreal question—Italic, Germanic, Slavic, and Baltic; and the relatively close relation of the Slavic and Germanic stocks to the system posited for PIE. Aside from their semantic interest, such specific conclusions bear directly on fundamental questions of early Indo-European dialects and migrations, and on the value of lexical semantics as a potential source for dialectal groupings through the comparative method.

The monograph draws on several kinds of authoritative work. The ecological theory was summarized from standard texts such as Woodbury. For the paleobotany I relied primarily on three works: Firbas's *Waldgeschichte* for the region north of the Alps, and the monographs by Frenzel and Nejshtadt for the prehistory of the USSR. The descriptive botany was garnered from many handbooks and from the entries in three encyclopedias: *The Encyclopaedia Britannica, Der grosse Brockhaus*, and above all, the *Bol'shaja Sovetskaja*. The archaeological information comes mainly from recent syntheses by Marija Gimbutas.

For the philological side, certain etymological dictionaries proved excellent, and I usually accepted the author's judgment on the phonological and grammatical relations of his language and stock to the ancestor language—although at times I had to reinterpret or correct his semantic or botanical statements about trees. My authorities on the languages and stocks have been: Mayrhofer on Sanskrit, J. Friedrich on Hittite, Vasmer on Russian, Fraenkel on Lithuanian, Frisk on Greek, Pokorny on Celtic (as contained in his general Indo-European dictionary) and on Germanic, Kluge for German, and de Vries for Old Norse. Bartholomae was ideal for Old Iranian, and Morgenstierne has recorded valuable information on the contemporary Iranian dialects. Latin, although one of the most crucial sources of evidence, constituted a problem: Walde and Hofmann sometimes include improbabilities without a caveat, whereas Meillet, in Ernout-Meillet, is incomplete, although what he does cite is usually beyond dispute. I have been hampered by the absence of adequate etymological dictionaries for Tocharian (which, granted, has little arboreal data), for Albanian (although Meyer and Tagliavini are helpful), and for Armenian (although Hübschmann and Solta are usually satisfactory). In these and similar instances, I have simply had to use my judgment and the assistance of colleagues. Of the numerous articles, notes, and chapters on tree questions, those by Hoops, Osthoff, Meillet, Thieme, Benveniste, and V. V. Ivanov were particularly stimulating.

Numerous scholars have contributed in various ways to this research. I am indebted to Harold Gall, Stuart Struever, Homer Thomas, and Floyd Zwink for their helpful suggestions, and above all to Karl Butzer and Burkhardt Frenzel for their informed reading of the botanical portions of the manuscript. For critical assistance on specific philological questions I wish to thank Hans Güterbock (Hittite) and Manfred Mayrhofer (Indic). Penetrating and copious were the critiques by William Wyatt, Jr. (Greek and Latin), Maurits Van Loon (Greek and Anatolian), Ben Howe (Slavic), Alfred Senn (Baltic), Henry Hoenigswald (Greek, Germanic, and Sanskrit), and Eric Hamp (particularly Albanian and Celtic, but also general points, and some bibliographical gems). A discussion with Jerzy Kuryłowicz was most encouraging at a crucial point in the conceptualization. Additional help was provided by other scholars, many of whom are acknowledged in the text: Warren Cowgill, Zbigniew Gołab, Winfred Lehmann, George Metcalf, Jaan Puhvel, James Redfield, Thomas Sebeok, Nancy Spencer, and Antonio Tovar.

This work, finally, reflects a deep intellectual debt to Henry Hoenigswald and Murray Emeneau for their respective courses on Indo-European; to Robbins Burling, Ward H. Goodenough, Harold Conklin, and Floyd Lounsbury for their ideas on the semantics of paradigms and taxonomies; and to the archaeological anthropologist, Lewis Binford, for his often inspired thoughts on how to relate ecological factors to inferences about prehistory. I am indebted to Robbins Burling for a trenchant critique of an earlier version of chapter 1. Margaret Hardin Friedrich read the entire manuscript twice and contributed invaluably to improving the structure and explicitness of the argument. It should go without saying that none of these botanists, geographers, Indo-Europeanists, and anthropologists is responsible for whatever errors of fact, judgment, and organization occur in the book.

1 Methods and Concepts

Introduction

This short study deals with one small portion of the language-and-culture system of the speakers of the PIE dialects, who are assumed to have been scattered in a broad band over the steppe, forests, and foothills between the western Caspian area and the Carpathians (and possibly the north German plain), during roughly the fourth millennium and the first centuries of the third millennium B.C.

The taxonomic hypothesis to be presented and argued consists of three parts. First, that the PIE recognized and named at least eighteen units or categories of trees. Second, that the PIE language, or large groups of PIE dialects, contained at least thirty names of trees; these are attested in varying ways and degrees in languages of the descendent stocks, but particularly in Italic, Germanic, Baltic, and Slavic, and to a lesser degree in Celtic and Greek. Third, that the thirty tree names refer to categories of trees that in the main correspond to generic groups such as the birch (*Betulus*), but are limited in other cases to single species, such as the Scotch pine (*Pinus sylvestris*); some PIE classes cross-cut the familiar ones of the English language, or of the language of Linnaean botany, as when, for example, *Ker-n-* includes both the wild cherry (*Prunus padus*), and the cornel cherry (*Cornus mas*). The probabilities of at least forty-one species-level entities for the PIE will be demonstrated in the pages following.[1]

---

[1] In the following pages, *V*, *L*, *T*, and *K* stand, respectively, for a general vocalic nucleus, a liquid, a dentoalveolar stop, and a dorsovelar stop, the more exact shape of which is not being specified. With the exception of *maHlo-* and *bherHǵo-*, and a few other scattered points, I have not used or posited laryngeals; in some other place one might well

1

The Conjunctive Approach

The tree names, their meanings, and the botanical realities to which they corresponded are assumed to constitute a set of interdependent systems. The nature and interdependencies of these systems can only be discovered and interpreted by conjoining three approaches, or analytical systems.

The first approach is linguistic—above all, phonological. Although there do remain serious contradictions of evidence and conflicts of judgment, the phonology of IE and of PIE itself is today based on an exhaustive and theoretically sophisticated study of rich factual material. This phonology can provide the protosemanticist with the essential information on the existence of protomorphs, on their phonological shape, and on their symbolic notation, and with at least some of the criteria for making decisions about homonymy, synonymy, and so forth; the interpretation of a protosemantics depends significantly on protophonology. To a lesser extent, the semantic interpretation depends on morphology—on the theories of nominal root structure and on the patterns of declension and derivation. Syntax is of negligible relevance because of the absence of prototexts, and even—with a few exceptions—of protosyntagmas containing tree names. The phonological and morphological parameters of inference constitute the *linguistic system.*

Second, just as the shape of a morpheme is an abstraction from the tabulated phonological correspondences, so the denotation of a protoform is abstracted from the tabulated correspondences in meaning. But these semantic abstractions need to be interpreted by a combination of the traditional science of etymology, concerned with the unique histories of word and word families, and, on the other hand, the newer sciences of linguistic ethnography and structural semantics, which are concerned with relations of contrast and covariation between sets of morphemes and words, and with the semantic features which underlie such sets. These philological and ethnographic parameters of inference constitute *the semantic system.*

---

take up in detail the apparent relevance of this study for laryngeal theory, morphology, and the morphophonemics of stem formation. Following botanical practice, the Latin names of the genera are capitalized, and abbreviated to the first letter when followed by a species name, which is always in minuscule.

Third and last, the reconstructed lexicon may relate to data and systems that are neither linguistic nor semantic. Such data may range from archaeological site reports (e.g., containing oak beams), to paleobotanical pollen diagrams. The interpretive systems may range from the general concept of a Neolithic technology (e.g., where pastoralists cropped elm and linden shoots), to that of an arboreal ecosystem (e.g., that of eastern Europe)—a set of trees related to each other and to other biota, and to the climate, the soil, and space and time as part of a "trophic-dynamic equilibrium" (Lindemann 1942). The results of linguistic or semantic reconstruction may be tied outward to the up-to-date information from the humanistic sciences, as in the metrical analyses by Meillet, Jakobson, and Watkins, or to the social sciences, as in the mythological analyses by Dumézil and Littleton, or to the natural sciences, as in this book. This process of tying outward I would call disambiguation through contextualization. The entire field of nonlinguistic and nonsemantic information I would call the *external system*.

The conjunctive approach develops from the postulate that the science of linguistics is concerned with systems of sound and meaning in natural language and with the interconnections between these two levels of reality; linguistic (here lexical) meaning is assumed to be significantly related to natural habitat and human culture. The conjunctive approach rests less heavily on tight or stringent proofs using only one line of evidence, such as phonology, and seeks, rather, to exploit all relevant evidence in order to establish a hierarchy of probability. By taking account of diverse facts and analytical models, the conjunctive approach may reduce the indeterminacy or "nonuniqueness" of narrowly based solutions—particularly of those based on purely formal operations and purely internal textual analysis. The conjunctive approach may eventually lead us to rewrite many dictionary entries and—what is more interesting—to develop an adequate theory of PIE culture; that is, of the system of perceptual and conceptual values shared and transmitted by the members of this primitive Neolithic society.

Three Semantic Problems

Over- and Underdifferentiation

As with fieldwork in descriptive semantics, two of the major problems in inferring a protosemantics are over- and underdifferentiation in the relation between sets of things and sets of symbols. In overdifferentiation, two or more symbolic forms are found to correspond to what at first appears to be but one eligible or available referent. In underdifferentiation, the number of such minimal meaningful forms (or "morphs") is inferior to the number of referents which, for one reason or another, one would wish to postulate. My meaning may be clarified by several brief examples, the full details of which are treated in the etymological studies that make up the bulk of the book.

A considerable number of PIE morphemes or arboreal units have two or more alternate names or forms, as is obvious from the ratio of eighteen units to thirty names; specifically, the oak and the willow have three each, and five trees have two each: the yew, the apple, the maple, the elm, and the nut (tree)—although the latter is probably on a different level of taxonomic contrast and analogous to the notion of "fruit tree." In any case, the two forms for "nut (tree)" are complementary geographically; may one assume that the two protoroots, the western *knw- and the eastern *ar-, reflect a late terminological differentiation of what was a single unit at some earlier stage of PIE? In other instances, such as that of the yew unit, the reflexes of the two terms contrast in some stocks (Slavic, Greek, and perhaps Italic), although with different denotata. May one here postulate a contrast in early or pre-PIE between two species of yew (*Tacus baccata*, and some other), or between the yew in two distinct functions—as a tree in nature (*tV́kso-*) and as a material used in religious ritual (*eywo-*)?

In yet other instances, such as the maple, two terms are at hand for "one tree." Such cases of apparent overdifferentiation suggest that the two terms go back to one earlier antecendent that served to symbolize one earlier unit, and this, in turn, suggests a reexamination of the forms themselves; the two maple terms, *klen- and *akVrno- might go back to a pre-PIE *kL-n-. The correspondences diverge from conventional phonological and root theory, but they cannot be dogmatically rejected.

There are instances where one of the two terms has reflexes that are limited to two or three continguous stocks. One of the maple morphs just discussed (*ak Vrno-*) is reflected in the three western stocks, Celtic, Italic, and Germanic, and nowhere else. Does this indicate that a particular species of maple was limited to western Europe during the Subboreal (roughly 3000 to 800 B.C.)? In contrast with such discrete distributions, we find that the reflexes of the first maple name (*ak Vrno-*)overlap within Germanic, and only within Germanic, with the reflexes of the second name for this tree (*klen-*), which is otherwise reflected farther to the east and south. To what extent do the overlapping forms within Germanic reflect a synchronic taxonomic contrast between distinct species or two groups of species of maples? and how far back does the contrast carry into Proto-Germanic? And into Western or West-Central PIE dialects? And into PIE itself?

Somewhat less troublesome and frequent are the problems of semantic underdifferentiation, but examples are not hard to find. In at least parts of the PIE homeland of the fourth millennium, both the juniper and cedar were probably hardy. But these denotata show up in only one set of cognates, and one of the poorest (i.e., Proto-Slavic *jalovьtsь*, "juniper," Armenian *elawin*, "cedar," and Greek ἐλάτη "spruce, fir"). This imperfect set of forms contrast with other sets of forms, just as, in a much looser sense, the junipers and cedars are physically more similar to each other than either is to any other class of trees; in other words, there is enough formal and semantic correspondence and contrast to postulate a hypothetical morphemic nucleus. May we provisionally assign the denotation of juniper-cedar to late PIE *el-w-n-*?

Sometimes there is no term at all for a referent that may well have existed in the system. Are we to regard this as a "zero lexeme" (Goodenough 1956, p. 214) or accept one of the candidate roots on the basis of pattern congruity or paleobotanical evidence? It is well established that the larch was present in much of the PIE homeland, yet no protoform exists. The linden (*Tilia*) was ubiquitous throughout eastern Europe during the entire Atlantic (roughly 5500 to 3000 B.C.), yet the protoforms for the linden are precarious. Does this not pinpoint the need for new hypotheses, and for a detailed reexamination by stock specialists (e.g., Slavists and Celticists) of such possible reflexes of a linden term as Welsh *llwyf*, "elm, linden," and of Proto-Balto-Slavic *lēipā-*, "linden," and of the pan-PIE *lenTā*, "linden, linden qualities."

Denotation and Connotation

The idea of denotation is useful within universes of discourse where the referents are as clearcut as trees. In what follows, "denotation" is used for the class of individuals that is necessarily referred to by a name; those referents are necessarily botanical constructs, but one may reasonably assume that these latter correspond in some important sense to conceptual-taxonomic units in PIE culture. Clearly, my usage of denotation and connotation differs from that of either a medieval philosopher or a modern logician, both of whom have quite different motivations, and also from that of the ethnographer who seeks to elicit supposedly "objective" referents from live speakers. Let us now consider some problems in inferring proto-denotation.

Denotative relations may be paradigmatic. For example, the PIE terms for blood relatives were distinguished by generation, sex of relative, and patrigroup membership. Within this set the "husband's brother's wife (**yenHteːr*; Friedrich 1966, p. 10) and the "wife's sister's husband" (Old Norse *svilar* from PIE **sweliyo(n)-*; Cowgill 1960, p. 497) constitute a unique dyad sharing the feature of self-reciprocity—that is, two husband's brother's wives are both **yenHteːr* to each other.

I would assume that the tree names constitute a paradigmatic set discrete from other sets such as kinship terms, and composed of members distinguished from each other by unique combinations of dimensions such as leaf-shape, the yielding of fruit, and overall shape.

The denotation of proto-terms is characterized by various kinds of semantic relations: the color terms are on a gradient; the names for parts of a chariot or of a tree are related anatomically; various kinds of congruity may exist between symbol sets in the mythical pantheon and the social structure.

Denotation is often ordered in folk-taxonomies; that is, hierarchies of inclusion and exclusion (Conklin 1962). For example, Indo-European shows two terms for "fish": the

Western *pysk-* (Gothic fisks, etc.), and a central term reflected by Greek ἰχθύς, Armenian *jukn*, and Lithuanian *žuvìs* (see Winter 1965, pp. 104–5 for origins in a **uX*). Since the terms were complementary we may assume, for the sake of this discussion, that they referred to the same reality for Balts and Teutons in the north, and Greeks and Armenians on the Black Sea. The fishes referred to by these terms included the salmons (**laks-* is reflected in some stocks). "Salmon," in turn, was certainly divided into at least two terminologically differentiated species— the Atlantic trout and the salmon trout. Some eastern dialects probably distinguished another subspecies, the Caspian salmon trout; these latter taxa cannot be recaptured, but ichthyological evidence makes the presence of the species certain and the terminological distinctions likely. Similar taxonomic relations occur within the arboreal nomenclature, although suprageneric taxa are hard to recapture.

Connotation is often defined as a residual class, or metaphorically as a sort of verbal penumbra. In a sense that admittedly is only somewhat less inexact, I would take connotation to refer to the relatively less essential meanings of a name— to the associated meanings which only function in comparatively marked contexts. Such associations may arise through similarity or contiguity with the referents of other names or through the functions of the referents in various social contexts. Such associations are often patterned in complex and relatively structured sets. Connotation may be usefully distinguished from denotation, although drawing a sharp line necessarily obscures significant transitional phenomena.

The varieties and degrees of validity in protoconnotation are many. At one extreme, the reflexes in only one or two stocks suggest connotations that, because of other considerations, may be attributed to the parent speech community; Italic etymologies indicate that the term for "hornbeam" may be connected with a root for "cut, carve" (*qerep-, gerebh-*), and this is congruous with a widespread semantic association in modern languages ("iron wood," "skewer wood," etc.). In the second place, the reflexes in two or more stocks may have the same connotation, and this may be paralleled by the reflected connotations of a second term; thus, the reflexes for PIE "ash" (**os-*) variously connote or denote "spear," and the same holds for the reflexes of

7

"yew" in Celtic and Germanic; this case, which is actually transitional between strong connotation and secondary denotation, suggests the more general inference of some feedback between the names of trees and of the artifacts for which they are characteristically employed. In the third place, sets of names may denote trees that serve some common function, such as providing nuts (beech, oak, hazel, walnut); this function is a type of connotation.

Protoconnotation presents great problems of attestation. In general, I would posit a connotation for any late dialectal group such as "Balto-Slavic" or "Western" if it is reflected in two or more stocks, and for progressively earlier stages and larger dialect areas as there is an increase in the number of stocks, in their degree of noncontiguity, in the antiquity of the textual materials, and in correspondence to phonological laws. Also relevant, although less decisive, is the acceptability of the connotation in terms of the natural and social sciences, and its "naturalness" in terms of "common sense." The value of connotation in protosemantics should not be obfuscated by the timidity or reticence of contemporary ethnographers and semanticists in dealing with it (which is reminiscent of the former anxiety of American linguists about questions of "meaning"). I assume that paradigms, taxonomies, and other sets of terms often share sets of connotations that "hold them together," and that significantly influence the speaker's usage and the course of semantic change.

Prehistoric Culture and the Protomorpheme

To a Proto-Indo-European hewing down a tree with a stone ax, the physical differences between an elm and a linden, or even an English and a live oak, would be obvious—often painfully so. He would tend to symbolize these differences in words, probably roots. This simple premise about trees as semantic primitives underlies much of the reasoning in the analyses below. What further assumptions need to be clarified?

A primary assumption is that the PIE speakers shared a culture, in the sense of a unique and coherent set of percepts and concepts, of values, attitudes, and symbols pertaining to their economy, social life, religion, and the natural environment. I assume that all cultural systems have the structure of interlocking sets of symbolic features and forms.

A second assumption is that the cultural system partly includes a second symbolic system, that of language; I say "partly" because the degree of inclusion depends on the type of language subsystem. For example, the cult symbolism of Druidic oak worship is almost completely discrete from the question of laryngeal sounds or ergative clause types in PIE. In fact the subsystems of sound (the phonology), and of the linear ordering of referential units ("morphosyntax" in a narrow sense), are relatively independent of the cultural symbolic system.

The semantic subsystem of language is the system of meanings that can be inferred more or less directly from linguistic distribution and usage, be they grammatical or, as in this study, lexical. Many linguists and anthropologists today confuse semantics and semantic analysis with culture and cultural analysis, although the latter draws on any and all kinds of evidence—material, behavioral, and introspective as well as verbal. On the other hand, although isomorphism between language and culture is not possible, the semantic subsystem is without doubt significantly connected with the cultural symbolic system; for example, the symbols of a Druidic cult *are* dynamically reticulated with the connotations of the names for the oak, acorn, and mistletoe. Rather than construct a semantic account rigidly independent of culture, a principal motivation for working out the semantic subsystem has been to investigate and demonstrate or suggest congruities and covariation between it and the symbolic system of culture.

A third assumption is that a protolanguage is a realistic analogue to the sort of natural language the prehistoric people might well have spoken. As such, its semantic system is assumed to fall into types of subsets, of which "level" and "domain" are particularly important. The former term comprises any more or less homogeneous class of process or organization, such as the nominal root system or the derivational morphology; because my criteria are primarily semantic, I regard as gratuitous any assumptions as to the absolute number or rigid discreteness of these levels.[2] The "domain" is any set of features

[2] Bazell (1952) has shown that theories of sharply demarcated strata have been based on the implicit priority of phonetic-phonological criteria, whereas giving priority to semantic criteria leads to a much more finely graded hierarchy.

or forms that may be defined by a salient component, such as "denoting some class of tree." Surely, semantic analysis is concerned with the meanings proper to the domain, such as whether a morpheme refers to junipers or cedars. But semantic analysis is equally concerned with any and all other meanings of forms and features, because these meanings show how a symbol in a domain is concatenated with other domains; how the oak morpheme, for example, is related to the idiom of morality and the cultural system of religious beliefs.

Within the semantic system, the basic unit is the morpheme. Following Pike, I would assume that the morpheme is trimodal.

First, there are the forms or overt symbols, usually called morphs. A morph is a minimal meaningful unit represented by concatenations of phonological features—in this instance, those which are postulated for PIE on the basis of correspondences in the daughter languages; for example, the minimal idea of "beech" is represented by a string of phonological units in *bhāǵo-*, which, in their turn, are a shorthand for concatenations of phonological features. The second mode is that of the under-lying or covert features—the perceptual and conceptual values or symbolic differentiations which in various concatenations define the forms and differentiate them from each other; one or more such features were probably shared by the cornel and wild cherry (hence their grouping under one term). The com-bination of features defining a term is its signification.[3] The third mode is the concepts necessarily or usually referred to or associated with a form. Such referential or associative symbols can range from the connotation of "truth" (a possible referent of one tree form) to concrete denotata such as beech or horn-beam. In sum, the three aspects or modes of a morpheme are its forms, its features, and its referents and associations; ulti-mately, these are the minimal units of the semantic system.[4]

[3] For structural semantics in principle, I prefer the notion of "sense"—the general meaning inferred from the types of use of a refer-ential symbol, and the patterning of its relations, both syntagmatic and paradigmatic, with other such symbols in the language. For this study, however, which involves restricted contexts and paradigmatic relations, I am using the more limited analytical notion of signification (Lyons 1968).

[4] In the following discussion I have used "form, name, term, morph," and "protomorph" as stylistic variants for this first mode of the mor-

Partly because the system is five thousand years old and partly because there are no living speakers, one often finds it realistic to group forms, features, referents, and associations somewhat more loosely than is customary in linguistics. The three modes contrast and complement each other in various ways and at various levels. For example, one or more features may define a form that is actually lacking, as for the larch, which is well attested paleobotanically. Or denotata may be lumped or split on the basis of criteria which are partly cultural, as when we posit an additional oak morphemes instead of rejecting *ayg-. Or, to take a final example, the two late PIE terms for "nut (tree)" complement each other geographically but cannot go back to a common form, whereas *klen- and *akVrno-, although contrasting in Germanic and diverging significantly in their correspondences, probably go back to a common antecedent pre-PIE *kL-n-, "maple." Rather than the "tight" or "rigorous" morpheme as "a class of noncontrastive, semantically similar morphs," I would prefer to regard the morpheme as a nucleus or cluster of overt forms defined by covert features and related to various denotations and connotations; the ultimate reality is contrast with other morphemes

---

pheme. For the second mode I have usually employed "feature" and "component," but sometimes "discrimination, dimension," and "covert symbol"; for the aggregate of such features I have used "signification" or "meaning." For the third mode I have used "referent" and "denotatum" as more or less equivalent, and "reference" and "denotation" as more general or inclusive terms. "Connotation" and "association" or "secondary association" have been used for the second type of referential meaning described above. "Meaning" has been used on occasion for either the second or third mode—although I think the exact sense has always been clear from context. "Root" and "symbol" usually refer to a protomorpheme, but have in some cases been used for protomorphs. "Arboreal unit" is used for individual morphemes or clusters of two or more morphemes which refer to a major arboreal category (e.g., the birches, the cherries) in contrast with other such units. Given the present state of semantic theory, I have found it more communicative and stylistically convenient to have several labels for each of the three modes of structure (without, I believe, any sacrifice to precision). Incidentally, the stylistic problems in discussing PIE trees make one aware of the plethora of arboreal metaphors (mainly dead ones) in the literature of linguistics—stems, offshoots, roots, genealogical trees, branching diagrams, derivational trees.

within the field that lies between form and meaning. As Bazell has said, "The morpheme, as the central unit of language, bridges the asymmetry of content and expression, but stands itself in a relation of 'reduced' asymmetry to each of these levels" (1949, p. 226). In this specific sense, the morpheme is also a crucial point of theoretical intersection between cultural anthropology and structural linguistics (including Indo-European structuralism).[5]

[5] Theoretical discussions of the morpheme sometimes gain a specious operational rigor at the price of at least two theoretical fallacies: building morphemic theory on the model of phonemic theory; and building a model for semantic reconstruction on the model of a synchronic description of distributional relations within morphology.

2 Botanical Ordering

Introduction

This book, and particularly this chapter, is partly a criticism of the lack of systematization in protosemantics, particularly the treatment of semantic units as unordered sets; there is even less theoretical justification for ordering protomorphemes on the basis of the protosound with which they begin than there is for a purely alphabetical ordering of the phonological units in a protolanguage; in neither case is a convenient finding scheme any substitute for a statement of systematic interdependencies.

When it comes to the protonames for trees, the tripartite model proposed above makes possible at least three kinds of scientific (as against alphabetical) ordering. First, tree names may be arranged by their overt form, in terms of criteria such as the variations in linguistic evidence; this has been done in the conclusions at the end of the book. Second, the inferred tree names might be ordered in terms of their signification or underlying meaning; a folk taxonomy, for example, involving the distinctive features by which native speakers differentiate or claim to differentiate the phenomena in question. To a very limited extent this has been attempted for certain subsets, as when the PIE ash and elm are defined as, in part, "plants which can be harvested for fodder," or when the pine, spruce, and fir are lumped as "conifers," or when the oak, ash, and yew are classed as "yielding wood for bows." But for the PIE tree names in general it has not been possible to perform a total semantic analysis that results in an elegant hierarchy with an internal differentiation of all its members; in large part this is because the informants are dead.

Third and last, the referents in the arboreal system can be ordered in terms of an external system, such as the botanical "facts"—in Ralph Linton's wry sense of "the consensus of those in a position to know." Such external ordering of the PIE names for trees can be carried out in at least two ways. First, in terms of the paleobotanical facts on the presence and absence over space and through time of the genera, species, and sometimes even varieties. The second kind of ordering combines the data of the first within the larger framework of the general theory of biological succession. I have followed this combined approach in the present study, which concerns the arboreal history of central and eastern Europe during the middle and late Atlantic (about the middle of the fifth to the beginning of the third millennium), a period which corresponds roughly to the last two millennia of PIE speech unity, or at least of mutual dialectal interintelligibility. I regard as only somewhat less relevant the paleobotany of the following thousand years—the first millennium of the Subboreal—particularly since several tree names may be late dialectal and are attested in only three or four stocks (for example, the hazel, *kos(V)lo-* and probably one of the elm words, *Vlmo-*, are both limited in their generally accepted attestation to Western Indo-European—Celtic, Germanic, and Italic).

Pollen and Area in Paleobotanical Ordering

A paleobotanical ordering of the arboreal system raises numerous and disturbing questions rgarding the use of   pollen as evidence, questions I want to make explicit at the outset so that the Indo-European philologist will retain a due skepticism of "hard science."[1] First, trees produce enormously varied amounts of pollen; for example, the hazel yields three times as much as the hornbeam, eight times as much as the oak, and twenty times as much as the linden; in general, the hazel, alder, birch, and pine produce a great deal. Second, pollen varies greatly in its ability to survive in fossil form; the maple is notorious for

[1] The following discussion has been synthesized from Butzer, Kubitski, Straka, Tansley, and Woodbury, and, more particularly, from Firbas, Frenzel, and Nejshtadt. Since I do not pretend to be making an original contribution to botany, I have kept footnotes to a minimum (although there are many bibliographical references in the detailed statements below on the individual trees)

leaving few traces. Third, the pollen of genera can be identified with differential ease and accuracy; for example, the fir is easy, whereas the ash and larch are difficult. Fourth, the species of a tree genus are always difficult and usually impossible to identify. Fifth, analyses are usually done of the pollen from moors and similar ecological niches, and as a consequence often fail to represent realistically the conditions in a given space. Sixth and last, datings in the Soviet area, so crucial for PIE questions, are relative and based primarily on geological criteria. As of 1966, only a small number of carbon 14 determinations had been made, and these were for central and northern European Russia; and we also lacked interlocking pollen diagrams such as characterize the studies in Germany, the Netherlands, Scandinavia, and the British Isles.

For all its battery of natural scientific instruments, the field of paleobotany often entails precarious and problematical inferences and depends heavily on personal judgment about data that is often inadequate and variables that are numerous. My own opinion is that the pollen-based inferences of the paleobotanist about the Atlantic period in eastern Europe are of about the same order of accuracy and validity as the inferences, based mainly on ancient texts, of the paleolinguist working on PIE. Granted these qualifications, I still think that the Indo-Europeanist can safely turn to the paleobotanist for answers on whether a genus was present or absent in a general area such as Germany or the Ukraine over a long period of time such as the late Atlantic. I also suspect that if we get more Carbon 14's from the USSR, they will not greatly alter the picture of what trees were present in the PIE homeland during the Atlantic.

This brings us to the second general problem in the paleobotanical ordering of a tree inventory: the determination and characterization of the area in question. For central and eastern Europe during the Atlantic the four main considerations are as follows. First, the natural boundary between the forest and the (forest-) steppe of the Russian plain was established during the mid-Holocene, probably the early Atlantic. Second, the southern line of this forest-steppe extended about two hundred miles north of the Caucasus, merging with the northern forest line somewhere just east of the Volga; presumably a narrow deciduous belt continued eastward to the central Asiatic uplands.

15

Third, the north German plain (and also much of what today is Poland) was significantly warmer than today, and the entire east European area enjoyed a moister and essentially temperate climate. Fourth, the arboreal attributes of the great river systems of "southern Russia" are important for this paper and have been vividly summarized by Nejshtadt (1957, p. 221): scattered but often large forests and groves of pine and hardwoods (oak, linden, willow, hornbeam, maple, beech, alder, hazel) were found along the southern Bug and the Dnieper, and similar mixtures grew along the Don and Volga all the way to the Sea of Azov and the Caspian Sea. In sum, from the foothills and steppe north of the western side of the Caspian westward through what is now the Ukraine and on northwestward into the north German plain there ran a fairly continuous and fairly homogeneous ecological zone—by and large one of temperate climate, open plains, and mixed hardwood forests. I assume that it was precisely in this east European area during the Atlantic period that speakers of Proto-Indo-European were distributed in a block of dialects about three hundred miles wide and five hundred or more miles long: the area may have been only a third as large, but in any case probably included the central and eastern Ukraine. Subsequently, during the last of the late Atlantic and the first part of the Subboreal, the speakers of at least three dialects (Celtic, Italic, and Germanic) entered, crossed, or occupied central Germany and adjacent areas to the west, south, and north.[2]

Rather than pinpointing a homeland as Thieme does, my main contention is that most of the PIE were living in an area rich in virgin forests, meadow groves, and wooded riversides. I think it reasonable to assume an "arboreal orientation" in the relatively prosaic sense that the speakers knew and used many trees and were keenly aware of their properties; it is concomitantly reasonable to try to correlate the results of linguistic and botanical reconstruction. The tree names reconstructed linguis-

[2] These three stocks, plus Baltic, Slavic, and Greek, yield most of the linguistic evidence on the arboreal system and this, as a sort of practical felicity, happens to match the intensive study and dating of pollen sites in Germany and its peripheries, notably as summarized by Firbas. The "arboreal orientation" needs to be more fully investigated in its archaeological associations—wood axes, acorn leaching, tanning, and so forth.

16

tically as pan-PIE should occur during the Atlantic in eastern Europe; vice versa, those genera which are evidenced in the pollen should show up in the inventory reconstructed by linguistics and philology. Methodologically, the paleobotanist and the paleolinguist are in a position to perceive and generate interesting hypotheses for each other.[3]

Biological Succession

In addition to establishing distributional correlations between tree names and pollen-inferred trees, my goal is to order the arboreal inventory within the framework of the biological concept of "succession." Such succession refers to the relatively systematic ways in which the members of some population succeed to each other and realign over space and through time. Successional change is studied in relation to the climate, the soil, and the contingent dependencies of the biota upon each other. Specifically, as an area is colonized by trees there is a fairly predictable sequence of changes in the composition of its arboreal communities, involving the rate of reproduction, effective seed yield, need of light, the creation of shade, soil richness, and so forth. Often, the climax of a given genus or group of genera is followed by its entropy, and the dominance of the next in line. However, I would emphasize that—as will become amply clear—the future or past dominants are often present as minority members of mixed communities, and that the concept

---

[3] Aside from PIE and Atlantic eastern Europe, I think that a similarly interesting correlational study could be carried out in the New World, involving, for example, Central States paleobotany and Proto-Central-Algonkian, with reference to the middle and late Woodland culture (about 200 B.C. to A.D. 800). Both fields have been relatively well studied (e.g., Leonard Bloomfield's Proto-Central-Algonkian). See now Siebert's brilliant and comprehensive analysis, which correlates the paleozoological evidence with fifty-three items of fauna and flora in Proto-Algonkian, and uses the intersection of their distribution to determine "the earliest residence" of the speakers. Another equally brilliant and yet more recent analysis is that by R. Gordon Wasson, who has now apparently demonstrated that the diverse Rig Vedic descriptions of the mysterious *soma* correlate neatly with the known stages or aspects of the (psychotropic) fly-agaric mushroom (*Amanita muscaria*). Wasson's work appeared after *PIE Trees* went to press, and I have only been able to see Weston La Barre's fine, detailed review of it (to appear in the *American Anthropologist*).

of succession is largely a statistical one; succession is a concept, or a way of perceiving biological phenomena that is not only biologically "realistic" but provides the linguist-botanist with an economical way of ordering trees and of stating their contingent interrelations—particularly in terms of competition and symbiosis.

Succession through time is of two main kinds. First, *ecological* succession refers to the way trees follow each other after drastic or accidental changes such as fires and floods, usually within a few scores or even hundreds of years. Ecological succession is thus a constant feature of any environment, and various "pioneer" genera such as the willow or birch will remain present as a sort of biotic reserve force to emerge and play a salient role after natural catastrophes. Moreover, within any large area such as the postulated PIE "homeland" there is always considerable ecological variation—from swamp to river bank to dry flatland to moist foothill to mountain ridge.[4] Therefore, any people characterized by an efficient collecting adaptation (whether mobile or sedentary) can be expected to know and use many genera of trees and plants which are not dominant or well represented physically.

This study is primarily concerned not with ecological succession, but with *geological* succession—that is, with the replacements, realignments, and changing frequencies over long geological time spans. As has been recognized, the historically established order of geological succession in Europe, after the dissipation of the glaciers, closely followed the usual order in local, ecological succession—for example, the transition from birch-pine to alder-hazel to mixed oak to beech-spruce. But the close parallel must not be overemphasized, because it was strongly modified on a regional or local scale by special climatic changes, initial soil conditions, human agency, the distance of migration from tree refuge areas, and other partly unpredictable factors.

---

[4] As a relevant ethnographic example, the Tarascan Indians of San José de Gracia in southwestern Mexico live close to three entirely distinct ecological zones: the temperate plain, the contiguous rocky "badlands," and the high pine sierra to the south. They know the properties of the many trees in each zone and have Tarascan words for the properties and the trees.

Arboreal Succession in Eastern Europe

Let us now briefly review the order of geologically defined arboreal succession in central and, more particularly, eastern Europe and southern Russia—the putative PIE homeland. Reference will be to the Boreal, Atlantic, and Subboreal periods, but above all to the middle and late Atlantic—the last two millennia of PIE unity.

The alder (*Alnus*) and the aspen (*Populus*) actually may have been hardy among the melting glaciers. The first tree to enter directly after their retreat was the juniper (*Juniperus*), which today still extends far north as an understory in open coniferous stands and even on open tundra. About the same time came another tough pioneer: the moisture-loving willow (*Salix*). The highly adaptive aspen increased its distribution. Both genera can withstand exposure and great cold, do well on poor and dry soil, and seed rapidly (having among the highest pollen yields). But both of them are also short-lived and intolerant of shade, and were soon pushed back or crowded out by the birch (*Betula*) and the pine (*Pinus*). These two genera more or less together developed stands that, depending on the region, dominated during the Preboreal (8500 to 7200), and even later. The willows, aspens, and poplars persited as minorities in birch and pine forests or clustered along bodies of water as aggressive pioneers in ecological succession. With the pine and birch other genera may have entered, albeit on a relatively reduced scale: first, the larch (*Larix*), limited to highland areas, including the Caucasus and the Carpathians; second, the alder, which probably penetrated new zones about this time, pioneering in wet and unpopulated areas, or spreading as an understory to the other genera; third, the bird cherry (*Prunus padus*) and the wild apple may have penetrated and spread during these millennia, although the paucity of evidence makes this very conjectural.

The transition, at about 7200 B.C., between the Preboreal (8500 to 7200) and the Boreal (7100 to 5500), although not a climatic one in some areas, was generally marked by increased dryness, and coolness.[5] During this transitional period the

[5] A more up-to-date discussion comes from Butzer (personal communication, 1969). The transition from the Preboreal to the Boreal was not a contemporaneous phenomenon throughout Europe but was a mat-

hazel, which could tolerate the shade of its forerunners while reducing their regeneration, apparently increased phenomenally, becoming dominant—sometimes overwhelmingly so—during the subsequent "hazel time" of the later Boreal and early Atlantic. Since the species of hazel cannot be distinguished palynologically, and since the climate was warmer, these climax stands may have included or even featured the relatively large *Corylus mas*, or even *Corylus colurna*, the so-called Turkish hazel.[6] Before this advance of the hazel the birch yielded rapidly, but the pine considerably less so. The maple (*Acer*) entered and diffused, but the meager pollen evidence for this genus precludes a clear picture.

By its very dominance, the hazel created conditions for its successional replacement: "The weakness of pioneer species is their high light requirement and short life span. Consequently, they succumb easily in competition with so-called climax species. The latter reproduce slowly, but are notably tenacious, and they tolerate as well as provide ample shade" (Butzer 1964, p. 408). During the "hazel time" the oaks were entering, followed by the elm (*Ulmus*) and possibly the frost-sensitive ash. Mixed-oak forests formed gradually. For a time the combination of oak and hazel was characteristic.

Polynologists use the term Atlantic for the approximately three millennia of relative warmth and moisture that began about the middle of the sixth millennium (5500 B.C.). The maple increased somewhat and persisted thereafter as an important minority. More diagnostic was the elm which, possibly

---

ter of succession dominated by ecological factors and rates of migration—in particular, the arrival of the hazel. Radiocarbon dating of the Preboreal to Boreal transition indicates a time span of 7900 to 6900 B.C., depending on the area, with the Preboreal dating from 8500 to 7200, and the Boreal from 7200 to 6200. Some paleobotanists prefer to consider the Preboreal and Boreal as a single phase in the succession.

[6] The hazel maxima of the earlier interglacials seldom attained the prominence of the later Boreal and Atlantic. I think that the tree was propagated or at least favored by man; the nuts were probably an important food, and have been found in some Mesolithic sites (incidentally, they were also an important food for the essentially Mesolithic middle and late Woodland Indians of the eastern United States). Since hazel, pine, and birch all produce comparatively large amounts of pollen, the paleobotanical reconstruction of their *relative* frequency is apt to be fairly reasonable.

in response to climatic change, began a dramatic rise, often accompanied by the linden (*Tilia*); the two rather similar trees formed climax forests from Germany to the Caucasus and, frequently admixed with the oak, extended as far north as the White Sea. However, both the elm and the linden retreated rapidly during the late Atlantic and the early Subboreal—possibly because of the decline in moisture and warmth, possibly because they were heavily harvested as fodder, and certainly because their saplings required more light than was being obtained under the ever increasing oak and two relative newcomers, the coniferous spruce and fir.

Other important growths and declines marked the middle and late Atlantic. The alder spread west into Germany and reached climax percentages in many parts of the Ukraine. Various species of the hornbeam (*Carpinus*) increased north of the Caucasus and, after disseminating over much of European Russia, eventually attained maxima of 30 percent or more in the pollen spectra. The spruce became more frequent in the moist highlands and three mountainous zones: the Alps, the Carpathians, and the Balkans. The cornel cherry is sporadically reported, and the cherry proper probably entered areas north of the Alps. The maple reached its optimum development, with maxima of 5 to 10 percent (probably involving the Norway, sycamore, Tatar, and other species). The beech increased somewhat. The Atlantic, in short, witnessed an efflorescence of the hardwoods unparalleled before or since: the deciduous belt in the USSR was over eight hundred miles wide—more than twice its width today. This is another ground for postulating an "arboreal orientation" for the PIE speakers.

At the core of the new arboreal environment was the oak, which expanded at the expense of the elm, hazel, maple, ash, and pine, often mixing with them over protracted periods. The main species was the brown or English oak (*Quercus robur*), which, more or less during the fifth and part of the fourth millennium, covered with great forests the landscape of Germany and the Ukraine, and intervening and contiguous zones. The oak line extended about three hundred miles north of its present position, with giant exemplars of the genus in far northern Russia. Mixed with the hazel, maple, and beech, it dominated most of the Caucasus, which is today the Eurasian area

21

with the greatest subgeneric differentiation—a total of nine species (seventeen according to one Soviet authority, whose criteria for the line between species and variety are obviously different). The paleobotany of the oak relates to several fascinating problems in the linguistic and semantic interpretation of several PIE terms (*ayg-*, *perk*$^{\omega}$*-*, *dorw-*).

Scientists differ considerably about the date of the transition from the Atlantic to the Subboreal; expert judgment ranges from about 3400 to 2500. Perhaps the most reasonable position at this point would be a compromise at about the beginning of the third millennium.

The transition was marked by climatic change that was considerable and may have been relatively abrupt. The winters grew colder. In the Ukraine the cold of the Subboreal was less distinctive than its aridity. The beech was considerably reduced. But this same beech (*Fagus silvatica*) became frequent or dominant in many western regions, extending from England to the middle European and north Mediterranean highlands. This was during precisely the millennia of the early and middle Subboreal, when the early Indo-Europeans were migrating westward and southward. Much of the Caucasus continued to be covered by climax forests of beech.

The spread of the beech was concatenated with other arboreal changes. During the second half of the third millennium and the first half of the second, the shade-tolerant hornbeam, which had already penetrated most of southeastern and eastern Europe, advanced rapidly into western and central Europe, where it flourished as an understory beneath the beech and the oak. Competitors such as the birch, hazel, alder, maple, and elm were often reduced or practically eliminated by the dense shade of these trees and of the rapidly spreading spruce and fir (*Abies*), which often formed stable communities. The new dominants least affected the oak—partly because *Quercus robur* is also a shade-tolerant, climax species, partly because the huge, heavy-seeding old oaks outlive the beech; two thousand years after the "Beech Age," Caesar and Tacitus described the huge and somber oak forests of what is now southern Germany.

Three other genera have been reported from European (e.g., Swiss) Neolithic sites.[7] Of these, the wild apple and the yew

[7] A valuable dimension could be added by systematically combing

(*Taxus*) were frequent minority members of hardwood forests in historical western Europe and probably in the Caucasus, although palynological evidence is lacking. The walnut (*Juglans regia*) entered or was carried in by man from Asia Minor and the Balkans in very late Atlantic times.

This concludes my ordering of the PIE tree inventory in terms of the concept of geological succession, or, to be more accurate, of a simplified version of succession in central and eastern Europe between the retreat of the glaciers and the Subboreal—with particular attention to the last millennium of the Atlantic. As a mnemonic aid, the main geological periods are shown in table 1 (adapted from Butzer 1964, p. 407).

TABLE 1

GEOLOGICAL PERIODS

Name	Date	Vegetation	Inferred Climate
Younger Subarctic	9000–8500	tundra and forest (birch, pine, larch, willow, poplar)	arctic
Preboreal	8500–7200	birch and pine dominance	continental, somewhat warmer
Boreal	7200–5500	pine, some mixed oak; hazel dominance	continental, warmer
Atlantic	5500–3000	early: mixed oak; elm and linden climax; firs middle, late: oak dominance	warmer and maritime
Subboreal	3000–800	beech dominance (cum hornbeam), spruce, mixed oak	more continental, drier

Let us now turn to the etymologies of some thirty tree names, and to the philological-semantic and botanical inference of the genera and species to which they probably referred. The tree names will be listed roughly in the order of the geological succession of their presumed referents, except that the oaks are taken up last.

all site reports for central and eastern Europe and the north Caucasus from about 3500 and 1500 and carefully recording all the genera and species identified by archaeologists, paleobotanists, and other scientists.

TABLE 2

Synoptic View of Important Reflexes in the Twelve Stocks

Stock	*bherHg̑o-	*pytw-	*pu/u̯K-	*el-w-n-	*osp-	*sVl̥sk-	*uyl-	*urb-	*ăbVl-	*maHlo-
1. Slavic (Russ.)	berĕza		pĕklo (OR) pьkolъ	jálovets	osína		vit'	verba	jábloko	
2. Baltic (Lith.)	béržas		pušьs	ĕglé (?)	āpušé		vytìs	viřbas	obuolỹs	
3. Greek		πίτυς	πεύκη	ἐλάτη	ἄσπρις (?)	Ἑλικών	Ϝῑτέᾱ			μῆλον
4. Italic (Cl. Lt.)	fraxinus	pīnus	pix, picea, Umb. peřu			salix	vītis	verbera	Abella	mālum
5. Celtic			(MIr.) ochtach			(OIr.) sail	(Ir.) fēith		(OIr.) uball	
6. Germanic	(OE) berc		(OHG) fiuhta		(OE) æspe	(OE) welig	(OE) wīthig		(OE) æppel	
7. Indic	(V) bhūrjá-	(Sk.) pītu- (?)			(V) sphya-; Wakh; Fiák.		(Sk.) vĕtasáḥ			
8. Iranian	(Osset.) bärz						vaētay			
9. Albanian		piśé								mōlle (?)
10. Armenian				el-ew-in						maɫa-
11. Anatolian (Hitt.)						u̯elku (?)	gi (?)			
12. Tocharian										(A) mälan (?)

Stock	*ḱlen-	*akVrno-	*alyso-	*kos(V)lo-	*knw-	*ar-	*Vlmo-	*uyg̑-	*lenTā- (?)	*lēipa-
1. Slavic (Russ.)	klën-		ol'khá	Proto-Slavic *lĕsko		orekh	ílem	vjaz	lutъ	lĭpa
2. Baltic (Lith.)	klēvas		álksnis	kasùlas		ríuošutĭs		vìnkšna	lentà	líepa
3. Greek	κλινό-	ἄκαρνα	Ὀλιζών (?)			ἄρυα (H.)			ἐλάτη (?)	ἀλίφαλος (?)
4. Italic (Cl. Lt.)		acer	alnus	corylus	nux		ulmus		lentus	(MW) llwyf-en (?)

		*alisa (?)				(OH.) lem	(E) wych	(OHG) linta	
6. Germanic	celyn (OE) hlyn	(OHG) ahorn	(OE) alor	(OE) hæsl	(OE) hrutu	(ON) almr			
7. Indic		(V.) akráþ (?)					(Kurd.) vīz vith		
8. Iranian									
9. Albanian					arrë			l'ëndë	
10. Armenian									
11. Anatolian									
12. Tocharian									

	*os-	*grōbh-	*bhāgo-	*k(e)r-n-	*eywo-	*iVkso-	*gʷelH-	*ayg-	*perkʷ-	*dorw-
1. Slavic (Russ.)	jásen'	grab	buziná	cherëmukha	íva	tis	zhëlud'		(OR) Perunŭ	dérevo
2. Baltic (Lith.)	úosis	skrúoblas (?)		Kìrnis	ievà		gìlė		Perkūnas	dervà
3. Greek	(H.) ὄξυ-	(H.) γβάβιον	φᾱγός	(H.) κρανεία	ὄα, οἴη	τόξον	(H.) βάλανος	αἰγι-		(H.) δρῦς
4. Italic (Cl. Lt.)	ornus	Grabovius (?)	fāgus	cornum	ūva	taxus	glans	aesculus	quercus	dūrus
5. Celtic	(MW) onn-en		(Gaul.) *bāgos (?)		(OIr.) eó				(Gaul.) Hercynia	(OIr.) daur
6. Germanic	(OE) æsc		(OE) bōc		(OE) íw			(OE) āk	(OE) furh	(OE) trēo
7. Indic							gulah		(Sk.) parkatī-	dāru
8. Iranian						taXš				(Av.) druvō dru
9. Albanian	ah	shkozë (?)	bunge (??)	θανε (?)			l'ëndë (??) katin		Perëndija	
10. Armenian	haçi				aigi (?) eyan				(?) orot (??)	tram taru or
11. Anatolian									perunaš	
12. Tocharian										

3 Eighteen Arboreal Units

1. The Birch: *bherH-ĝ-o-

The birch is usually treated as one of the basic, pan-PIE morphemes, one of those "sound etymologies" which serve as a basis for formal theories; for example, Lehmann includes it in his discussion of PIE phonology (1953, p. 53).[1] In part this has been because of the distribution through at least six stocks, and in part because, like the willow, the birch is one of the few tree names with reflexes in both Iranian and Indic (the maple and pine are far less certain).

Let us begin with Indo-Iranian. Iranian contains several reflexes, such as *bärz* in Ossetian (from **barzā*; Abaev 1958, p. 253), and other forms in at least four other languages (e.g., Wakhi *furz*). As for the Indic evidence, the fact that the birch is not hardy in the Indus Valley originally led Hirt (1892, p. 476) to argue that only certain recently attested dialects of the Himalayas contained reflexes of *bhūrjás*; other scholars have since come to the same decision. In fact, *bhūrjá-* is attested in the Kaṭhaka version of the Black Yajurveda and therefore—although late—is Vedic. Moreover, numerous cognates have been found in the Dardic dialects of northwestern Indic: Phalūra *brhuǰ*, Dameli *brũš*, "all historically connected with that which appears in the Aśokan inscriptions" (Morgenstierne 1947, pp. 147, 152). The conformity of most of the Dardic reflexes to the proper metathesis of liquids greatly reduces the possibility of borrowing and generally strengthens the Indic attestation.

[1] Except for Nehring's apparently unique suggestion of an "Asiatic borrowing" (1954, p. 20). Some form of the PIE birch name appears to have been borrowed into Basque, as still reflected in contemporary *buruki*, according to Antonio Tovar (see Múgica for the forms). I am indebted to Jaan Puhvel for his personal communication on the philology of the birch name.

26

The PIE form is also well represented in Italic, Germanic, Baltic, and, above all, Slavic, as in Russian *berëza*, Ukrainian *bereza*, Polish *brzoza*, Bulgarian *brěza*, Serbocroatian *breza*, and almost all other languages of the stock.

The PIE birch name is also generally accepted as having a sound etymology because of the formal correspondances between the many cognates. For the initial voiced, aspirated stop and for the medial liquid these correspondences are essentially regular, and for the final *ǵ* they are nearly so (e.g., Slavic *z*, and Iranian *z*, but Sanskrit *j*). The Balto-Slavic *bērža-*, the Germanic forms such as Old English *berc/birce*, and the European cognates in general, all indicate a full vowel in the root. A laryngeal, on the other hand, is indicated by the forms supporting a long syllabic *r*, such as Sanskrit *bhūrjá-*. Both Meillet (1923, p. 197) and Vasmer following him, posited a thematic vowel *o*. Also reasonable is Meillet's feminine gender, considering the *o*-stems in Sanskrit and Lithuanian, the feminine long *ō*-stem in Germanic, and the feminine *a*-stem of Slavic. In sum, a PIE feminine *o*-stem with the shape *bherH-ǵ-o-*, seems indicated. In five stocks—Indic, Iranian, Slavic, Baltic, and Germanic—the reflexes denote birch, usually the white birch (*Betula pendula*).

A semantic problem, commented on by many Indo-Europeanists, is the apparent parallelism between the birch name and phonetically similar verbal forms meaning "to shine, shimmer, gleam, become white." Do the parallelisms in five stocks demonstrate that the Proto-Indo-Europeans conceived of the birch as somehow quintessentially white, shimmering, and the like? The suggested protoconnotation and etymological relation is interesting because of the geographical spread and noncontiguity of the stocks, and because of the well-known poetic and religious connotations of this tree in the ritual and folklore of northern Europe (especially Germanic and Slavic, but also Finno-Ugric; Holmberg 1927, p. 266). I have argued below (note 1 to chap. 4), on the basis of congruous grammatical, lexical, and cultural gender categorization in Germanic, Balto-Slavic, and Indo-Iranian, that the birch has been a female-virgin symbol for many Indo-Europeans for over five thousand years. The particular question of physical brightness is highlighted by the obvious white, creamy, or silvery bark of most birch species.

The best evidence comes from Germanic, where Old Norse *bjǫrk*, "birch," can be lined up with *bjartr*, "bright," and Old High German, where *birihha* is similarly aligned with *beraht*; Kluge (1963, p. 78) adds, "Die Birke ist nach ihrer hellen Rinde benannt."

As for Baltic, Fraenkel says that the cluster of birch words such as Latvian *bḗrzs*, Lithuanian *béržas*, Old Prussian *berse*, and also Lithuanian *bìržtva*, "birch grove," may indeed be related to the Latvian *birkstis* ("glimmernd oder auch nur heisse Asche"), and a set of related forms. But Balticists generally agree that the form usually cited in these discussions—Lithuanian *beršti*—cannot contribute to the set, as was originally proposed, because its original meaning was, not "to lighten, whiten, be bright," and so forth, but rather "to bear, ripen."

Numerous Indo-Iranian and Latin forms have been adduced. Late Vedic *bhūrjá-*, "birch," has been aligned with Classical Sanskrit *bhrájate*, "it shines," and Ossetian **barzā*, also "birch," with Avestan *brāz*, "to shine," and *brāza*, "to glitter, flash, shimmer" (Bartholomae 1904, p. 972). Latin *farnus* and *fraxinus*, both meaning "ash," and deriving from **far(a)g-(s)nos*, have been similarly paired with *fulgor*, "brilliance, brightness," and *flāgro*, "to blaze, glow, glitter," but this connection in Latin is most unlikely.[2]

The Indo-Iranian and Latin forms can be interpreted in one of two ways. On the one hand, they all may belong with the Germanic (Old High German) *birihha/beraht* dyad, and even with Baltic (Latvian) *bḗrzs/birkstis*, and go back to PIE *bhereg-*, "bright." On the other hand, all the forms referring to brightness, glittering, burning, and the like—but not to birch—may go back to a distinct PIE root, *bhel-g-, bhl-eg-*, "bright, shine," which is also reflected in Greek *phlox, phlégō*. This second alternative would disassociate the tree from its quality in these three stocks, and leave in isolation the Germanic pair (and the Baltic, if the latter is admissible at all). Some of the most widely cited of these moot correspondences are shown in table 3.

---

[2] The Latin forms illustrate the common Indo-European pattern whereby tree names yield adjectives, here by the suffixation of *no* and *ino*; the adjectives eventually come to be used as nouns for the object; Fraenkel 1913, p. 45, based on Osthoff; see Szemerényi 1960 and 1962 for this and other morphological points.

TABLE 3

THE BRIGHT BIRCH

	Birch	Bright
Latin	*farnus, fraxinus*	*fulgor, fla:gro, flamma*
Latvian	*bęŕzs*	*birkstis*
Old Norse	*bjǫrk*	*bjartr*
Old High German	*birihha*	*beraht*
Iranian	**barzā*	*brā́z*
Indic	*bhūrjá-*	*bhrájate*

The evidence certainly suggests some folk etymological or connotational link between the birch names and the various roots for associated qualities; trees so often yield the names of colors and similar properties (ashen, piney, and so forth). Yet here one can determine neither the nature of the relation nor the direction of derivation, and all the arguments, both pro and con, seem inconclusive.

A second semantic problem, as interesting as that of the connotation of "white, bright," is posed by the shifts in referential meaning. To begin with, no reflexes occur in Celtic, Armenian, Anatolian, Tocharian, or, be it noted, Greek or Albanian. In some northeastern and Siberian dialects of Russian what was originally an adjectival derivative, *bérestъ*, underwent a shift to "elm"—possibly because of a functional similarity between the uses of elm bast and birch bark. Whatever the motivation, the shift was considerable, since the two trees bear little resemblance to one another.

In Italic (i.e., Latin) the birch reflex shifted to "ash," usually the common or European ash (*Fraxinus excelsa*), although Walde and Hofmann mention the "wild mountain ash" (*wilde Bergesche*), which could mean either the flowering ash (*F. ornus*) or the mountain ash (*Sorbus aucuparia*). The shift to "ash" in Latin, like the total loss in Greek, is often thought to have been motivated by the absence of the birch in these climes (except in some highland niches).

The Albanian tree name, *bredh/bredhi*, is usually glossed as "fir, pine," or even "larch," and was correctly described by Meyer (1891, p. 45) as the source for Romanian *brad*, "Scotch pine, white fir" (the form is probably a back-formation from earlier *braz*). As the same author continues, "Lautlich ist mit *bredh-* der europäische Birkenname fast identisch ... Aber man wird selbst den Albanesen nicht soviel naturwissenschaftliche Verwahrlosung zutrauen, dass sie den Birkennamen auf ein Nadelholz übertragen hätten." But as has been shown, the shift of the birch name to other genera would not be without at least two precedents, in Slavic and in Italic. Phonologically, Albanian *dh* may go back to a PIE *ǵ*, the preceding *re* to a long syllabic (and early PIE *rH*), and Albanian *b* to PIE *bh*. Thus, Albanian *bredh*, like Sanskrit *bhūrjá-*, may stem from PIE **bhrHǵ-*. A similar derivation has been proposed for Albanian *bardhë*, "white," with an implied connection between the word for the tree and for its main connotation. Given the regularity of the phonological correspondences, and the plausibility of the shift in reference, Albanian could be added as the seventh stock supporting PIE **bherHǵo-*, although many scholars, including the author, would regard *bredh* as a loan from Greek (βραϑυ, *Juniperus sabina*, itself a Semitic loan; Frisk 1954, 1: 263).

Covariation between the reference of names and the ecology of tribes brings us to the "birch line" arguments. Various scholars have used the presence of the birch term in PIE to argue for a southern boundary for the PIE speech community. Thieme in particular (1953, 1964) has conjoined such a "birch line" (today running approximately from Bordeaux to Bucharest), with a "beech line" (roughly from east Prussia to Bessarabia), and a "turtle zone" (the turtle is absent from Scandinavia), to box the PIE into the north German plain. However, the birch is of relatively little power in these demonstrations because of its shifting habitat; during the Subboreal (about 3000 to 800 b.c.), the birch line extended a good deal south of its present position, and the genus has always been present in the Ciscaucasian area. Otherwise, the beech is one of the basic arboreal components of the Caucasus, and flourished far northward during the warmth of the Atlantic. At this same period the turtle was probably present in Scandinavia, and the Cossak steppe of south Russia was and remains today an area of relatively great turtle differentiation, with the steppe turtle, the swamp turtle, the Caucasian turtle, and so forth. In sum, none of Thieme's well-known criteria support his homeland hypothesis.

30

Let us turn to the botany of the birch. Cold-hardy *Betula* came in early, probably with or before the pine, and dominated in many areas through much of the Preboreal and Boreal, often providing 80 percent to 90 percent of the pollen deposits; the genus produces enormous numbers of minute two-winged "seeds" (nutlets) which, after lying at winter temperatures for several months, will germinate in the melting snows of spring. During the Atlantic the birch receded rapidly before the advance of a main competitor, the hazel, but, together with the willow, it became more prominent again in the Subboreal. The birch has persisted ever since, either as an ecological pioneer or as a minority member (10–20 percent of the pollen spectra) along rivers as far south as the southern Volga, or as a prominent or dominant tree in northern forests. Today it is present throughout the northern hemisphere, primarily in temperate to arctic zones. Three species are important in the central and east European region being discussed: *pubescens* and *humilis*, but particularly the widely spread and rapidly growing white birch (*B. pendula*). Many of the types in the USSR are limited to very particular regions; three are distinctive of the Caucasus. The birch has often profited from the presence of man, who—as would hold also for the PIE—cuts out valued hardwoods or allows cleared land to revert to the ecological pioneers.

2. *The Conifers: *pytw-, *py/wK- (*pyk-, *pwḱ-)*

The classification and naming of the conifers in contemporary northern European languages manifests two distinct if not quite contradictory tendencies. First, within any one dialect, such as Standard German, numerous terms, simple, compound, and complex, serve to denote not only the principal genera (*Kiefer, Tanne,* and *Fichte*), but many of the species (e.g., *Schlange-, Hänge-, Trauer-,* and *Schimmelfichten*). Between two or more dialects, on the other hand, and also in borrowing, there is a great deal of cross-referencing and terminological overlap. For example, in German the word for spruce (*Fichte*) is often replaced by "red fir" (*Rottanne*), and was borrowed earlier into Russian to denote the fir (*pikhta*); in scientific nomenclature, one species of fir (*Picea*) is called the "spruce fir" (*Picea abies*); finally, the Scotch pine is often called "fir" in British English, and was the *fura* of the Vikings. Reconstruction within the

31

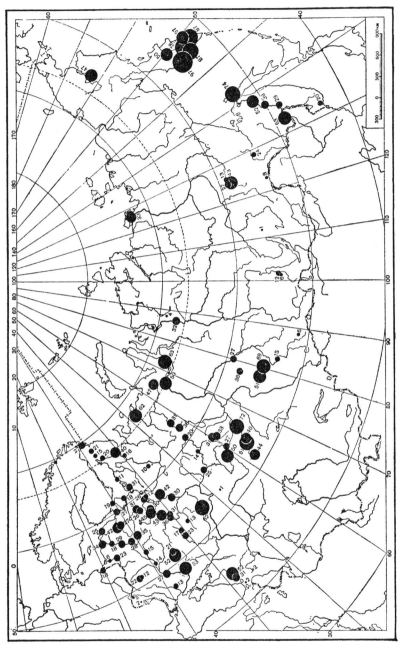

MAP 1. Distribution of *Betula* in the middle Holocene (from Nejshtadt)

The Conifers: **pytw-*, **py/wK-(*pyk-*, **pwḱ-*)

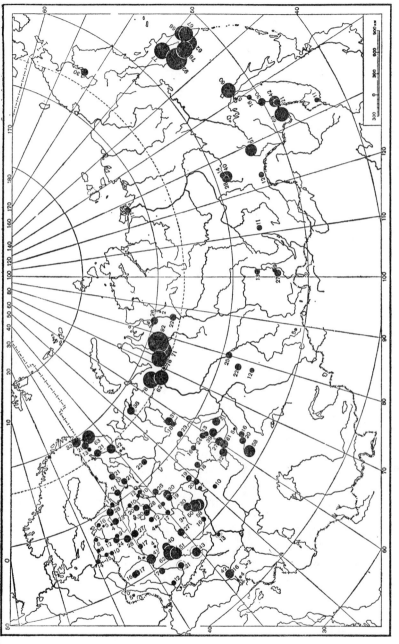

Map 2. Distribution of *Betula* in the late Holocene (from Nejshtadt)

33

various stocks also indicates cross-referencing of the conifers with each other, and with tar, pitch, and resin, a pattern which apparently goes back to remote times. This has intrigued scholars such as Specht, and raises interesting questions about the PIE: Was there an arbitrary and "culturally specific" lack of concern with the conifers? Or was there a dearth of coniferous species in the PIE environment? Or were there drastic differences between the coniferous environment of the PIE and the areas into which the speakers of the daughter stocks moved?

One PIE word for a conifer may be reflected in four stocks, of which Indic is the most questionable. Sanskrit *pītu-dāru* is generally rendered as a kind of pine, or fir, or resinous tree (Ernout and Meillet 1951, p. 901), and as the Deodar tree in post-Vedic sources. Mayrhofer (1956, 2:293) evaluates it as an isolated name for "a kind of tree" that cannot be derived from a verbal root. There is great variation in the attested forms (Benveniste 1955, pp. 30–31). Kuiper (1954, p. 248) suggests that the first element is of Dravidian origin, and originally meant "gum, resin" (compare Telegu *pisunu*), whereas the second segment was a suffix -*du*-, later folk etymologically restructured to -*dru*-, "tree." A "Pamir dialectal" *pit* is cited as "spruce" (e.g., Walde and Hoffmann 1938, 2:308); as Benveniste has pointed out, the sole evidence for this is an addendum on the last page of a monograph on the Ghalchah languages (Shaw 1876, p. 278).

Three apparent cognates occur in the Mediterranean area. Homeric Greek πίτυς denoted the pine according to some (Cunliffe), the spruce according to others (Hofmann), and both (or either?) according to Frisk, who also mentions the stonepine. Latin *pīnus*, "pine, fir," may descend from **pīt-snus*, and be related to the Greek. Finally, there is the Albanian *pišé*, "spruce, pine, fir," which G. Meyer (1891, p. 340) derived from **pīt-s-i̯a* and related to *pešk(ve)*, "tar, resin" (the cluster -*kv*- is a contamination-formation); see also Jokl (1923, pp. 32, 215), who relates the suffix to other nominal formations in Albanian.

After considering these four stocks, some would agree or at least sympathize with Benveniste's purge: "Rien ne doit faire présumer que cette dénomination ait appartenu au lexique indo-européen commun." I would accept **pytw*- as a weak and chronologically late PIE tree name denoting some sort of conifer, probably the pine. Possible evidence of its antiquity are the alleged loans into Finnic (*petäjä*).

A second word is attested in four stocks. (1) Middle Irish *ochtach* meant the kingpost of a house, in the Book of Lecan (Stokes 1895, p. 73), and is certainly a cognate of *octgag*, "pine," and *octhgacha*, "fir" (*ochtach* comes from **puktākā*). (2) Old High German *fiuhta, fiehta*, meant "spruce" (Modern German *Fichte*); the Germanic reflexes are limited to the Continent, both insular and peninsular languages lacking them because of the absence or relatively late arrival of the spruce in these areas, according to Kluge and others. (3) Greek πεύκη, "spruce, spruce, forest, spruce faggot, pine." (4) Lithuanian *pušìs* means "spruce" or "pine." On the basis of these correspondences I would posit a PIE **pewḱ-* or **pwḱ-*, denoting "pine" or "spruce."

A third set of correspondences occurs in three stocks: (1) Greek πίσσα, "tar, resin"; (2) Latin *pix, picea*, "tar, pitch, pine," and *picea*, "spruce," and Umbrian *peiu*, "spruces" (from **pik-ye-*); (3) Slavic, as in Old Russian pьkъlъ, "pitch, tar," Serbocroatian *pàkao*, Polish *piekło*. The Latin *pix* was widely borrowed, and appears in Old High German *pëh*, Lithuanian *pìkis*. I would posit a PIE **pyk-*, and suggest that it is derivationally related to the second conifer word. The second conifer word and the word for "tar, pitch, pine, spruce," and the like, are treated in the conclusions as evidence for a strong second PIE tree name[3]; for convenience, the two terms are represented by the single **py/wK-*.

How are these conifer forms to be correlated with the numerous types of conifers purported to be in the environment? First, in all stocks the denotata of the two words are limited to the spruce-fir-pine set, and in no case do they include the juniper, cypress, cedar, yew, or any other evergreen. This is evidence that the Indo-Europeans since early times have dichotomized sharply between the first three conifers and all other evergreens. Like the status of the elm and linden as "crop trees," this is one of the few "middle range" taxonomic groupings, located between "tree" and the score or so of generic-level taxa that can be

---

[3] Two other points deserve mention. First, Frisk says that the denotation of Greek πεύκη was *Pinus laricio*, and might be a substantivized adjective meaning "needle tree." Second, Hirt (1892, p. 478) suggested that the corresponding forms for "woodpecker" (Latin *picus*, German *Specht*, Sanskrit *pika*) were derived from the tree name, "since this bird primarily dwells in forests of spruce and feeds on the insects which live beneath its bark." This strikes me as farfetched.

inferred for the PIE arboreal system (Berlin, Breedlove, and Raven 1968). The exceptions to the coniferous/nonconiferous dichotomization are discussed below under the junipers and cedars. In the second place, the philological evidence alone would permit one to infer that either of the conifer words, and probably the pitch-tar word also, could have denoted any one of the three conifers, or simply "conifer." At this juncture, the paleobotanical evidence provides some help.

Judging from the absence of its pollen, which is produced in large amounts and is readily identifiable, the fir (*Abies*) was absent in the fourth millennium from all the central PIE homeland. In certain higher and peripheral zones the pollen which has been found—although useless for subgeneric differentiation—can nevertheless be assigned to one of three species on the basis of the facts of contemporary distribution; fir species are geographically limited to an unusual degree. First, the wind-resistant Caucasian fir (*A. Nordmannia*) was probably present at least shortly after the glaciers and, during the Atlantic, crowded out the oak in some areas; but *Nordmannia* grew not in the Ukrainian forest-steppe, nor even in the Caucasian foothills, but in the mountains at altitudes of twelve thousand to seventeen thousand meters. A second species, the Siberian fir, was present in Siberia. Finally, the white fir (*A. alba*) generally prefers temperate, hilly, or mountainous zones with moist soil and without late spring or early autumn frosts. The silver fir was present over parts of southern Germany, central Poland, the Balkans, and the Alps (Walter 1954, p. 195). Its silvery or gray bark produces large amounts of resinous turpentine. Partly because of this bark, and the whitish effect created by two narrow stripes under each needle, the tree has been dubbed the "noble fir" or "silver fir" in German and other languages. During the Subboreal and later it attained maximum development, often flourishing in stable coexistence with the beech. But firs were generally absent from central and southern European Russia until well after the dispersal of most of the PIE.

Let us turn to the second genus. The spruce (*Picea*), like the fir, has readily distinguishable pollen and also was absent from the central PIE homeland during the fourth and third millennia. The common or European spruce, botanically *Picea excelsa* or *P. abies* (the "fir spruce,"), grew on the edges of the PIE area and was certainly known to some of the speech community. It was found in the western Caucasian highlands, together with the Eastern spruce (*P. orientalis*), and ran north of the forest-steppe boundary until mingling with and eventually yielding to the Siberian spruce (*P. obovata*). The Siberian spruce, in its turn, was scattered across central Russia, and attained its greatest growths in the Carpathians.

The reddish-barked spruce dislikes the excessively arid air of summer droughts, which kills its young fruits and flowers. Climatic factors such as increased precipitation presumably caused the tree to spread greatly during the middle and late Atlantic; pollen has been found not in the Ukraine, but in Armenia and on the southern Volga and the Pripet-Desna. The spruce expanded with the pine, by which it was greatly out-numbered. During the greater aridity of the Subboreal it again withdrew, yielding to the beech and fir. Today it is concentrated in five separate zones, all moist and cool: the Carpathians, the Balkans inland from the Adriatic, the Alps, the central German highlands (it is not hardy west of the Vosges), and the area extending east from the Baltic Sea through central and northern Russia.

In contrast to the spruce and fir, the third main conifer—and a particular species at that—was present throughout the PIE homeland during the entire Atlantic. Trees of the pine genus (*Pinus*) produce more pollen than any other, with a "gray rain" that may cover the forest floor to a depth of 1.5 centimeters; this pollen is easily identified. Several species have been present in central and eastern Europe at least since the early Holocene; for example, the mountain pine (*P. mughus*) in the Carpathians and Alps, and the "crooked pine" (*P. hamata*) over all the Caucasus, often as dominants in the earlier millennia.

By far the most widespread and frequent has been the common or Scotch pine, a distinctive tree with blue green needles and bright orange bark. This Scotch pine (*P. sylvestris*) dominated central and northern Europe during the Boreal and extended in copious stands along the valleys and shores of the southern rivers to the Black Sea (Nejshtadt 1957, p. 248). It was forced back somewhat by the hardwoods during the Atlantic, a retreat which was completed before the later advance of the beech, fir, and hornbeam (Firbas 1949, p. 140), with which

37

the pine often formed stable communities. The pine remained a conspicuous and frequent component of forested areas all over central and eastern Europe during the Subboreal as well. Its millennial strength is due to many factors—relatively rapid growth, abundance of pollen, and perhaps the idiosyncratic fact that some cones require the heat of a forest fire to open them fully, when they release vast amounts of viable seed to completely restock areas that have been burned over; in short, the pine is both an ecological pioneer and capable of competing with the large hardwoods. Today the Scotch pine forms great forests in Scandinavia, Germany, Poland, and the USSR, often with little admixture of other trees. Large amounts of turpentine are extracted from the bark, and tar is made from the roots.

Let us conclude. First, the reflexes of neither *pytw-* nor *p(e)wk̑-* denoted fir, and *Abies* itself was absent from the PIE area; individual dialects developed fir terms after their westward expansion and the coterminous spread of the silver fir (*A. alba*) during the Subboreal (3000 to 800 B.C.). Second, some early Indo-European dialects, particularly Greek and Germanic, had forms descended from *p(e)wk̑-*, which were applied to the pine, or to the spruce in the highland areas. Third, PIE and all the early IE dialects had terms similar or related to *pytw-*, *pwk̑-*, or *pyk-*, which were applied to the dominant species of pine, *Pinus sylvestris*. On the Carpathian, central Russian, and Caucasian peripheries, the silver fir, the eastern and Siberian spruce, and the crooked and mountain pines presumably were labeled by derivative formations, such as a conifer word plus a modifier. After the dispersal of the PIE about the beginning of the third millennium, various descendent forms were adapted to the several varieties of conifer found in any given area. In particular, numerous labels were evolved by the Balts and Teutons for the varieties of conifer in the northern arboreal zones into which they migrated.

3. *The Junipers and Cedars: *el-w-n-*

One protomorpheme rests on fairly good correspondences between two stocks. The Armenian word for "cedar" is *el-ew-in*. The Proto-Slavic cognate is *jalovьtsь* (Vasmer 1950–58, 3:488), as in Russian dialectal *jálovets* and Polish *jalowiec*, both of which mean "juniper." As for the correspondences between these cog-

The Junipers and Cedars: *el-w-n-

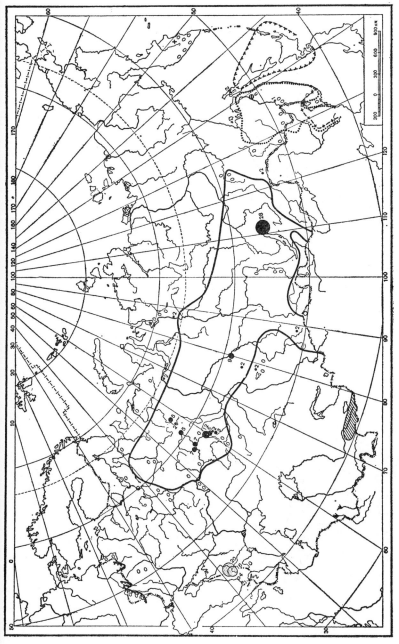

MAP 3. Distribution of *Abies* in the middle Holocene (from Nejshtadt)

39

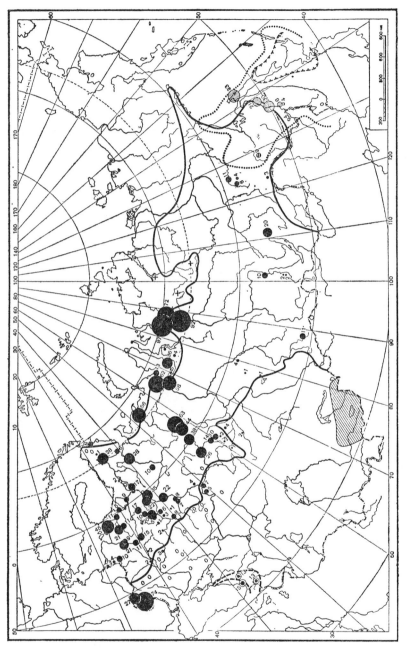

MAP 4. Distribution of *Picea* in the middle Holocene (from Nejshtadt)

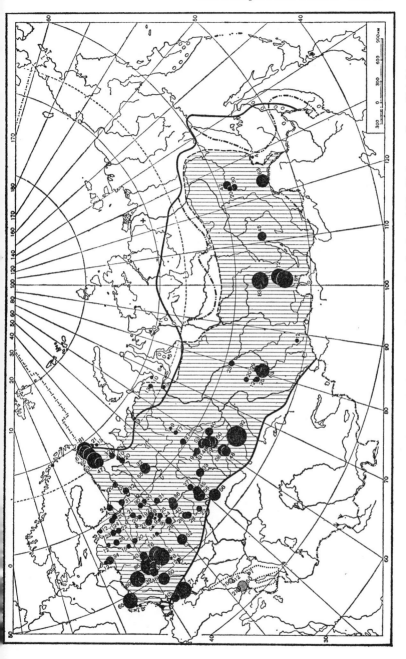

MAP 5. Distribution of *Pinus sylvestris*, *P. hamata*, and *P. mughus* in the middle Holocene (from Nejshtadt).

41

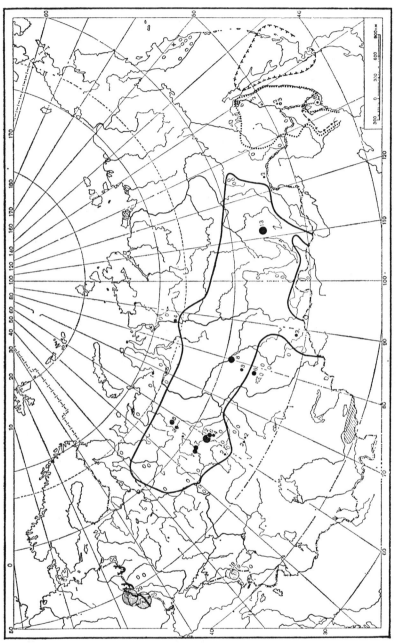

MAP 6. Distribution of *Abies* in the late Holocene (from Nejshtadt)

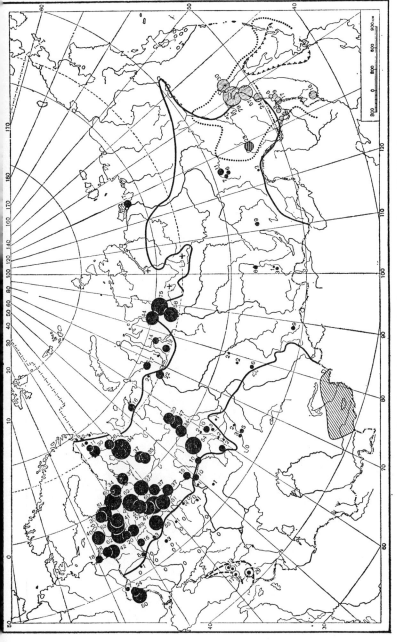

MAP 7. Distribution of *Picea* in the late Holocene (from Nejshtadt)

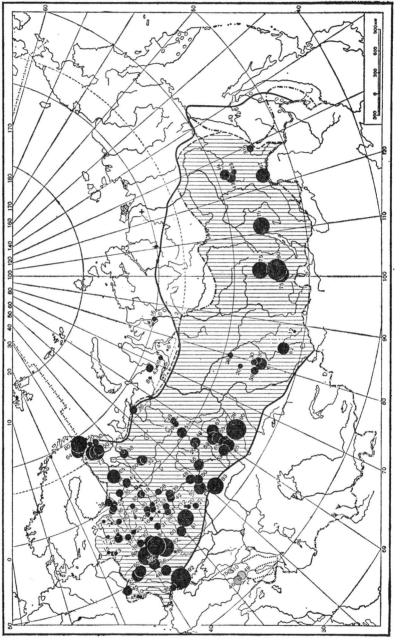

MAP 8. Distribution of *Pinus sylvestris*, *P. hamata*, and *P. mughus* in the late Holocene (from Nejshtadt).

nates, the following points are most relevant. First, the liquid
and the *w*-stem formative of the Armenian matches the Slavic.
Second, the alternation of initial *e/o* is shared by other tree
names (compare the alder and the second yew name). Last, the
-in- of Armenian corresponds to the *-en-* of some Slavic forms
such as White Russian *jelenets*; both are reflexes of a PIE suffix
that is also found, for example, in the term for ash. Armenian
and Slavic thus justify the postulation of a protoform, **el-w-n-*,
that, although limited to the central dialects, is in two respects
a typical tree name.[4]

The distinct denotations of "cedar" and "juniper" reflect a
widespread tendency to confuse or cross-reference these trees—
probably because of the many similarities in the berries, wood,
and general appearance. One word may be used for both trees,
as in the Theophrastian χέδρος, or two obviously related forms
may be employed, as in the Old Slavic *smrěchъ*, "juniper," as
against the similar *smřcha*, "cedar." In fact, the so-called red
cedar wood of our cedar chests and mothball closets comes from
what is botanically a species of juniper (*Juniperus virginiana*),
and in some American English dialects is called the "red cedar
juniper."

To the Slavic and Armenian there corresponds the Greek
ἐλάτη, which has been derived from a reconstructed **el-n-*, plus
the suffix *-tā* (Lidén 1905–6, pp. 491–92). 'Ελάτη, anomalous on a
number of semantic grounds, raises a fascinating question of inference. First of all, it denoted "spruce" or "fir," although both
the juniper and cedar are present in Greece; these meanings also
fly in the face of the general tendency in Indo-European to
discriminate sharply between the conifers and the nonconiferous
evergreens. Finally, Greek ἐλάτη also denoted rowboat or canoe
(*Kahn*), and oar or rudder (*Ruder*; Frisk 1954, p. 481). Assuming
that ἐλάτη is related to **el-w-n-*, how can we account for the shift
of the arboreal denotation to spruce or fir, and of the non-
arboreal denotation to rowboat and so forth?

The speakers of the dialects transitional between PIE and

[4] Several Slavists have tried to relate the name for juniper to *jálov-*,
meaning "barren," on the grounds that the juniper tree, with its male
blossoms, might suggest this property—farfetched, to put it mildly!
Others have argued for the same connection because of the tree's green
fruits—still farther-fetched! (see Vasmer for the literature).

Proto-Greek probably lived in the western part of the PIE homeland—probably in and between the Crimea and what is now the Hungarian plain. In this area both the juniper and the cedar were probably present, whereas both the spruce and the fir were absent (as was shown above under the conifers). The Pre- and Proto-Greek antecedents of ἐλάτη were used for the juniper and cedar, from which boats and oars very probably were fashioned.

Such exploitation is widespread in primitive technology. Speaking of the American Indians and the American "northern white cedar" (*Arborvitae*), Harlow wrote (1957, p. 71): "The wood is soft, light, and very durable (cedar fence posts) and is used in boat and canoe construction, for shingles, and for making fire by friction . . . this rubbery toughness makes the wood particularly useful for canoes, particularly those in river work where rocks cannot always be avoided. Gibson says the Indians made canoe slats by pounding the wood with a stone maul until it separated along the annual rings."[5]

After the Proto-Greeks entered Greece, the referents of the antecedents of ἐλάτη presumably oscillated for a time between the juniper-cedar and the spruce and fir; this inference is supported by a comparison with Baltic forms such as *paĕgle* and *ĕglĕ*, which refer to trees in both the juniper-cedar and spruce-fir categories (Fraenkel 1962, p. 117). Eventually, the Greek form came to denote the more readily available spruce and fir—from which boats and oars continued to be fashioned just as they had been formerly from the juniper and cedar. That this was still true in Homeric times is neatly evidenced by part of the boat-building scene in the *Odyssey* (5:237–40):

> She led the way to the end of the island, where the tall trees grow, alder and black-poplar and fir, that reaches toward heaven, long-dried, very [? an unidentified element], which would sail for him lightly.[6]

[5] Botanically, the *Arborvitae* is neither a cedar nor a juniper, but the *Thuja occidentalis*. However, despite the differences in the reproductive organs (to which so much attention is paid in the Linnaean system), this *Arborvitae* shares many properties with the cedar and juniper—hence the terms "white cedar," or northern white cedar.

[6] I am indebted to James Redfield for calling my attention to this passage. Murray's translation is:

My conclusion is that the Greek meanings of oar, rudder, canoe, and rowboat represent archaisms that have been carried down from an earlier period. They are related to the meanings of juniper and cedar as part is to whole, that is, metonymically. The transferred meanings of spruce and fir are related to those of juniper and cedar on the basis of shared properties, that is, metaphorically. The history of Greek ἐλάτη thus exemplifies two of the basic processes in semantic change: metaphor and metonym (Jakobson 1956). Otherwise, the Greek shifts are congruous with the fact that almost half of the seventeen to twenty-one PIE tree names reflected in this stock have shifted their denotata.

The PIE juniper-cedar term may be related, by a second hypothesis, to a cluster of arboreal terms that is limited to Baltic and Slavic. First of all, the Lithuanian *paēgle,* "juniper," is probably related to *ēglé,* "fir." Second, a Proto-Slavic *edlā* has widespread reflexes in Russian *el',* and Polish *jódla,* both meaning "fir," and Serbocroatian *jéla,* "spruce," and other languages of this stock. Taken together, the forms in Baltic and Slavic may descend from a Proto-Balto-Slavic *edlī- or *edlā- (although the latter probably reflects subsequent, differentially motivated shifts in the two stocks); the Baltic forms then went over to *e*-stems, and shifted in a regular fashion from *d* to *g.* The Proto-Balto-Slavic forms obviously resemble Greek ἐλάτη, and could be the result of metathesis, although most specialists would probably agree with Hübschmann that the phonological difficulties are "insuperable"—particularly the "inadmissible" correspondence of Armenian *l* and Balto-Slavic *dl* (1:442).[7] The interpretation of Armenian *l* and *w,* moreover, is fraught with more difficulties than implied by the summary statements above. The apparently close connection between the Armenian and Greek forms, on the other hand, like the cognates for "goat," is a valuable lexical isogloss linking these stocks.

Then she led the way to the borders of the island where tall trees were standing, alder and poplar and fir, reaching to the skies, long dry and well-seasoned, which would float for him lightly.

[7] Here and elsewhere in this monograph "Balto-Slavic," "Italo-Celtic," and similar terms are to be taken as convenient labels for specific shared features and forms, and do not imply a commitment to tribal or national entities.

There is a third interesting hypothesis. Balto-Slavic *edlī-* corresponds well to the Italo-Celtic *edhlo-* that is realized in Latin *ebulus*, Gaulish *odocos*, and Old Irish *aidlen* ("fir"), although the latter presents formal as well as semantic difficulties (Ernout and Meillet 1951, 1:338). The semantic connection between Balto-Slavic and Italo-Celtic, however, is extremely tenuous because the Italic and Celtic forms denote neither junipers, nor cedars, nor conifers, nor evergreens, nor even the lowly elder (*Sambucus nigra*), but rather the dwarf elder (*Sambucus ebulus*), a six-foot, white-flowered, deciduous bush with an unpleasant odor. I would agree with Benveniste (1955) that the relation between *edlī-* and *edhlo-* is a case of "Indo-European homonymy."

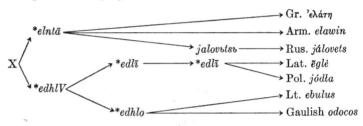

Chart 1. Proposed cognates for *el-w-n-*

The juniper and cedar are generally ignored in the paleobotanical sources (e.g., Nejshtadt), although on the basis of their present distribution and botanical characteristics I would think that both trees entered not too long after the glaciers; today, they extend north beyond the tree line into the frozen moors and tundras of Russia and Scandinavia. Juniper pollen is widely spread in east European pollen deposits of the Atlantic and Subboreal, but the pollen of the cedar is difficult to distinguish from that of the pine. Both junipers and cedars occur throughout eastern Europe, usually as an understory in coniferous stands or as pioneers on dry, barren ground. The European junipers include some sixty species of the cypress family, of which two are particularly important. The junipers are ubiquitous and are physically distinctive in many ways—the scalelike leaves, the silver gray to cadet blue berries, the reddish, shreddy bark, and the medicinal qualities of the leaf extracts and the berries. From remote times the PIE speakers probably had a ready label for the junipers and cedars.

Because of the many unsolved problems presented by the PIE
juniper-cedar hypothesis, and particularly because of the complexity of the relations between the reflexes, I have chosen to
summarize the proposed cognates in chart 1.

4. *Populus:* *osp-*

Osp- is attested in three central and east European stocks,
where several closely related words denote different species of
the genus *Populus*. The white poplar was denoted by the Old
English *æspe*, and the North Sorbian *wosa*, whereas Lithuanian
ãpušė or *ēpušė* refer to the black poplar. The quaking aspen is
labeled by the Latvian *apse* and the Russian *osína*, the latter
deriving from Proto-Slavic **opsa* (Vasmer 1950-58, 2: 282).

There is disagreement about the sequence of medial consonants. Kluge (1963, p. 175) cites the Germanic forms for wasp
such as Old English *æspe* and Modern German *Wespe*; presumably, Germanic **wesp-*, "wasp," is to Slavic **wopsā*, also "wasp,"
as German *Espe*, "aspen," is to Proto-Slavic **opsa*, also "aspen."
Kluge thinks that a Germanic populus form with *sp* came from
an earlier form with *ps*. Other scholars think that the *sp* form is
earlier, and that it was the Balto-Slavic forms which resulted
from metathesis. In fact, as originally shown by Walde, the
Germanic "wasp" forms, like their cognates in Slavic, Baltic,
and Iranian (e.g., Middle Persian *vabz*), ultimately derive from
the PIE root for wasp, **wobhsā*, which comes from the root for
"to weave," **wobh-* (Szemerényi 1952, pp. 52–53), with later
metathesis in Latin *vespa* and the Germanic languages. The
wasp set did not provide a model for metathesis of the spirant
and stop in the tree word.

A larger framework to the problem of the ordering of the
consonants would appear to be provided by the non–Indo-
European evidence; **osp-* looks suspiciously non–Indo-European
to some Indo-Europeanists. Many languages of southern Siberia
contain strikingly similar forms: *ausak* in Tobol, *apsak* in Altai
and Lebed, *aspak* in Kumandu, *ëvës* in Chuvash, *o/ōs* in Sagai,
and so forth. Shapes such as the latter may represent a late
borrowing from Slavic, whereas those with *p* may have been
borrowed very early from Iranian; many Turkic languages attest
both a late Slavic and an earlier Iranian level of borrowing

(Hoops 1905, pp. 122–4; although in this case there do not appear to be any Iranian cognates). On the other hand, both Pedersen and Lidén (1905–6, p. 491) thought that the Turkic forms had been borrowed from early Armenian, a hypothesis which remains to be related to the tantalizing but unexplicated form of Armenian *op'i*, "white poplar" (cited in a footnote by Eilers and Mayrhofer 1962, p. 89, in their article on the beech). Finally, Vasmer simply asserts that **ops-* was borrowed from an "eastern Indo-European language." I would conclude that during the third and second millenia both Indo-European and non–Indo-European languages shared forms with both orderings of the medial consonants that referred to poplars and aspens. **Osp-* was an areal term shared and borrowed in one form or another by the members of a *Sprachgruppe* of interacting speech communities in eastern Europe and southern Siberia.

The Greek evidence involves an interesting but, I think, fallacious equation. The common word for buckler or shield in the language was ἀσπίς, as in the Iliadic passage (3. 347): "First Alexander hurled his far-shadowing spear and smote the son of Atreus' shield." This ἀσπίς was related by Schrader to a similar word, ἄσπρις, the name for a specific kind of oak (*Q. cerris*). According to his hypothesis, the PIE populus term shifted to oak in Greek, and some variant of the oak term then shifted to shield. In support of this etymology Schrader cited the apparently parallel αἰγίλωψ (from αἰγί?), meaning "oak," and a word occasionally used for "shield," αἰγίς. The four terms can be set in an equation:

ἀσπίς (shield) : ἄσπρις (oak species) : : αἰγίς (oak shield) : αἰγί (oak)

The equation is weak on two grounds. To begin with the second half, the form αἰγί (oak) is definitely not related to αἰγίς (shield), which previously meant "breastplate," and before that "goatskin," and ultimately stems from the word for "goat" (αἴξ). To turn to the first half of the equation, the meaning of ἄσπρις as a particular species of oak could be explained on the grounds that the poplar is absent in Greece, or that shields are fashioned from oak wood, or that in Greek tree names tend to shift to particular species of oak. Frisk (1954, p. 169) was probably warranted in denying that ἄσπρις (*Quercus cerris*) descended from PIE **osp-*, and in categorizing ἀσπίς as a foreign loan. Greek ἀσπίς : ἄσπρις remain as possible but improbable cognates.

Populus: **osp-*

If the Greek forms could be accepted, they would disambiguate the initial vocalism. As it stands, Slavic *o*, Old English *æ*, and Lithuanian and Old High German *a* can reflect either PIE *a* or PIE *o*.

A daring and cogent attempt to broaden the Indo-European character of the otherwise narrowly areal **osp-* was made by Thieme (1953), and has since been bolstered by Janert in a learned and well-organized article (1964). According to their hypothesis, the PIE term for populus was **asp(h)i-o-* or **osp(h)i-o-*. This term underlies or is at least genetically connected with a second form which has descended as *sphyá* in Sanskrit, and as obviously related forms in other Indic languages.

The meanings of the *sphyá* family of words are diverse, but connected. First, some denote the front oar on a boat, as in "will become quite useless, like a front oar (*sphyá*) or a rudder on dry land." The more usual association is between *sphyá-* as the front oar in contradistinction to *aritra-* as the back or stern oar; *sphyá* may also have denoted a pole for poling boats (the common denominator for pole and front oar being that both are used to propel).

The second denotation of the Indic forms is that of shovel, or some other agricultural tool, and the third denotation is shoulder blade. Apparent reflexes with the meanings both of shovel and of shoulder blade have been found in modern Indic languages such as Nepali, and also in modern Iranian (Wakhi *fiák*, "shoulder," Persian *fah*, "oar, paddle"). The correspondences are acceptable phonologically, and the oar-shovel-scapula concatenation seems semantically plausible—the shovel and scapula pair has well-known parallels in other languages (Russian *lopáta* and *lopátka*). One is inclined to accept the postulated early Indo-Iranian (*s*)*phiya-* (Janert 1964, p. 108), denoting oar or shovel and, probably by a metaphorical shift, shoulder blade. But the possibility must also be entertained that the original meaning was scapula, which then shifted to shovel and similar tools; the shoulder blades of deer and other animals are utilized as shovels in many primitive technologies.

The fourth and final meaning found among the Indic forms is that of a sacred instrument (*Gerät*) used for cutting or furrowing the soil before a sacrifice, and often but not necessarily in the shape of a sword or a pointed blade; actually, in the last

51

century Böhtlingk and Roth (1855–75, 7:1381) defined Vedic *sphyá* as "ein Holzspahn, messerförmig zugeschnitten, armeslang, zu verschiedenem Gebrauch beim Opfer dienend." The hypothesis relating this Vedic meaning to PIE **osp-* and the cognates in modern Indic would run as follows: The early (eastern) Indo-Europeans revered *Populus*, found many poplars and aspens about them, or for some other reason customarily fashioned some sort of paddle- or shovel- or sword-shaped ritual instrument; because of its shape and its ritual functions, and possibly because of its emotional connotations, this religiously charged blade may have served the early Indo-Iranians as a model for other artifacts of similar shape; eventually the original arboreal denotation was lost altogether, and even the meaning of ritual tool did not survive beyond Old Indic days. We need not be disturbed because Vedic *sphyá* occurs only once; it is a philological fact that the Indic evidence for many PIE words, including, for example, several kinship terms, is often limited to one or two forms in the oldest texts.

The etymological argument advanced by Thieme and Janert is phonologically reasonable. The Sanskrit *sph*-forms would reflect a morphologically justified zero grade of the initial segment, and there are plentiful cases of *sCh* in the same language corresponding to *sC* or *C* elsewhere. Regarding the alternation in *sphya-* and *æspe*, Hoenigswald writes, "The initial laryngeal might in some cases be to blame" (1965, p. 95). On the semantic side, a bit of Finno-Ugric (Cheremis) ethnography might be construed as a link between the Balto-Slavic arboreal referents and the Indic ritual ones: speaking of "magic affecting evil powers," Sebeok and Ingemann (1956, p. 266) write, "An aspen stake driven into the ground at the grave is supposed to prevent a corpse from leaving the coffin."[8]

The components in the foregoing discussion are summarized below:

North-Central-European	Indo-Iranian
*osp-	**sphiya-*
aspen/poplar	shovel, sacred instrument, etc.

[8] This is the only reference to the aspen in their apparently definitive study. I am indebted to Thomas Sebeok for several pointers on Finno-Ugric ethnography.

The wood of the aspens and poplars is hard to differentiate from that of the willow, and the pollen deteriorates rapidly under most conditions. However, some species endure great cold, and seed and grow rapidly. The genus may have survived the glaciers, and certainly did appear shortly after them as a pioneer in geological succession, coexisting for some time with the willow and birch before being crowded out or severely reduced by the birch-pine complex. During the Atlantic and later they probably persisted as pioneers in ecological succession—after forest fires and the like—and as a characteristic feature of shorelines and the banks of streams. Today three species (the black, white, and gray poplars *M. nigra, alba, canescens*) abound in central and southern Europe; but it is the quaking aspen (*P. tremula*) which for centuries has been salient in the east and northeast. Huge forests cover many Baltic regions, and this is *the* tree of trees along much of southern Siberia, where the seeds, buds, twigs, and shoots provide food—particularly in the winter—for many wild animals such as the deer, rabbit, and bear. I think that *Populus* was well known and economically important to both eastern and western Proto-Indo-Europeans in their Cis-Caspian-Caucasian and Ukrainian homeland area.

5. *The Willow: *s/wVlyk-, *wyt-*

The first Indo-European form for the willow is limited to the three western stocks, plus Greek, and very problematical outliers in Anatolian. Latin *salix* is certainly related to Old Irish *sail* (genitive singular *sailech*) and Middle Welsh *helygen*; Meillet derived these Italic and Celtic cognates from an ancestral **sᵒlyk-*. The Germanic evidence includes Old High German *salah(a)* and Old Norse *selja*, which have been derived from a Proto-Germanic **solk-*. All these forms denote willow in some botanical sense, and presumably descend from a (late?) Western-Indo-European **salyk-*, with the same referent.

The Greek data raises a paradox of contrast and complementation. First, 'ελίκη meant "willow" in Arcadian (according to Theophrastus), and the place name, 'Ελικών, has been interpreted as "willow hill" by Frisk (1954, p. 494); both must be entertained as cognates of the Western-Indo-European set. However, in sixth-century B.C. poetry there occurs ϝελικών— instead of 'Ελικών; there are similar cases elsewhere in Greek involving an initial digamma and rough breathing (on their relation to the presence or absence of a prothetic vowel, see Cowgill 1965, p. 153). These Greek forms are probably cognates of a distinct Germanic set of forms denoting "willow," that includes Old English *welig* and Middle High German *wilge*. The paradigm is summarized below:

Greek	Germanic
Ἑλ ικών	*salah* (*a*) (Old High German)
ϝελ ικών	*wilge* (Middle High German)

The words in the second row are identical in meaning and patently similar in form to those in the first, but few Indo-Europeanists (particularly Germanists) would accept them as cognates, because of the contrastive relation between *s* and *w* in Germanic.

The main conflict above is between the criterion of meaning—practically identity of meaning here—and the criterion of sound—of regular phonemic contrast in the daughter stocks. A third criterion is that of the morphophonemics of the mother language; specifically, the initial consonants of the willow forms appear to have formed an alternating set in PIE. Meillet (1937, pp. 171–72) pointed out that an initial *s*- plus a consonant or sonant could alternate with that same consonant or sonant, and specifically posits an alternation between *sw*-, as in Greek 'ϝὲξ and *s*-, as in Latin *sex*, and *w*-, as in Armenian *veç*, although "dans un cas de ce genre, la forme complete peut par hasard ne pas être attestée." On the acceptance of this inference, the Greek and Germanic forms in the paradigm can be brought together with each other and with the remaining cognates from Western-Indo-European. In addition to the initial alternation, the several reflexes attest the full range of vocalic grades. In sum, I would posit a western and central *$s/wVlyk$-, which may have been a consonant stem, but may also represent a *k*-extension added to an old *i*-stem (Specht 1943, p. 58).[9] For convenience, the form *$sVlyk$- is often used hereafter in the text.

---

[9] After the PIE period distinct meanings came to be attached to the variants, at least in Germanic, where the form with *s*- ended up denoting a particular species of willow (*Salix caprea*), and the *w*- variant was used for willows in general. In Old High German the two reflexes were compounded to yield *salewīde*; today the initial segment of the descendent *Salweide* has become a "cranberry morph," with no independent meaning aside from its contrasts with *Weide*, *Bachweide*, etc.

The initial alternation of *s-* and *w-* argued by Meillet opens two very hypothetical possibilities of a connection with Hittite. First, Hittite *úellu*, "meadow" (J. Friedrich) may be a cognate of PIE *sel-, "wet place" (as reflected in Greek *helos*, from which Solmsen (1901, p. 15) attempted to derive an *s*-variant of the willow). Second, the Hittite word for "meadow" may be a cognate of a Hittite word for "grass," *úelku*, as in the following quotation from "The Soldier's Oath" (Pritchard 1955, p. 354):

> Let not his wife bear sons and daughters!
> Let his land [and] his fields have no crop,
> And his pastures no grass [*ú-el-ku-wa*]!
> Let not his cattle [and] sheep bear calves [and] lambs!

Both *úellu* and *úelku* may be related to a *w*-variant of the willow form. Willow leaves, long, thin, and often lanceolate, do resemble blades of grass (note the modifier "willow-leaved"), and some species of willow are shorter than many grasses, such as the tall steppe species of the prehistoric Ukraine. In sum, Proto-Indo-Anatolian *s/wVlyk-* may have shifted in Hittite to some kind of long grass, and then to grass in general. If either of these admittedly improbable Hittite connections is valid, then the willow form is carried back to the Proto-Indo-European of the early or middle fourth millennium, before the breaking off of the Anatolians.

The willow had a second name, one of the most widely attested units in the PIE vocabulary. The evidence from nine stocks includes: (1) Sanskrit *vētasáḥ*, "willow, rod, switch"; (2) Avestan *vaētay*, "willow, switch" (Bartholomae 1904, p. 1314); (3) Greek *οἶσος*, a kind of willow, and *ϝῑτέᾱ*, "willow, a shield woven of willow shoots" (and the obviously related *ἴτυς*, "felloe, rim of a shield"); (4) Latin *vītis*, "grape, tendril, shoot, willow" (and the again obviously related *vitus*, "felloe," and perhaps *vitex*, "the chaste or hemp tree"); (5) Irish *féith*, "fiber, cord"; (6) Old Norse *víþir* or *víðir*, "willow" and Old English *wīðig*, "withy, willow"; (7) Armenian *gi* may belong to this set, since *g* is the normal reflex of *w*, and the PIE *t*-extension could have been dropped; the meaning of *gi* as "juniper" could have resulted from the use of its branches for baskets, nooses, and so forth (Lidén 1905–6, pp. 494–97), paralleling the use of willow osiers for similar purposes. Particularly good is the match between Baltic and Slavic, as in Lithuanian *vytìs*, "willow switch," and *žilvitis*, "willow" (Fraenkel 1962, p. 1268), and Russian *vit'*, "a woven object," and *vetlá*, "willow."

In all nine stocks, the cognates indicate that PIE **wyt-* referred not only to the willow, but to willow withies or shoots, and to artifacts woven or twisted out of them; as Meillet concluded, "en réalité, il s'agit de la branche flexible qui peut être utilisée de toutes sortes de manières" (1937, p. 397). The various nominal forms have been derived from a PIE verbal root **wy̆-*, "bend, twist," and the like, as reflected in Sanskrit *váyati*, "wound," and Lithuanian *výti*, Russian *vit'*, "to twist (e.g., a cord)"; the Baltic and Slavic forms, in particular, support this interpretation. By similar reasoning, the first willow word, **s/wVlyk-*, has been derived from a verbal root for "wind, twist" (PIE **selk-*).

A third willow form, **wrb-*, as in Latin *verbera* and Latvian *vìrbs*, "rod," and Slavic *verba*, "willow," may be derived from a third root for turn or twist, **wer-* (Meillet 1937, p. 396). Ultimately, all three forms for willow (**s/wVlyk-*, **wyt-*, **wrb-*) may go back to a pre-PIE root, the exact form of which cannot be recaptured.[10]

A set of four interconnected considerations leads to the PIE binary classification of willows. First, as already noted, the tree is etymologically linked to notions of weaving or twisting, and this is congruous with the pliability of willow wood, and the possibility, suggested by other linguistic evidence, that the early Indo-Europeans used willow osiers, shoots, and branches for weaving baskets, fences, and making felloes (I have not been able to determine whether willow wood was preferred or is particularly appropriate for felloes). Second, there were at least two willow words for part of the speech community, since contrasts occur in four stocks: Celtic, Germanic, Greek, Latin. Third, in both scientific and folk botany the willows fall into two great categories: the osiers or bush willows (e.g., the golden, purple, and pussy willows), some of which are only one or two

[10] The terms for the willow, perhaps more than those for any other tree, have been subjected to etymological reduction (deriving them from some other root). In addition to the derivations already mentioned, the first willow form has been traced to a word for "yellow" (e.g., as reflected in the Old High German *salo*)—presumably because some willows have relatively light leaves.

inches high, and the tree willows, which normally range to twenty or thirty feet, like the common *Salix alba,* although some giant Siberian varieties attain over 110 feet. Most of the one-hundred-odd species of willow fall unambiguously into one of these two categories. Fourth, PIE **wyt-* (and possibly **wrb-*) may have denoted the osiers, or the shoots of tree willows, since all its reflexes in the daughter stocks involve some notion of weaving or bending. Complementing this, PIE **s/wVlyk-* might have been limited to the tree willows. This would seem a felicitous correlation between two reconstructable terms, and a clear dichotomy in the phenomena referred to.

Paleobotany is not particularly helpful regarding the willow. The major problem is the inability to differentiate species. In addition, willow pollen, although yielded copiously, does not carry far, and has often been hard to distinguish from that of the wormwood (frequently reported in Frenzel). Nevertheless, the available deposits of wood and bark indicate that this tree probably came in with the birch and pine, spread during the moist and cold Preboreal, and was present all over the USSR during subsequent millennia (Njshtadt 1957, p. 266). The species *S. alba* and *S. vitellina* were probably present.

The wide attestation and general validity of the two main terms is probably connected with the residence of so many PIE speakers along or near the great rivers of "southern Russia," particularly the Dnieper, Don, and Kuban, as well as other stream banks, lake shores, and swamps—all favored habitats of this moisture-loving tree. Given its great practicality, the number of species and hybrids, and the extraordinarily wide distribution—from the tropics to the arctic, and from the lowlands to the treeline—one is surprised that not more than two or three PIE roots can be reconstructed; an idea of the taxonomic richness possible is conveyed by Russian folk speech, where about seven types of willow are designated by at least twenty-one names (most of them complex forms).

6. *The Apple: *ăbVl-, *maHlo-*

The inference of the PIE words for the apple rests to an unusual degree on external, nonlinguistic criteria. Although little is said in paleobotanical sources (mainly because the evidence is practically nil), we do know that the apple is hardy throughout a large Eurasian zone that provides the required minimum of cold for its winter dormance; in much of Europe, the Caucasus, and Anatolia, the common wild apple is a typical minority member of mixed hardwood forests. I assume that varieties of the wild apple diffused over much of Europe, especially northern Europe, between the Preboreal and the early Atlantic.

In contrast to the wild apple, the common cultivated apple was probably developed in the highland region south of the Caucasus (close to the PIE homeland postulated by some); this was but one of several fruits whose domestication was an important component of the Neolithic revolution in the Near East. The cultivated apple soon diffused to other parts of Eurasia. For example, there is considerable evidence of it in the early Neolithic sites of southern Great Britain, and in the pile dwellings of Switzerland (Firbas 1949, p. 189), although this information remains to be adequately assessed. After the penetration of Roman horticulture, the apple was in many areas the only tree fruit to retain its indigenous name—possibly because of its dietary and economic importance (it has high caloric value and its easily preserved by drying). Cato recognized seven varieties of the cultivated apple, and in some ancient languages the word, such as Latin *mālum*, was often used as a general designation for fruit. Speaking of the tribal Germans, Tacitus (*Germania* 23) wrote: "Their diet is simple: wild apples [*poma agresta*], fresh venison, and curdled milk. They banish hunger without sauce or ceremonies." (Although cited by Kluge under "Apfel," *poma agresta* might refer here to wild fruits in general.) Finally, in the folklore and mythology of many Indo-European peoples—particularly the Celtic, Greek, Slavic, and Germanic (Scandinavian) divisions— the apple is a fruit of social, magical, and religious ritual connotations; at times it seems the northern analogue of the grape. I think—even on the basis of the rudimentary fragments just advanced—that the apple was a well-known fruit and that it figured as prominently as the nuts (walnut and hazel) in the PIE diet. It is on the basis of such considerations that I am taking a positive stand regarding the sometimes highly problematical linguistic evidence.

As possible PIE names for the apple, two protoforms must be entertained. The first is reflected in at least four northern stocks:

Celtic, Germanic, Baltic, and Slavic. The dietary importance
of the apple may be indicated by the presence of a distinct set of
correspondences for the fruit as against the tree. The following
tabulation sums this up:

	Pre-Celtic	Old English	Pre-Baltic	Old Slavic
apple	*abalos*	*æppel*	*ābū l*	(*j*)*ablъko*
apple tree	*abal-n*	*apuldor*	*ābeles*	(*j*)*ablanъ*[11]

In addition to these four, Meillet and many others have
accepted as an italic reflex of the first apple term the name of an
Oscan town, Abella—allegedly so called because of its copious
apple harvests, as referred to in the *Aenead* (7. 40), "maliferae
. . . moenia Abella." Abella may be a vestige of the early intru-
sion of apple-cultivating and apple-trading Italic-speakers from
the north where, as I have posited above, the wild apple was
highly valued.

On the basis of the five cognates cited, a North-Indo-European
ăbVl- may be posited, with full and reduced grades evidenced
in some degree for both vocalic segments—which is an argument for the Indo-European status of the term. The shape is
divergent, however, in at least two ways: the *l* of the *l*-stem
(which may represent a suffix), and the *b*, particularly a medial
one, since *b* is relatively rare in PIE, appearing in no suffix, and
otherwise only in onomatopoeic words or in secondary elements
of words (Meillet 1937, p. 89)—the *b*'s that do occur are often
explained by borrowing. Yet these divergences from a norm
do not vitiate the opinion of Pokorny and of Meillet that
the two sets of correspondences, for the tree and for the fruit,
are close enough to establish that some term of the shape proposed did exist to designate the apple of the ancient people
of Indo-European speech in northern and western Europe
(Ernout and Meillet 1951, 1: 15). In the four more northern of
these stocks—Celtic, Germanic, Baltic, and Slavic—the reflexes
of *ăbVl-* were the only names of tree fruits to survive the cul-

[11] On the relation of Pre-Baltic and Baltic forms, see Leskien 1884,
p. 270. Some of the cognates supporting these protoforms include Old
Irish *ubull*, "apple," and Middle Welsh *afallen*, "apple tree," Latvian
âbuolis, "apple," and *âbels*, "apple tree," and finally, Russian *jábloko*,
"apple," and *jablónъ*, "apple tree."

tural and terminological impact of Roman horticulture. Regarding the shift in Italic to *mālum*, Meillet said, "ce mot désignait une pomme cultivée; ici se manifeste la substitution de la civilization méditerranéenne et hellénique à celle de l'Europe du nord qui était originairement celle des Latins et des Osco-Ombriens" (1937, p. 398).

The second word for the apple is attested—depending on one's caution or credulity—by anywhere from zero to five Indo-European stocks. First, the Greek forms, Dorian μᾶλον, Attic (and Homeric) μῆλον may descend from PIE, or reflect a borrowing from a non-Indo-European or another Indo-European language. Second, Latin *mālum* corresponds point for point with the Greek, but may be a loan from the latter. Third, Albanian *mölle* might be a descendent from PIE, but might also be a loan from Latin (Tagliavini 1937, p. 195), and might also belong to a small group of names for flora borrowed from Greek at a very early stage (Eric Hamp, personal communication). I do not know how to decide conclusively between these alternatives.

The fourth candidate as a reflex of the second apple term involves an improbable but, I think, logical argument. In brief, the Albanian word for apple occurs in a fixed and frequent expression for "apple cheeks." In Greek, the apple word meant "fruit" or "apple" in Homer, but was used later poetically with the meaning of "cheek.' Finally, Tocharian A *mālan* meant "cheeks," and only "cheeks," and, on these grounds, has been proposed as a cognate. If accepted, the Tocharian form would complete an axis running from Italy, where the apple abounds and is called *mālum*, to the Balkans, where in both Greek and the contiguous Albanian there are cognate forms which denote apple and connote (or denote) cheek, and on to distant Chinese Turkestan, where the form survives with the transferred and originally metaphorical meaning.[12] Because of the agreement between the three eastern stocks, I would posit an early connotation of "cheek," and, from the agreement of all four forms, a PIE apple word with the tentative shape of **mālo-*.

---

[12] I think that apples are relatively unimportant in Chinese Turkestan, but have not been able to ascertain the exact facts. (I doubt if there *are* many paleobotanical facts for the periods in question.)

The fifth and last stock to be considered takes us into laryngeal theory, where the apple and the birch are the trees to have figured with the most prominence. The meaning of "apple" was assigned to *mahla-* by the original decipherer of the Hittite texts—Hrozný. He was followed by Kuryłowicz (1927), and Sturtevant (1928, 1931), and others, who were quick to point out that the form fit the common pattern of correspondences whereby words in Hittite with a vowel plus a medial *h* often had cognates with a long vowel in other Indo-European languages; both types of vocalic nuclei presumably reflected an earlier vowel plus laryngeal. Then, in 1933, Ehelolf apparently demonstrated that Hittite *mahla-* meant not apple but grapevine. After this most Indo-Europeanists, with the signal exception of Sturtevant, ceased to regard it as a cognate of Latin *mālum* and Dorian *μᾶλον*; J. Friedrich gives the denotation "Rebe, nicht Apfelbaum."

Ehelolf's new gloss was based on a subtle but, I think, very precarious exegesis. First, he knew there was a Hittite law against stealing something called *mahlaš*, and assumed that the object could not be apple trees, but probably was grapevines. Was his judgment not biased by the biblical legal tradition? In fact, primitive peasantries sometimes have rules against stealing or damaging young trees. In the second place, his crucial evidence was a single formula for sympathetic magic: "Wie eine Sau viele Ferkel hervorzubringen pflegt, so soll auch jede einzelne Rebe (*ᵍⁱˢma-a-a-h-la-aš*) dieser Weingarten wie die Sau viele Trauben (*mu-u-ri-uš*) hervorbringen." Since the meaning of *mu-u-ri-uš*, the second word, had been shown to be grape elsewhere Ehelolf naturally deduced that the linked *mahlaš* denoted grapevine. But why not assume that this key word, *mahlaš*, could have denoted any tree or plant that bore fruit, including either grapes or apples?

Some affinity between grapes and apples is implied in many Indo-European language and culture systems. Several languages show a link between grapes and a particular type of apple known as the "honey" or "must" apple (Latin *melimēlum*). The juices or pulp of either may be called by the same name—such as Germanic *must* (a Latin borrowing). These meanings indicate that the transition between grape and apple may be more gradual than is generally assumed. It is possible that at some point in Hittite a word originally used for the (honey) apple (tree) could have shifted to "fruit-bearing tree or plant."

My conclusion regarding the second apple term is that an early Proto-Indo-European masculine stem, **maHlo-*, was shared by some southern dialects, and that it could be used to denote varieties of the apple, most probably the honey apple (*mālum musteum*). The term was still shared by about the middle of the fourth millennium B.C., before the separation of the Anatolians and after the domestication of the applie in the highland Near East, south of the Caucasus.

Having reviewed the evidence for both apple words, how are we to evaluate their status vis-à-vis the other trees, and PIE speech unity? Aside from the two moderate hypotheses just entertained, of accepting a northern **ăbVl-* and a southern **maHlo-*, there are two extreme positions: to reject both terms, or to regard both as descended from a common earlier form. Let us briefly entertain each in turn.

One may adhere to a "strict, cautious" position, and assume that the so-called sound laws are highly regular, and that the roots of PIE conform to certain "canonical forms." Because of its anomalous shape, one would then want to reject *ăbVl-* as a "suspiciously non-Indo-European" borrowing from an unidentified (and unidentifiable?) non-Indo-European language.

As for the second apple word, the majority of Indo-Europeanists would probably reject the "apple cheek" argument for Albanian and Tocharian, evaluating the latter as a coincidence and the former as a borrowing from Greek. The Latin form may also be from Greek. With the sister stocks lacking cognates, Greek μᾶλον is invalidated as a reflex of the PIE apple term.[13] Many scholars actually do regard *mālo-* either as limited to Greek and Latin, or to Greek alone (e.g., Meillet), or as one of the many floral terms borrowed by some southern IE tribes, not including Hittite, from some unidentified (and unidentifiable?) non-Indo-European language(s) of the Mediterranean. So much for the two negative positions regarding the "Finnic and Minoan" apples.

[13] In this and some other cases, such as PIE *wk-*, "wife," reflected only in Latin *uxor*, one can, I think, make a reasonable argument in terms of semantic space and similar criteria for positing a PIE form on the basis of a single reflex.

The alternative extreme position is not to reject either term, but to accept both and argue for their provenience from a common source. This can be done only within the context of more permissive premises about sound correspondences, and a reminder that the names of fruits not infrequently diverge from the "canonical forms."

The relation between the two apple terms would be as follows. First, the reflexes apparently indicate a long *ā* (Meillet 1937, p. 102), although the southern term probably reflects a laryngeal. The differing position of the vocalic vis-à-vis the labial might be the result of a metathesis—but this is admittedly ad hoc. The liquids are identical. The stop and nasal are both bilabial.

Bilabial stops have developed regularly from the homorganic nasal in two Indo-European stocks. In the south, Greek shows βλάξ, "slack, dumb," from *mla-*, and βλωθρός, "tall, high-grown," from *mlōthrós*, and so forth (Frisk 1954, 1: 240, 246); the shift was presumably from *ml* to *mbl* to *bl*. This shift is not directly related, of course, to the *ăbVl-* terms.

In the north, there was a historically attested shift in Irish at about A.C. 800 of *ml* to *bl*, and similarly in prehistoric Gaulic and British Celtic. Pokorny (1959, 1: 716) lists PIE *mēl-*, "to beat, grind," going to Old Cornish *blot*, Middle Irish *blăith*, and so on in other languages. PIE *melg-*, "to wipe off," is reflected in Middle Irish *bligim*, "I milk," and *buigid*, "he milks, presses," and Welsh *blith*. This "drift" of *m* to *b* at various periods in distinct Celtic languages makes somewhat more likely the sporadic shift for a Pre-Celtic apple term. Germanists and Celtologists, such as Thurneysen, have long argued that the apple term—whether or not originally Celtic—was borrowed from this stock into Germanic, and then into Baltic and Slavic, when the speakers of the latter dialects were in contact with Celts on the lower Danube; there has been some disagreement as to whether the Baltic forms were borrowed from Slavic or vice versa. Oscan *Abella*, finally, would reflect an early period of contiguity between the Italics and Celts, before the invasion of the Italian peninsula.

Berger (1956, pp. 26–33) has gone yet further, and argued that both the apple terms ultimately come from an Iranian *man-* (e.g., Wakhi *ma ṇa*), with a dissimilation of *n* to *l*

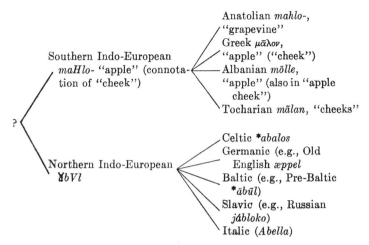

CHART 2. Proposed cognates for the apple terms

before a former plural, and of *m* to *b*, and a route of diffusion of *ăbVl*- forms from Slavic to Germanic to Celtic, and from Baltic to Illyrian to Italic. He even adduces Basque *mandaka* as of the same provenience.

Despite the interest of the diverse hypotheses relating **ăbVl*- and **maHlo*-, I have concluded that they do not descend from a common etymon and that the evidence does not permit a solution to the question of borrowing from a non-Indo-European language.

7. The Maples: **klen*-, **akVrno*- (**kL-n-?*)

The first of the two PIE maple morphemes is reflected in four stocks: Baltic, Slavic, Celtic, and Germanic—with Greek as an improbable fifth. The Baltic reflexes include Lithuanian *klēvas* and Latvian *klavs*. Proto-Slavic **kleno*- is reflected in all three branches of the stock, including, in South Slavic, the Serbocroatian *klĕn* (genitive *klĕna*) and *kljĕn* (Vasmer 1950–58, 1: 562). The Celtic evidence comprises cognate forms with distinct referents: compare Welsh *celyn*, "maple," and Old Cornish *kelin*, "holly." Old English has the same two referents in *hole(g)n*, "holly," and *hlyn*, "maple"; both of the Old English forms, and also the Old Norse *hlynr*, "maple," go back to a Proto-Germanic **hluniz*. Another Germanic set includes *lin-*

boum of Old High German, reflecting a shift in that language of
initial *hl-* to *l-*, about A.D. 800.

The Greek evidence is limited to the corrupt κλινό-τροχος, the
first element of which comes from Theophrastus (*History of
Plants* 3.2. 2), whereas the second is foreign and may have
meant "tree"; the construction thus would parallel the Old High
German *lĭn-boum* cited above. Γλεῖνον, also in Theophrastus,
was thought to have been borrowed into Greek from "Old
Macedonian" by G. Meyer, and appears again in Pliny (15.15)
as *glinon, alinon* (see G. Meyer 1891, pp. 19–29). My own conclusion is that Macedonian γλεῖνον is totally problematic—for
one thing, the *g* would normally be a reflex of *g, gh.*

In sum, the Baltic, Slavic, Celtic, and Germanic forms are
certainly cognate, and go back to a stage, probably a late one,
of the northern dialects of PIE. The nuclear vocalism remains
uncertain and imperils the etymology, but three stocks (all but
Germanic) more or less indicate *e*; PIE *klen-* was probably
masculine in gender, and may have been a consonant stem in
final *-n,* although the Baltic indicates a *w*-stem; the original
may also have been a biliteral *kl-,* to which the *e*-grade of an
n-extension was added.

The second maple morpheme is *akVrno-.* The solid evidence
is restricted to three stocks: Italic, Greek, and Germanic. The
Latin cognate is *acer,* which Osthoff (1901, p. 187) derived from
a postulated *acernos.* In the Greek stock, a Hesychian gloss,
ἄκαρνα δάφνη, displays an *n,* and supposedly referred to either
"sweet bay or Olympian maple." This ἄκαρνα stands beside
ἄκαστος, which may have meant maple (Hesychius), although
Meillet says flatly that "les glosses grecques n'enseignent rien."
Ἄκαστος, according to Hofmann (1950, p. 9) and Frisk (1954,
p. 51), comes from ἄκαρστος.[14] In Germanic, finally, the widespread reflexes include Danish-Norwegian *ær,* from an earlier
ahira (apparently without *n*), whereas the Old High German
ahorn goes back to *ahurna.* Drawing together the substantial
evidence from Medieval Germanic, Greek, and Classical Latin,

[14] The *-stos* ending of both the latter forms was probably added by
analogy with the word for plane tree (πλατάνιστος; Chantraine 1933,
p. 302). In addition to the three stocks here discussed is the "Gallo-
Roman" *akar(n)os,* which calls for a critical inspection by the relevant
specialist.

I would posit a central dialectal *o*-stem, probably masculine, and with the shape *ákVrno-*, and showing evidence for both full and reduced grades; several forms indicate that variations in the vocalic nuclei were correlated with accent.

The form as posited resembles Basque *azkar*, which may reflect borrowing from early Indo-European. Depending on the dialect, the Basque name denotes "maple" or "oak," with the secondary meaning of "strong," thus paralleling PIE *dorw-*, "tree, oak," but also "firm, fixed, strong." The PIE *ákVrno-* also has a shape that resembles the problematical *ăbVl-*, "apple," discussed in the previous section.

This concludes the reconstruction of the two forms. The remainder of the maple discussion will concern three speculative but significant hypotheses: the Vedic *akráḥ*, the binary opposition between the two maple words in Proto-Germanic, or earlier, and last, the possibility of a single (Pre-?) PIE maple word, *kL-n-*.

The Indic form *akráḥ* appears only once, but in the Rig Veda (10.77. 2), in a passage which Ludwig translated as "Des Himmels Söhne haben sich angestrengt wie Hirsche, wie Säulen wuchsen die Aditya in die Höhe" ("the sons of heaven strained like stags, the Aditya grew into the heights like pillars"), and Grassmann rendered as "Die Söhne des Himmels gingen wie Hirsche gereiht, sie, die Aditya, wuchsen wie Heeresbanner empor" ("the sons of heaven went arrayed like stags, they, the Aditya, grew upwards like the banners of an army"). The Sanskrit dictionaries also give "banner," although some cite "wall, fence," and one gives "big animal (elephant)."

Sharply contrasting with these specialists, Brunnhofer (1901, pp. 108–9), in what remains a brilliant speculation, argued as follows. First, the pressed drops of Soma allow Indra to grow like the branches of a tree. Second, Indra allowed mankind to grow like the branches of a tree. His third point, which sounds ad hoc as he puts it, was that the maple "grows to giant size." Finally, there is the phonological correspondence with the *akVrno-* forms in western Indo-European languages. Vedic *akráḥ*, therefore, meant maple, and the correct translation is: "The Aditya grew upward like maples."

Most Indo-Europeanists would reject this solution, or stigmatize it as the intriguing but unprovable inspiration of a poetic philologist. Thieme, on the other hand, picked up the *akráḥ-* "maple" connection, and has been referred to uncritically by Kluge. Although personally skeptical, I think that this metaphorical Indic reflex must be entertained for several reasons. First and foremost, the Vedic form corresponds fairly well with "good cognates" of the *acer*: *ahorn* set, the important exception being that a Sanskrit *k* is not the normal reflex of PIE "simple" *k*. Second, as noted above a number of words with excellent Proto-Indo-European etyma also occur only once in the Rig Veda, and lack attestation in the later dialects of Indic; rather than abruptly ruling Brunnhofer's suggestion out of court, we might fruitfully search the Prakrits and similar evidence.

Third, it is true that the European maples are in general not particularly large; they are slow-growing and inclined to lowland areas and even swamps, and would therefore be an infelicitous choice for comparison with the Aditya. On the other hand, one species of maple does display the properties implied by the Vedic passage: the "mighty maple"(Russian *klën velíchestvennyj*) has leaves a foot wide and soars upward to 120 feet or more. The mighty maple grows in the central and eastern Caucasus, where, during the Atlantic, the speakers of the eastern PIE dialects may quite well have been located. During the centuries after their migration to India the pre-Vedic poets—precisely by the nostalgic, reminiscent, archaic metaphor that marks the primitive bard—might well have compared the mighty maple to the sons of heaven. So much for the *akraḥ* hypothesis.

Let us turn to the binary opposition between the two maple words. The attestation of **akVrno-* and **klen-* is somewhat restricted geographically, and the assignment of physical meanings may never be satisfactory. Nevertheless, several lines of reasoning are relevant.

First, the late, central PIE **akVrno-* may have denoted the Norway maple (*Acer platanoides*). In many contemporary European languages this species is designated by compounds that refer to the relatively sharp or pointed quality of the leaves (German *Spitzahorn*, Russian *óstrolístnyj klën*, and so forth). Moreover, there may be an etymological connection between **akVrno-*, and the root for "sharp" that is reflected in Greek ὄκρις and Latin *ācer*, although this is unlikely; in addition to the difference in the length of the initial vowel, the Latin words in

67

question belong to different stem classes. Pokorny (1959, 1: 20) thought that the formation *acerabulus* represented *acer*, "maple" or "sharp," plus *arbor*, "tree," or be a derivation paralleling *digitabulum, acetabulum*, and so forth. Meillet suspected a Gaulish *-abolos*. Finally, a derivational relation between "sharp" and a "sharp-leaved" or "sharp-pointed" plant may exist elsewhere in Indo-European, as in Greek ἄκορνα, "type of nettle." On the basis of these and similar considerations, some scholars think that late PIE **akVrno-* may have referred to the class of maples perceived as having sharp leaves.

The second hypothesis rests on two related facts. First, the two maple words are in complementary distribution except in Germanic, where both are reflected, and presumably contrast (Proto-Germanic **hluniz* and **ahirna-/*ahurna*). In the second place, it is also in Germany and the immediately adjacent country that the zones of two species of maples overlap: the area contains both the Norway maple, which does (did?) not grow west of a line from Auverne to Belgium (Firbas 1949, p. 184), and also the so-called sycamore maple (*Acer pseudoplatanus*), which is hardy in the north Mediterranean and middle European highlands, but absent in the Ukraine. In sum, the presence of two contrasting terms is correlated with the presence of two physically distinct referents.

Having established this correlation of contrast, let us now explore its history. Some Medieval Germanic dialects such as Old High German may show a binary opposition between the Norway maple (the *līn* in *līnboum*, botanically *A. platanoides*) and the sycamore maple (*ahorn*, botanically *A. pseudoplatanoides*), although Kluge (1963, p. 10) asserts that the specific meaning of sycamore maple was a learned innovation. The sycamore maple, however, is often hard to distinguish from the sycamore proper or "plane tree" (*Platanus*), and in some folk taxonomies the two are classed together and set off against the maples.[15] Possibly the medieval Germans—like contemporary botanical taxonomists—had a series that was graded partly on leaf shape and ran from the Norway maple to the sycamore

[15] The contamination of the Greek word for maple by that for plane tree has been mentioned in the footnote above. The Modern German for sycamore maple (*A. pseudoplatanoides*) is *Bergahorn*, literally "mountain maple," which must not be confused with the American mountain maple (*A. spicatum*).

maple to the sycamore. Also, one cannot ignore the most wide-spread species, the common or field maple (*Acer campestris*), which has been identified in Neolithic sites and extends today from England to the southeast Russian steppe and on into Asia. In conclusion, the precise physical referents of **akVrno-* and **klen-* cannot be recaptured, but the existence of terminolog-ical-perceptual contrast between two or more kinds of maple would seem likely within Medieval Germanic and Proto-Ger-manic.

The early Germanic contrast may have carried back into PIE, at least the later stages of PIE. Botanically, the Norway maple probably had been present in central Europe since the early Atlantic, and the sycamore maple since the Mesolithic. In the general Caucasian area maples were present during the entire period in question, with maxima in the pollen spectra of about 8 per cent during the Atlantic; today the greatest diversification of the genus is in the Caucasus, with a range from the bushy Tatar maple (Walter 1954, p. 174) to the above mentioned mighty maple; the area with the greatest growths of maple in the USSR is the Bashkir republic. This long presence and sub-generic diversification of the maples in the Ciscaucasian foot-hills and steppe and the lands to the north—within or overlap-ping with the PIE homeland—would be congruous with the probable presence of at least two maple names in the PIE language.

The discussion up to this point has emphasized the presence of the maple in peripheral areas, largely on the basis of con-temporary distributions. In fact, the maple is characteristically underrepresented in the pollen records because the little pollen it produces deteriorates rapidly. As a result, the history of the maple during the Atlantic is poorly understood. Frenzel (1960, pp. 387–97) does not report it for the Ukrainian area, where many of the PIE were located. The alternate hypothesis might therefore be advanced tentatively that the maple was relatively unimportant to the PIE, and that the two established forms, **akVrno-* and **klen-*, go back to a single root. The **klen-* would reflect a zero grade of the first vowel, and a full grade of the *n*-extension; the **akVrno-* would reflect a prothetic *a-*, and a zero grade the *n*-extension. Both forms would go back to a (Pre?)-PIE **kL-n-* (using *L* to symbolize a liquid sonant).

8. The Alder: *alyso-*

The evidence for the alder is strong in four stocks, mainly limited to personal and place names in a fifth, and quite problematical in a sixth. Baltic provides Old Prussian *alskande*. In Lithuanian *aĺksnis*, *eĺksnis*, and others, and the almost identical Latvian forms, the *k* is secondary, and the original form is *alisnis*, and ultimately *alisno-*. Both stocks show a suffix that is found with other tree names (e.g., *glúosnis*, "willow").

Slavic shows cognates in all three branches: for example, Bulgarian (*j*)*elkhá*, Czech *olsha*, and Russian *ol'khá*. For Proto-(or Common?) Slavic, Vasmer (1950–58, p. 226) followed Meillet in positing a pair of forms with alternation of the vocalic nucleus: *jélъkha* and *ólъkhá*. The second of these is presumably original, whereas the *je-/o-* alternation reflects a later development. *Ólъkha* derives from an earlier *alysó-* or *alysá-* by a series of regular sound changes: Slavic *o* may go back to a PIE a; Slavic *l* goes back to *l*; ъ goes back to y; *kh* goes back to *s* when following *y*, *w*, r, k, and preceding a back vowel, and *a* may go back to ō or ā.

Latin *alnus* is derived by most authorities from a reconstructed *alsnos* (described as a "morphological monster" by Szemerényi (1960, p. 229), who argues for *alisnos*, *alisinos*). It may also come from *alenos*, thus paralleling *farnus* from *farnos* (Specht 1943, p. 61). Within Latin, *alnus* could also denote certain artifacts of alderwood, and with these denotations has survived in the Romance languages (Ernout and Meillet 1951, p. 41). The use of alderwood for ships is evidenced in Virgil.

The many Germanic cognates include Old High German *elira* and, by metathesis, *erila*, with the *e-* reflecting *i*-umlaut in either case. In a second language, Old Norse, *ǫlr*, "alder," contrasts with *jǫlstr*, "laurel willow," and with *ilstre*, "willow." Szemerényi, disagreeing with the usual derivations of Old Norse *ǫlr* and of its Old English cognate, *alor*, from *aluz*, derives both from an earlier *alaru*, preceded by *aleru*, and ultimately by *alizā-*; "Nor do the other Germanic forms justify anything but the Common Germanic *alizā-*" (1960, p. 228). A Gothic *alisa* has been set up as a source for Spanish *aliso*, "alder." Proto-Germanic *alizā-* illustrates Verner's Law, with the *z* coming from an intervocalic *s* when not preceded by stress. The Proto-

The Alder: *alyso-

Germanic form came from an earlier *alisō- (Kluge 1963, p. 172).

Let us sum up. The e's and o's of the initial segments can be accounted for in various ways, whereas an original a is indicated by the bulk of the evidence from the four stocks with the best evidence. The root has taken an n-suffix in Latin, and both an n-suffix and a k-suffix in Baltic. The PIE name for the alder probably was *alysō- or *alyso-, an ancient feminine o-stem, according to Meillet.

The Celtic evidence primarily involves place names and personal names on the Continent. Alisanos was probably the name of a god (Holder 1961, 1: 94), and has been glossed as "the Alder God," and taken back to a Proto-Celtic *alisa (Walde and Hofmann 1938, 1: 31). Pokorny cites a Pre-Gaulish *alisā, with the meaning of "alder," and attested by the place name Alisia; a second, unlikely cognate here is the French alise, "sorb-apple, beamtree berry." *Alisa, "alder, service-tree," is a component in Gaulish personal names (Evans 1967, p. 291). Finally, an Iberian Celtic *aliso has been documented by Lejeune (1955, p. 67). A Proto-Celtic *alisa seems a good deal less certain than the *alysō- discussed above, but more certain than the Greek, to which we now turn.

The Greek forms are generally problematical. The etymological discussions include reference to a Macedonian ἄλιζα, "white poplar" (ἄλιζα· 'η λευκη in Hesychius), which may derive from *elisā-. I would agree with Frisk that this so-called Macedonian form was borrowed from a language farther to the north. One basis for the shift in reference would have been the light color of the underside of the leaf, a conspicuous feature shared by the white poplar and the white alder.

The second Greek reflex is the place name Ὀλιζών (home of the Iliadic Philoctetes). Fick interpreted Ὀλιζών as "the place of alders," and Kretschmer described the shift of a to o as an Äolism. A third Greek reflex, the place name Ἀλιζῶνες (Iliad 2. 856), shows an initial segment that has suggested a laryngeal explanation to some scholars. The word may at some time have referred to alders, but may just as conceivably be connected with the Haliṭu of the Urartian inscriptions, or the Halys River (mentioned in Homer), or the Khaldoi region cited in Xenophon (M. Van Loon, personal communication). The three

71

potential Greek cognates—ἄλιζα, Ὀλιζών, Ἀλιζῶνες—bear some similarity to the Basque *altza*, "alder" (or "elm"—there is some question about the gloss).

What was the botanical referent of PIE *alyso-?* Four species are involved: the gray, the bearded, the mountain, and the black alders. Some botanists have argued that the gray alder (*A. incana*) has always been the most prominent species in the north, and that even as long ago as the Boreal period, it extended to the polar line. Today it is a generally northern and highland tree, ranging from England to western Siberia, and southward into the Caucasus. But in both the Cis- and Transcaucasus, the dominant species is the bearded alder (*A. barbata*); in the early Holocene the pollen of the alder—presumably the bearded one—exceeded that of all other Caucasian trees except the chestnut, and during the Atlantic its pollen generally was in the majority (Nejshtadt 1957, p. 293). Third, the mountain or green alder (*A. viridis*) has long been present in many highland zones of eastern Europe. Finally, in Germany, Poland, and European Russia the most frequent and widely distributed species has probably always been the black alder (*A. glutinosa*), which today is found everywhere west of the Urals except southern Spain and the southeast Russian steppe. The black and the bearded alders easily attain heights of over sixty feet, although usually constituting the shrubby understory of deciduous communities in moist lowlands. All these facts on the four species are extrapolations based on present distribution. Despite some experimental successes in distinguishing the gray from the black alder, the paleobotanical account is basically that of the genus.[16]

The copious pollen produced by the alder carries far and is readily identified. Judging from the remains of this pollen, the alder existed in and among the last glaciers, and then multiplied vigorously as a geological pioneer together with the pine and the birch, and has been on the Eurasian scene ever since. During the early Holocene it thrived in central and middle Russia, and during the Boreal extended its spread throughout Poland. During the same millennia it migrated southward along the Bug and

[16] In various folk or scientific terminologies the alternative terms for the species are: *incanus* = gray = white = hairy; *viridis* = green = mountain; *glutinosa* = sticky = black.

Dnieper rivers to the shores of the Black Sea and, as I have already noted, was ubiquitous in the Caucasus. The alder became yet more prominent during the late Boreal and early Atlantic, generally advancing in the same general area as the hazel but occupying a complementary ecological niche—the moist soil of moors, lowlands, and floodplains, and the wet sections of forest floors. *Alnus* pollen attained its maxima during the humidity and precipitation of the middle Atlantic, about 5000 to 4000 B.C. Although rarely the dominant member of climax forests, its percentages in the pollen spectra did range from 24 percent to over 40 percent; 33 percent is reported from the southern Bug, and one maximum of 58 percent was reached in the central Russian plateau (Frenzel 1960, p. 387). It was also during the middle Atlantic that the alder spread into Germany. Clearly, the success of the genus as a whole was congruous with climatic change.

The Subboreal witnessed a sharp decrease in the frequency if not the areal distribution of alder pollen. This was probably for three reasons. First, the aridity. Second, the spread of the fir and of the alder's "main competitor—the spruce (Firbas 1949, pp. 200–203). The third cause was probably man, who often cleared out river bottoms and other favored alder habitats. Since the Neolithic and subsequent millennia the alder has remained as an ecological pioneer in flooded plains and wet lands that have been burned off; short-lived alder forests have sometimes formed.

I think it particularly significant that the alder apparently flourished during the last millennium of the Atlantic, which I regard as more or less equivalent to the last millennium of PIE unity. In addition, the alder flourished precisely in those ecological niches where—according to be best archaeological evidence—many PIE speakers preferred to dwell, namely in river bottoms, along river banks, or in swampy depressions sheltered from the winter winds (Gimbutas 1966). In light of the congruities between botanical and archaeological factors, one is not surprised by the wide linguistic attestation of the alder: five (or six?) stocks.

9. *The Hazel:* **kos(V)lo-*

The hazel is attested by correspondences in three stocks that are identical in meaning, and regular phonologically. Latin *corulus* or *corylus* reflects the regular rhotization of intervocalic *s*, but

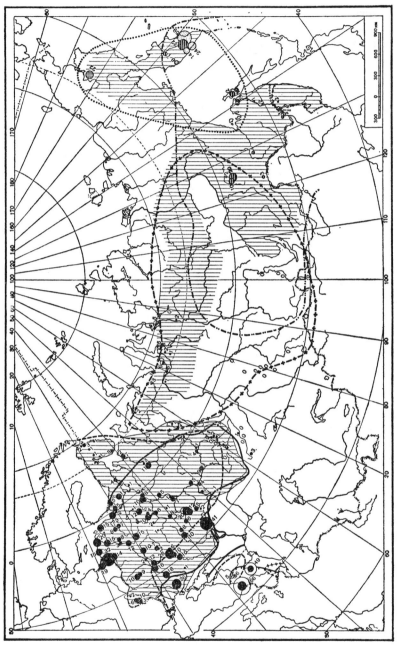

MAP 9. Distribution of *Alnus* in the late Holocene (from Nejshtadt)

does not permit a sure inference of the second vowel. Germanic shows the regular shift of *k* to *h* which forms part of Grimm's Law; the alternation of *l* and of the same sonant preceded by an unpredictable anaptyctic vowel is not unusual in such cases in this stock (Old English *hœsl* and Old High German *hasal(a)*); Kluge posits **kós(e)lo-* as the Proto-Germanic form. Third and last, Middle Irish *coll*, Middle Welsh *collen*, and Old Breton *limn-collin* go back to a Proto-Celtic **kosl* (Pedersen 1909, 1:84). One may posit an early Western-Indo-European masculine *o*-stem of the shape **kos(V)lo-*, which served to denote trees of the genus *Corylus*; it has been cited as evidence of an early western *Spracheinheit* by Krahe and others.[17]

The distribution of the strong linguistic evidence corresponds to some extent with the paleobotanical conclusions. The hazel appeared in central and eastern Europe during the Preboreal, if not earlier, and, like the alder, coexisted with the pine and birch during their long domination. Then, during the Boreal, the hazel spread sensationally. The late Boreal and early Atlantic of many zones such as northern Germany are described as "the hazel period." During these same millennia the hazel developed vigorously in the Baltic, the Carpathians, and along the southern reaches of the Bug, and extended into the central part of what is now the USSR (albeit very little south of what is now the forest-steppe boundary; Nejshtadt 1957, p. 282). From Germany to the Caucasus there were large stands and even forests of hazel trees, although to a considerable extent they also flourished as a bushy understory beneath the maple and other hardwoods. These estimates of "the hazel period" have been made while taking full account of the fact that its pollen yield is comparatively large.

Species of hazel cannot be distinguished by their pollen (Firbas 1949, pp. 150–51), but on various grounds it seems likely that the great hazel maxima of the Boreal and Atlantic involved not only the common hazel (*C. avellana*), but also the now more southern Turkish hazel (*C. colurna*) and the *Corylus maxima* of the Crimea and the Caucasus; both of latter regularly attain heights of over thirty feet. In the Caucasus there also flourishes *Corylus caucasica*.

The hazel tree was probably an important food source in

[17] I am indebted to Warren Cowgill for a valuable critique of an earlier version of this section.

central Europe, according to several scholars. "In the Low Countries, one early Atlantic site is known, de Leijen. It is situated on the shore of a depression which was still open water at the time of the habitation. People collected hazelnuts and also waternuts." "There is no botanical evidence for food production before the introduction of wheat and barley from southwestern Asia. Still, there is the hazel, the fruits of which are extremely common in some culture layers, and the postglacial spread of which was so rapid that Firbas has suggested that man played a part in its spread. Of course, it would be easy to promote hazel growth by cutting down other shrubs. But man would only do so if he could be sure of coming back regularly. This might be the case in the Maglemosian area." (Waterbolk 1968, pp. 1096, 1101).

Let us conclude with two final bits of philological evidence that seem moot. In 1902, Niedermann (pp. 97–98) advanced as cognate the Lithuanian *kasùlas*, "hunter's spear," not necessarily for wild boars, but, as Pokorny points out, possibly for hares and other small game. Precisely this "hazel/spear" relation shows up in another Baltic set: Lithuanian *lazdà*, "stick, hazelbush," and Latvian *lazda*, "hazelbush," but Old Prussian *laxde*, "spear-shaft" (Pokorny 1959, 2: 660). The tough, branchless shoots of the hazel have in fact long been utilized for artifacts such as canes, barrel hoops, fishing poles, and the like. Hazel shoots were employed during the Middle Ages of Ireland and elsewhere as spits for roasting—as in one text where "he was brought nine, long-pointed spits of white hazel" (Niedermann 1902, pp. 97–98). Great antiquity probably attaches to the use among Germanic peoples of hazel shoots for wands to ward off lightning and symbolize legal authority. Speaking of the Western IE *kos(V)lo-*, "hazel," Meillet (in Ernout and Meillet 1951) concluded that the reflexes "without doubt" included Lithuanian *kasulas* (he does not include the accentuation).

Although it seduced Niedermann, Pokorny, and Meillet, the tempting *kasùlas* hypothesis has also been rejected. First, the meaning of "hunter's spear" is only attested in the eighteenth century work of Mielcke and—according to Senn (personal communication)—is actually of unknown accentuation. If it ever existed at all, it could just as well have belonged with *kàsti*, "to dig," or with *kasulà*, meaning "bundle, clot, hank, bunch"

(Fraenkel 1962, 1: 226). Because of these and probably other considerations, Balticists stand arrayed against Neidermann's "phantasmagoria."

The second bit of moot evidence involves a possible Slavic cognate. Machek (1950, p. 54) has argued that Slavic *lěsko*, "hazel," resulted from a metathesis that was motivated by the association with the word for "nut," *orěkhъ*: the *lěsko* of *lěskovъ orěkhъ*, "hazel nut," would go back to **losko*, which in turn goes back to early IE **koslo-*. The argument is ingenious and would significantly increase the Indo-European character of the hazel name, but it has hardly won general acceptance. On the hypothetical connections between Baltic **lazd-*, "hazelbush," and Slavic *loza*, "switch, withy," and *lěsko*, "hazel," and Albanian **lazd-* or **laǵ-*, "hazelbush," and even Armenian *last*, "beam, ship, board," and so forth, see Jokl (1923, pp. 203–4).

Lithuanian *kasùlas* and Slavic *lěsko* raise a methodological question: given excellent correspondences in three stocks and the admissibility of cognates which are not identical but reasonably similar in meaning, as long as they correspond phonologically—just what are the chances of dredging up a pseudocognate in the scores of remaining languages in the other nine stocks, not to mention Illyrian, Messapian, and so forth? The PIE hazel form would seem to call for Meillet's injunction (1937, p. 41), that "les rapprochements valent seulement dans la mesure òu ils sont soumis à des règles strictes"—with the addendum that "strict rules" should refer not only to phonology but also to morphological structure and grammatical and lexical semantics.

10. *The Nut (tree)s: *knw-, *ar-*

The evidence is good that there were two terms for the nut or the nut tree.

One such term is reflected in the three western stocks. The Italic reflex is *nux*. The several Celtic cognates include Old Irish *cnú*, from **knūs* (Pokorny 1959, p. 558), and Middle Cornish *knyfan* and Middle Welsh *cnau*. The Germanic forms such as Old English *hnutu* go back to a Proto-Germanic consonantal stem, **hnut*, which, together with its Celtic and Italic cognates, goes back to a Western PIE **knw-*. Several authorities, including Pokorny and Kluge, have tried to derive this *w*-stem from a verbal root for "to squeeze, crush" (**ken-*, **knew-*).

77

Knw- was western, as was a second term already analyzed above: **kos(V)lo-*. But this second term denoted hazel tree, and it was the hazel which definitely flourished in western and west-central Europe during the entire Atlantic. I would postulate that **knw-* denoted the hazelnut in a botanically generic sense, from late PIE times in the west until the end of the Proto-Germanic period (i.e., down to about the time of Christ). In subsequent millennia, the reflexes acquired more varied meanings.

For many PIE speakers there was probably a close link between the nut and the apple, and in some stocks such as Italic (Latin), either word could be used in some contexts for any edible fruit. Morphologically, the western nut term resembles the term for the apple in the irregularity of its inflection, according to Specht (1943, p. 61).

The second nut term is reflected in four nonwestern stocks. Many Slavic languages have cognates: Russian *orékh*, and Bulgarian *oréh*, meaning "nut" (usually hazelnut in the north, and walnut in the south). Serbocroatian *òrah* (genitive plural *òrâhâ*) partly matches Lithuanian *ruošutỹs* (also *riešas*, and Latvian *riẽksts*; Fraenkel 1962, p. 731). The Greek forms include the Hesychian ἄρυα (αὔαρα), and κάρυον, "nut." Hofmann (1950, p. 134) also lists καρύᾱ, "nut tree." Chantraine (1968) thinks κάρυα could be a false variant of ἄρυα, but that, if authentic, the relation would parallel that between Greek κάπρος, Latin *aper* and other such sets in Indo-European. Finally, Albanian *arrë*, meaning "nut" or "nut tree," has an alternate, *harrë*, which, according to Jokl, relates it to the Greek κάρυον (Kretschmer 1921, p. 27). G. Meyer (1891, p. 17), on the other hand, said that the *h* was not significant, and that the two words could not be related on these grounds. The Albanian *rr*-forms may go back to *rs*-forms.

A protoform for this putative second nut term is difficult or impossible to reconstruct; according to Frisk (1954, p. 157), "Das nähere Verhältnis dieser Wörter zueinander bleibt noch aufzuklären." Some have suggested that the apparent cognates were early (Fraenkel) or late (Frisk) borrowings from a non-Indo-European language, or languages of the east Pontic or west Caucasian areas—Tomaschek even cited some Caucasian source forms (reference lost). My own opinion is that there existed an early central PIE term with the shape *ar-/arV-*, although, as

Specht (1943, p. 62) has pointed out, only the radical *r* survived in Baltic.

A quite unusual problem in establishing the meaning of *ar-* is that its reflexes are widely glossed as either "nut" or "nut tree," or both. The glosses are also ambiguous in that one cannot be sure whether the *Nuss* and *Nussbaum* in Vasmer, Fraenkel, Meyer, Frisk, and others, refer to "nut" and "nut tree" in general, or to the walnut—as would probably be sure of Albanian *arrë*, or to the hazel—as would appear to be true much of the time in Slavic dictionaries. Today, German *Nuss* is usually taken to mean walnut or hazelnut or both, but before and during the nineteenth century the terms for "nut" in European languages north of the Mediterranean usually meant "walnut."

Let us turn to botany. The walnut (*Juglans regia*) requires considerable warmth and light, and does concommitantly well in the Crimea and the Caucasus, often growing wild with the alder, beech, hornbeam, and so forth (Nejshtadt 1957, p. 267). It is believed to be native to a strip that runs from the western Caucasus (Lazistan) to the Pontic area and on into the Balkans. *Juglans* pollen has been found in Atlantic sites of the southern Volga (Frenzel 1960, p. 391), but not in the Ukraine or central Europe, whence it was probably spread or carried by man. A small-nutted variety was cultivated in Switzerland from the Neolithic onward (Firbas 1949, pp. 271–72).

The second major nut tree is the chestnut (*Castanea sativa*), which attains heights of over one hundred feet, massive girths, and life spans of over one thousand years. Within the USSR, chestnut pollen, although produced in abundance and easily identified, has been found only in the southern and western Caucasus; maxima were reached during the Boreal, when the chestnut may actually have been dominant. The pollen counts for the Atlantic drop phenomenally, with percentages rarely exceeding 5 percent (Nejshtadt 1957, p. 318). Simultaneously, however, *Castanea sativa* spread gradually into the Circum-Mediterranean. Both the Caucasian recession during the Atlantic, and the southern distribution at all times, make it likely that only some PIE speakers were aware of the chestnut, and that only some southern dialects had a name for it. The Greek word, κάστανος, "chestnut," which spread into other languages, was probably a loan (Frisk 1954, 1: 799).

Let us sum up. The possibility cannot be excluded that either or both the nut terms (**knw-* and **ar-*) were used for nut and nut tree in the general sense, and that particular genera were referred to by descriptive compounds, as illustrated by the contemporary English "walnut" and "chestnut." On the other hand, I think it more likely that the western **knw-* was limited to hazel, whereas the central **ar-* referred to the walnut, or to both the walnut and the chestnut. In any case, the sum total of linguistic and botanical evidence makes it certain that most of the PIE had the notion of nut and nut tree and some term for it.

11. The Elms: **Vlmo-*, **wyg-*

Like several other trees, the elm involves two reconstructed morphemes. The evidence for the name of the first of these, **Vlmo-*, may be limited to the three stocks of Western-Indo-European: Italic, Celtic, and Germanic.

Latin *ulmus* is the ancestor of several Romance *o*-forms (French *orme*, Spanish *olmo*, and so forth), and goes back to an earlier Romance **olmos*, which in turn goes back to a zero grade **lmos* (Vries 1961, p. 7), or to an *o*-grade **olmos*.

Within Germanic, Old Norse *almr* (from **olm*) denoted both elm and bow, and both denotations were combined in *elmr*, "elmwood bow" (Vries 1961, p. 7). To these Old Norse forms with initial *e-* and *o-* may be added the *i*-form of Middle High German *ilm* and the *u*-form of Old English *ulmtrēow*. Thus, four vocalisms are reflected in this one stock. (There is a flat contradiction, however, between scholars such as Kluge and Pokorny as to whether the Medieval Germanic forms with *u* were inherited from PIE or borrowed from Romance dialects, and Vanichek, at least, derived *all* the Germanic forms from Romance.)

The Celtic evidence is of two distinct kinds. On the one hand, Old Irish *lem* derives from **lemos* (Pokorny 1959, 1: 303), and this in turn comes from **lmo-*. On the other hand, Irish *lem* has also been derived from a posited **limā-*, whereas the alternate **leimā* has been posited as a source for the Middle Welsh *llwyf-en*, "elm, linden." Pokorny is among the scholars who have objected to including *llwyfen* in the elm set, because it "fällt aus den Rahmen heraus, da es auf Grund der Grundform *'leimā* wohl zu *ĕlei-*, 'biegen,' gestellt werden muss." Of course,

Welsh *llwyfen* also meant "linden," and resembles a set of cognates with that meaning, to which I will return in a later section.

Whether or not we include Middle Welsh *llwyfen*, the perfect correspondences between Classical Latin, Middle Irish, and Old Norse justify the positing of a Western-Indo-European feminine *o*-stem, **lmo*- denoting elm, and denoting or connoting bow. PIE **lmo*- has been derived from the root for "gray-yellow" (**el-*) and connected with the PIE alder term, **alyso-*, although neither of these interpretations strikes me as sufficiently motivated.

In addition to the three western stocks, the Slavic stock displays critical data calling for further analysis. Forms usually glossed as "elm" occur in Russian (*ílem, íl'ma*), Ukrainian (*ilém, lóm*), Czech (*jilem, jilm*), Polish (*ilm, ilem*), Polabian *jelm*, and so on. Most scholars such as Pedersen and Berneker appear to have agreed—without giving their reasoning—that all these forms were borrowed from Old or Middle High German. The Germanic forms do enter as constituents into an unusual number of Medieval Germanic place names stretching from Switzerland to the Baltic, and dating as far back as A.D. 800.

As against what appears to have become dogma, I would make several points. First, the relation of the vowels in the Slavic forms (*i-, e-*) to those in the Germanic ones (*i-, e-, a-, o-, u-*) is certainly inconclusive. Second, deriving the Slavic forms from PIE **Vlmo-*, does not violate an important phonological rule, although I can find no other case of PIE *l-* giving Slavic *el-* or *il-*. Third, deriving the same forms from Germanic does require us to somehow explain or "motivate" an unusual semantic process: the borrowing from numerous noncontiguous dialects of a neighboring stock into the noncontiguous dialects of a second stock of the name of a tree that has always been present to the speakers of the second; why, for example, should the speakers of Medieval Bohemian and Northern Great Russian (e.g., Novgorodian) dialects independently borrow the name for a particular species of elm—as against all other trees—from Germanic dialects as distinct as those of Saxony and Prussia?

Fourth, the antiquity of the Slavic symbol is suggested by its wide distribution through at least seven languages (albeit not including South Slavic), and also by its extraordinary frequency in Russian place names such as *Ilemno, Ilemna,* and river names such as *Ielemka* (Vasmer 1950–58, 1: 473).

Fifth, in Russian (and other Slavic languages?) *ílem* and its relatives denote not "elm", but the cold-hardy, highland "mountain elm" (*U. scabra* or *montana*), and this term contrasts with other terms such as Russian *bérest* and *karagách*, used for the common elm (*U. campestris*), and again with Russian *vjaz,* which is used for at least four other species (*U. laevis, celtidea elliptica* and *suberosa*). This taxonomy varies dialectally, but least of all with respect to *ílem = U. montana.*

My concluding opinion—which I offer as a hypothesis to the professional Slavist—is that Ukrainian *lom* and its Slavic cognates go back to a Proto-Slavic antecedent and on to PIE *Vlmo-*. In the introduction and conclusions to this monograph, I have compromised by calling *Vlmo-* a primarily or indisputably western term, and evidence of some sort of western *Sprachbund,* while at the same time linked to a probable Slavic cognate set.

The second elm name has the shape *wy̆ǵ-*, and is based on widespread correspondences in five stocks. Far to the east is the Kurdish *vīz,* "elm" (Bartholomae 1918), whereas in the west we find Low German *wīke* and English *wych* (or "witch") elm; both Iranian and Germanic indicate a long vowel.

The attestation is copious in Baltic and Slavic. The reflexes in two Baltic languages (e.g., Latvian *víksna*) derive from a Proto-Baltic *ving-snā* (Fraenkel 1962, p. 1257). The far-flung Slavic forms include Russian *vjaz,* Polish *wiaz,* and Serbocroatian *vêz,* and go back to a Proto-Slavic *vęzъ,* and ultimately to *venǵ-* or *vinǵ-*. The posited Balto-Slavic *vinǵ-* would have a short vowel. Most of the reflexes in these two stocks denote the common or European elm (*Ulmus campestris*).

Both Baltic and Slavic show a terminological link between the elm and bindings made of elm, usually of elm bast. Thus, in Russian both "elm" and "ligature, binding" are denoted by nearly identical words (*vjaz* and *vjaz'*). Old Prussian *wimino,* "elm," is etymologically connected with Latvian *vīmen,* "withy for weaving." Other Slavic and Baltic words for "elm," such as Lithuanian *gúoba* are similarly connected with verbs for "bend, weave," such as Lithuanian *gubúotis* (Jokl 1929, p. 74). Such linkage is congruous with the ethnological fact that Baltic

82

and Slavic peasants, and earlier, tribal peoples of the same area, used elm (and linden) bast for making mats and footwear and the like, a custom that may go back to PIE times.

The linkage between "elm" and "bind, weave"—to my knowledge a uniquely Balto-Slavic phenomenon—also raises the question of the direction of derivation, or at least of coloring or contamination between the two words. Of the two alternative solutions, the first—that the Balto-Slavic verbal root is primary —would yield an explanation for the distinctive nasalization of the Balto-Slavic elm word, *vinǵ-* (Vasmer 1950–58, 1: 244). But can one assume that the verbal root is primary? On the contrary, the verbal root—which is otherwise without an Indo-European etymology—may have been derived from the Balto-Slavic arboreal root, which in all probability goes back to PIE *wy̆ǵ-*. There are certainly enough parallels of a nominal root yielding a denominal verb.

Last, the Albanian *vith, vidhi* (Lambertz 1954, p. 213) may derive from **vinǵ-* or **viǵ-*. We cannot posit a borrowing from Slavic, since Albanian *dh*, as much as Slavic *z*, can come from PIE *ǵh* or *ǵ*; at the turn of the century Pedersen (1909, p. 335) asserted that "An eine Entlehnung aus dem Slavischen ist gar nicht zu denken. Zu bemerken ist der Schwund der *n* vor dem Spiranten; vor idg. *d* bleibt *n* bewahrt."

In sum, the five widely scattered stocks indicate a PIE consonant stem *wy̆ǵ-*, with a long or short nucleus, a quantitative variation which resembles that in other words of an agricultural nature, such as linen, flax (*ly̆no-*), and perhaps the northern apple word.

The linguistics of the elm words is related in fascinating ways to the paleobotanical and archaeological evidence on *Ulmus*. The areal distribution of the two names is partly complementary because the first word, **lmo-*, is primarily western, whereas *wy̆ǵ-* is pan-PIE with an eastern bias (i.e., an Iranian cognate). Reflexes of both forms occurred in Proto-Germanic and probably Proto-Slavic, suggesting that some Indo-European speakers differentiated and labeled two subdivisions of this genus. How is the linguistic subdivision correlated with botanical classes, and what are the botanical classes and their geographical distributions?

In Europe tree botanists distinguish three main kinds of elm, and numerous lesser kinds. The first of the main kinds, the mountain elm (*U. montana*, Russian *ílem*) probably grew in high country over most of Europe east as far as northern Russia (Firbas 1949, pp. 171—75); today it is absent from certain peripheries such as southern Spain, Sicily, and northern Scandinavia (Walter 1954, p. 161). Second, the European white elm (*U. laevis*, also called *effusa* and *pedunculata*), was distributed more to the east—from Greece to Finland, and on into European Russia where today it is the most frequent species. Third comes a species—better called a set of varieties—that is variously designated as the European, common, Scotch, field, or wych elm (botanically *U. glabra, foliacea,* or *campestris* and in Russian *bérest, karagách,* or *vjaz listovátyj*). During the Atlantic this common elm was probably more eastern and southern than the mountain elm, and today it flourishes all over northern Europe— the British Isles, Scandinavia, and northern Russia. Throughout European Russia are found not only the three main species just described (the mountain, white, and common), but three others: *suberosa, celtidea,* and *ellyptica*. As this paragraph implies, both scientific and folk taxonomies abound in what botanists call *nomina confusa*—synonyms, overlapping referents, and so forth.

What conclusions can be drawn from the botanical and linguistic distributions? The fact that reflexes of both elm words are found in both Germanic and Slavic languages implies that the contrast goes back through Medieval and Proto-Germanic and Slavic, when the ancestors of "wych" and *vjaz* may have denoted the common elm, whereas those of "elm" and *ílem* denoted the cold-hardy, northern mountain elm (the white elms might have been labeled by either of these terms, or by a third, now lost, or by some descriptive compound). The relatively certain binary opposition between at least two categories of elm may well carry back into late PIE, when speakers of the already differentiated Germanic and Slavic dialects, and probably speakers of the contiguous Italic and Celtic, employed yet earlier stages of the two terms to symbolize differences between the elms growing around them in the homeland area. The probability of the contrast is not greatly diminished by the difficulty of assigning the two terms to specific botanical classes. A tight correlation between "words and things" will never be demonstrated because, as already noted, the many species and transitional varieties of elm do not fall into two neatly discrete classes.

Let us conclude by turning to the botanical paleohistory of the elm. This tree was present in the Preboreal and Boreal in low percentages (1–7 per cent), when it extended as far north as Archangel. Then between Boreal and Atlantic times it increased rapidly, principally at the expense of the hazel, possibly because of the greater warmth of the climate; if, indeed, climate was the main cause, then the new, intrusive species may well have been the relatively sensitive common or "field" elm. In any case, many zones were dominated by climax forests of this tree, mixed with the linden (*Tilia*), the former achieving pollen spectra of 25 to 30 per cent in central Russia (Nejshtadt 1957, p. 320); abundant pollen has been identified from the southern Volga, the Caucasus, the Ukraine, the Pripet-Desna region, and the Baltic (Frenzel 1960, p. 393; Straka 1960, p. 313).

During the late Atlantic and Subboreal the elm declined drastically, yielding to communities of oak mixed with other hardwoods. The shift has been attributed to the aridity and cold of the Subboreal, but the decisiveness of climate has never been demonstrated in this case, particularly because in some areas (such as parts of Scandinavia) the decrease in the elm did not in fact coincide with a change in temperature.

New light has been cast on the entire question by Troels-Smith (1960) in his penetrating study of the use of elm by man. For Denmark and Switzerland he has established that the elm was the preferred fodder tree and was so used during the Neolithic, and that extensive polling and harvesting of the branches, leaves, and shoots affects pollen production catastrophically, mainly because the shoots must grow seven or eight years before they can flower again. The elm was not only a fodder plant, however; like the linden, its bark could be stripped off (often seriously damaging the tree) and utilized for the bast from which to fashion clothing, rope, mats, baskets, and so forth. The linguistic links between the words for elm and linden have been discussed above. It may be concluded that the abrupt decline of elm pollen, and, to a lesser degree, of the elm itself, was probably due to man—to the Neolithic and Bronze Age Indo-European tribesmen who were establishing themselves in central and western Europe and who are thought to have emphasized animal husbandry.

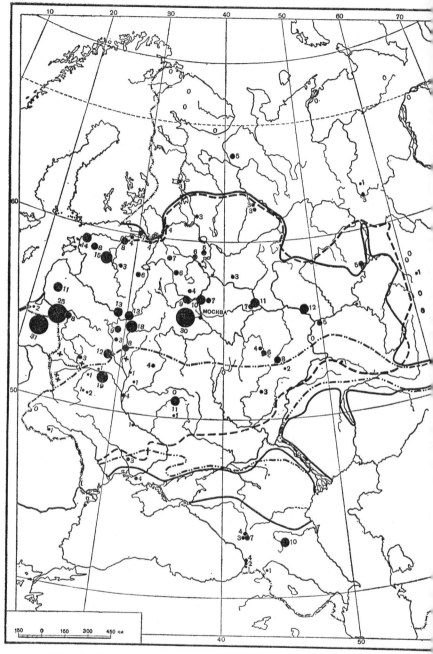

MAP 10. Distribution of *Ulmus* in the middle Holocene (from Nejshtadt)

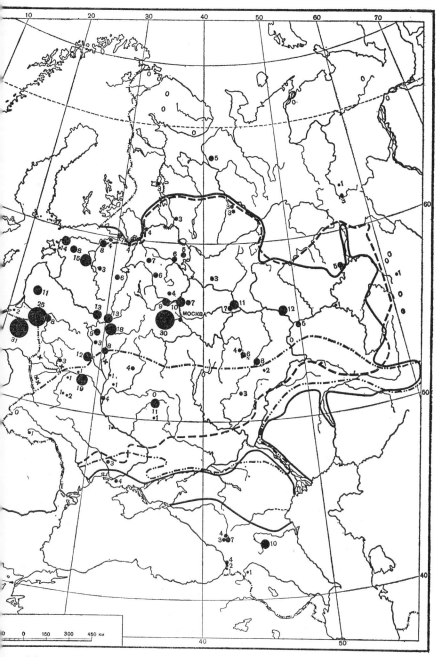

Map 11. Distribution of *Ulmus* in the late Holocene (from Nejshtadt)

12. The Linden: *lenTā-, *lēipā-, llwyfen (?)

The linden or lime trees of Europe belong to the same genus (*Tilia*) as the American bass(woods)—the latter name from Old English *bæst*, "bast." To an unusual degree, strong botanical arguments for the presence of the genus are coupled with philological arguments that are weak or not generally accepted.

The lindens are conspicuous for sticky, viscous inner bark, fiber (or "bast"), and soft and easily carved wood. They were present in the Caucasus and European Russia in the Preboreal, if not earlier, and were practically ubiquitous during the Atlantic, when their pollen reached 22 per cent of the total in the pollen spectra of some sites; they extended as far north as the Pechorin River (Nejshtadt 1957, p. 328; also Frenzel). In Germany and Poland the increase began somewhat later (toward the middle Atlantic), often after the elm and sometimes even after the oak (Firbas 1949, pp. 178–9). In both central and eastern Europe *Tilia* declined rapidly during the late Atlantic and Subboreal; although usually attributed to the advance of its competitors, the spruce, fir, and beech (Firbas 1949, p. 182), the linden retreat may also reflect depletions by man, including IE speakers. Even during the Subboreal, however, the lindens were still present in significant numbers, and have persisted ever since as a frequent and characteristic feature of European landscapes.

There are many species. Of the approximate total of twenty-five, two stand out. The most important of these is the small-leaved linden (*T. cordata*, the German *Winterlinde*) which ranges from southern England south to the northern Mediterranean, and east across southern Scandinavia and Germany, and on into central Siberia, with particularly high frequencies and even forest size stands in central and northern Russia. Although absent in the eastern Ukraine and most of the Cossak steppe (Walter 1954, p. 161), the small-leaved linden is hardy in the northern Caucasus and constitutes 52 per cent of the tree population of the Bashkir republic (both areas fall within or overlap with the putative PIE homeland).

Second in importance is the "large-leaved linden" (*T. platyphyllos*, German *Sommerlinde*), which has a more southern distribution, running through western and central Europe and on eastward into Greece and the Crimea.

In northern Russia it is *Tilia cordifolia,* which ranks after the small-leaved linden. Regionally limited species occur on the middle Dnieper (*T. tormentosa*), the Crimea, and the Caucasus. *Tilia dasystyla* ranges from southwestern Europe to the Caucasus and northern Iran.

Linden pollen carries far but—although the tree flowers when in full leaf—is not produced in large quantities. The pollen is easily and accurately identified, and is unique in that at least two species, the winter and the summer, can be accurately distinguished (with techniques developed by Z. P. Gubonina).

The linden (Russian *lípa*) is of great technological and economic importance: the soft, odiferous wood is a favorite with carvers; the blossoms have medicinal uses and yield an oil that is valued as a food; the bark fiber (Russian *lýko, lub*) was a major item in the material culture of the east European (especially east Slavic) peasants, who used it for baskets, mats, shoes of bast (*mochálo*), and so forth.

The linden had important ritual and supernatural meanings among the early Germans and other Indo-Europeans. Among the Finno-Ugric peoples, particularly those of European Russia, who are partly located between the eastern and western Indo-Europeans, the linden complex of interconnected magical and supernatural symbolism involved bast shoes, bast rope, and bast bridles for the sacrificial horses; linden spoons, linden trumpets, and linden bark and branches dripping with the blood of sacrificial animals; linden groves, categorical taboos against harming lindens, and finally, linden sacrifice trees, to which the oak and birch were distant seconds (Holmberg 1927, pp. 262, 266; Sebeok and Ingemann 1956, pp. 128, 135, 186, etc.).

With such a diverse reality in the relevant time or place, one might expect some linguistic corroboration in PIE. Such is not the case, although four groups of evidence have been advanced.

First, Greek πτελέα may have been borrowed into Latin (*tilia*), and certainly underlies Armenian *t'eli* (see Hübschmann); the Greek and Armenian forms mean "elm."

The second set of potential cognates comes from four stocks—Greek, Celtic, Baltic, and Slavic—which will be considered in turn.

Greek ἀλίφαλος was glossed as γένος δρυός by Hesychius, but Chantraine (1968, p. 62) thinks this is a false gloss for ἀλίφλοιος, which meant a kind of oak; oaks of course, differ greatly from lindens, and the formal status of this potential cognate remains most questionable.

The Celtic evidence is considerably less dubious. The scattered possible cognates include place names such as *Lĕmo-* and *Lĭmo-* (the latter from **leimo-*), and Middle Welsh *llwyfen*, which latter has recently been linked to Celtic **lemaria*, the source of Spanish *álamo*, "poplar" (Corominas 1955, p. 120). This Middle Welsh *llwyfen* means "elm" or "linden," and may come from a PIE verbal root for "to bend" (**eley-*). The more probable source or cognate, however, is the Western-Indo-European root for "elm" (**Vlmo-*) discussed above. The etymological discussions both of "elm" (**Vlmo-*) and of "linden" (e.g., Balto-Slavic **lēipā-*) tend to include Welsh *llwyfen*, which may represent a conflation of two PIE tree names (Eric Hamp, personal communication). This would be congruous with the technological and terminological-conceptual link between the linden and the elm, as was also indicated by the Greek πτελέα set above. The Welsh form remains as perhaps the most tantalizing enigma among the reflexes of the PIE arboreal terminology. The Celtic reflexes, speaking more generally, were probably influenced in their reference by the absence of the linden tree from Scotland, Ireland, and the Isle of Man.

The enigmatic Celtic forms and Greek ἀλίφαλος may also be connected with the standard Baltic words for linden: Lithuanian *lìepa*, and Latvian *liẽpa*. This strong Baltic set leads back to a Proto-Baltic **leipā-*. Cuny (1916, p. 199) argued that the correspondences between Baltic and Greek were "perfect," since, among other things, a prothetic vowel often appears before *l* in the former stock. But Fraenkel (1962, p. 366), with the advantage of more recent scholarship, asserts flatly that the Greek and Welsh have "nichts mit *lìepa* zu tun."

The Baltic forms are cognate with Common Slavic *lípa*, "linden," which has reflexes in eleven of the daughter languages, including Ukrainian *lýpa* and Serbocroatian *lȉpa*, both meaning "linden," and Polabian *leipó*, "linden bast" (Berneker 1908–13, 1: 723). The Slavic and the Baltic forms come from a Proto-Balto-Slavic **lēipā-* that in turn may be derived by a secondary vṛddhi formation from a nominal **leipo-*, or a verbal **leip-*, "to smear with fat, stick on, adhere to," which itself, by a primary vrddhi formation, derives from the well-established PIE **lyp-*, "sticky, slippery, to smear," and the like; the latter is also reflected in Sanskrit *limpáti*, Lithuanian *limpù-*, Greek λίπα, Russian *lípkij*, and so forth. Because its sticky bark was important technologically, the PIE may have called the linden "the sticky one," or even the "sticky elm" (compare the American English "slippery elm"), after which the qualifying adjective survived as the tree name, often in distorted form. There exists a historically known case involving the linden of a shift from a modifier-tree form to the modifier alone used for the tree. Old English *bæst trēow* shifted to Modern English "basswood tree," colloquial American English "bass"—which has not become standard, probably because it conflicts with the name of a type of fish in more or less the same dialects. The linden, or basswood, belongs with the hornbeam, or ironwood, as a tree which tends to acquire its name from its salient property.

Summing up the foregoing section, the second set of potential linden cognates includes a most improbable Greek ἀλίφαλος, the enigmatic Welsh *llwyfen*, and a strong Balto-Slavic **lēipā-*.

Let us turn to the third set of potential cognates. A Proto-Germanic antecedent would seem to underlie the set of forms meaning "linden" that includes Old High German *linta*, Icelandic *lind*, and probably English "lime" (with the *m* as a result of dissimilation). Since linden wood is typically preferred for carving, this set has been linked to a second one for "flexible," as in Old Saxon *līthi* and Modern English "lithe," and for "mild, soft," as in Old High German *lindi*, and Modern German *lind, lindern*; Danish *lind* means both "flexible" and "soft." Both Germanic sets, in turn, have been linked to Latin *lentus*, which means "pliant, slow, *but also* sticky, clammy"— all typical linden properties (Marchant and Charles 1955, p. 315). The Germanic and Italic forms for the linden and its essential properties have been tied to a Slavic set that includes Great Russian *lútъ*, "lindenbast," *lutókha*, "a stripped young linden," and *lutóje*, "a young linden ready to be stripped," and other cognates in Ukrainian, White Russian, Polish, and possibly Czech, and an Old Russian *lutovjanyj*, "cut from wood" (see Preobrazhensky; Vasmer; Fraenkel); these denotations

91

focus on linden in an interesting way, but the absence of *n* remains unexplained.

The third stock in the series, Lithuanian, yields *lentà*, "board," specifically of linden wood (following a source cited in Preobrazhensky); *leñtas*, "quiet, peaceful," although sometimes cited, comes through Polish from Latin *lentus*, according to Fraenkel. Last but not least, Albanian *l'ëndë*, "wood, material," has been derived from an earlier *lentā* or *lendā*, (e.g. Mann 1941, p. 20); the surviving *n* indicates a PIE *d*. The Baltic and Slavic forms may be related in some way to Greek ἐλάτη, discussed above under "cedar-juniper," or even to the Finno-Ugric *lud*, "sacred grove" (Holmberg 1927, pp. 143, 146), just as the Slavic and Germanic forms show some affinity to Welsh *llwyfen*.

Let us sum up this third set of cognates. They come from a total of five stocks, some of them noncontiguous. All have an initial *l*-, and all but Slavic a nasal *n* followed by an apical stop of some kind (*T*); Slavic shows only *t*; within the whole set the evidence for and against voicing of the stop is about equally strong. The correspondences for the root vocalism are impressive, since Latin and Lithuanian (and Albanian?) short *e* and Germanic *i* are regular reflexes of PIE short *e* (Meillet 1937, p. 100). I would posit a PIE morpheme with the shape *lenTā-*, the denotation of *Tilia* (primarily *cordata*), and generally signifying linden qualities. Most of the cognates are cited in any first-rate etymological dictionary such as Vasmer and Kluge, and Pokorny has *lenta* (1959, p. 677).

13. *The Ash:* *os-

Apparent cognates in eight stocks, or nine, if we count Illyrian, go back to a PIE *os-*, which denoted some combination of types of ash trees.

Of the eight stocks, three show reflexes with *n*-extensions. The botanist's *ornus* (i.e., *Fraxinus ornus*) today denotes the "flowering ash," but the "mountain ash" was denoted earlier, in Classical Latin, by this same word, which in turn probably descended from *os-en-os* (with syncope of the vowel following the regular rhotization). The second set of reflexes includes Old Irish *huinnius*, and Middle Welsh *onn-en*, both "ash," which come from Proto-Celtic *onnā*, which in turn derives from *osna*, ac-

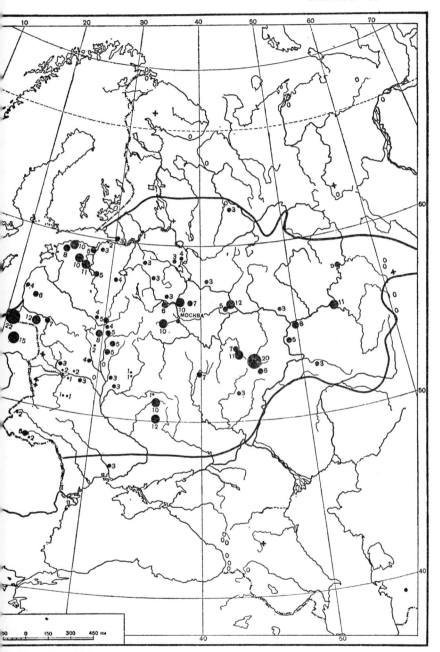

MAP 12. Distribution of *Tilia cordata* in the middle Holocene (from Nejshtadt).

93

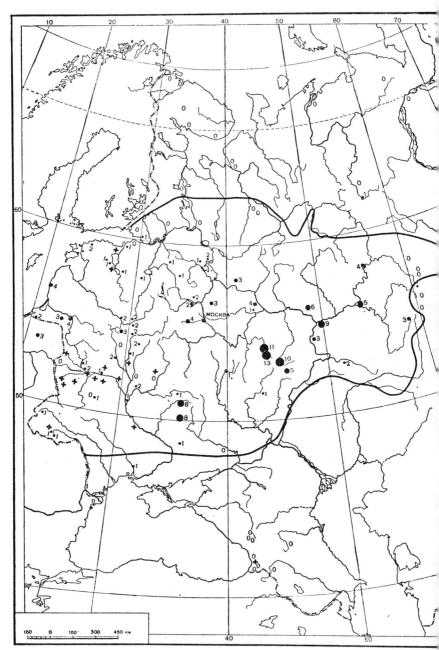

MAP 13. Distribution of *Tilia cordata* in the late Holocene (from Nejshtadt

cording to Pokorny (1959, 1: 782). With the Celtic is also cited the Ligurian *Oskela*, "Ashwood," but this is just a place name, transliterated from Greek. The Slavic cognates include Russian *jásen'*, Polish *jasień*, and Serbocroatian *jȁsen*; the forms reflect the Slavic prothesis of *j* before a front, unrounded vowel, and in this respect are paralleled by the Old Sorbian *jelъkha* as against the Czech *olsha*, both meaning "alder." The Slavic forms for "ash" all go back to a Proto-Slavic *ōs-en-*.

The reflexes in four other stocks share what has been called a *k*-extension: Albanian *ah* (from *ask-*, *osk-*), Armenian *hačʻi* (Hübschmann 1897, p. 464), Proto-Germanic *askiz* (Kluge 1963, p. 174), as in Old Norse *askr*, and Old English *æsc*, and finally, the Greek protoform, *oskes*. The Baltic reflexes for the ash, including Lithuanian *úosis* and Old Prussian *woasis*, go back to *ōsis*, which we may presume to be relatively close to the aboriginal PIE.

The Illyrian place names *Osi* and *Osones* may also contain a cognate (the word for ash also is relatively productive in the formation of place names in modern languages). Some linguists would regard the formal variation in the ash reflexes, particularly the *k*-extensions, as a "shining example" (*Paradebeispiel*) of dialectal differentiation (Solta 1960, p. 313), whereas to others the formal variation and the athematic root suggest a non-Indo-European provenience. The several Finnic forms such as Cheremis *oshko*, "ash," may have been borrowed from Indo-European, specifically Baltic, but the direction of borrowing may also have been from early Finno-Ugric into Indo-European.

As for meaning, the common or European ash (*Fraxinus excelsa*) is denoted by the Armenian, Germanic, Slavic, and Baltic forms, and by at least one of the Celtic reflexes (Welsh *onn-en*).

The denotations of the Greek and Albanian reflexes indicate parallel histories. The early Greek form *oskes* yielded Homeric ὀξυ-όεις, and ultimately the Classical ὀξύα, ὀξύη, with the meaning of the latter shifted to "a kind of beech, a spear-shaft made from its wood" (Liddel and Scott 1963, p. 491). Albanian *ah* also denotes "beech," and stems from an earlier *osk-* or *ask-*, according to Meyer (1891, p. 4; the word is not in Tagliavini's dictionary). These parallel shifts from an earlier "ash" to a later "beech" are congruous with the shift in the same two contiguous stocks of the reflexes of PIE *bhaǵos from "beech" to "oak."

Homeric Greek ὀξυ-όεις meant "made from beechwood," but also "sharp, pointed, epithet of spears" (Frisk 1965, p. 400). As just noted above, the Classical ὀξύα meant both "beech" and "beechwood spear shaft." (By the same patterning, yet another, formally unconnected word, μελία, meant both "spear" and "ash" [Cunliffe 1963, p. 261].) The parallel patterns for polysemy in the Homeric and Classical ὀξυ-forms, constitute an additional, semantic reason for regarding them as valid cognates of the PIE "ash" set—as against ἀλέρωίς, "white poplar," which is unlikely anyway on phonological grounds.[18] The Classical term for spear, ὀξύα, and the Homeric epithet for a sharp spear, ὀξυ-όεις, are presumably related either etymologically or folk etymologically to the common and standard adjective for sharp—ὀξύς (as in the name of the ash species, *Fraxinus oxycarpa*).

In addition to Homeric Greek, the other older evidence from Indo-European languages strongly attests a semantic hookup between ash and spear. In some Germanic languages the same word (e.g., Old Norse *askr*) denoted both the tree and the weapon. Latin *ornus* denoted both spear and mountain ash (which somewhat increases the chances that the denotation of the ancestral *osenos* originally included the common ash, used for spears). Finally, Latin *fraxinus* (coming, after a semantic shift, from the PIE birch term) denoted both the common ash and lance or javelin, as in Ovid (*Metamorphoses* 5. 143):

> Nam Clytii per utrumque grauui librata lacerto fraxinus acta femur.

> For through both thighs of Clytius went the ashen spear, Hurled by his mighty arm.

The ash cognates illustrate well the relation between the name of a tree and of the products manufactured from its wood; Moszyński was probably right that the widespread distribution and durability through time of the words for ash "were all surely motivated by the tree's extraordinary value in primitive

---

[18] About ἀχερωίς Frisk (1954, 1: 199) says: (since it) "in erster Linie als eine Ableitung auf -ίς zu beurteilen ist, kann das Element -ωίς (aus *-osis?) schwerlich direkt mit lit. *úosis* und anderen Baltisch-Slavischen Wörtern für 'Esche' verglichen werden." Chantraine (1968, p. 150) agrees that the relation to *úosis* lacks verisimilitude, although 'αχέρω- may be related to the river 'Αχέρων.

(and not only primitive) crafts ... spears ... bows" (1957, p. 27).

As for the botanical evidence, most authorities (e.g., Firbas 1949, pp. 182–84) assert that the pollen is difficult to identify and that species cannot yet be distinguished. Lemmon and Firbas disagree about the exact amounts of pollen produced by the ash, but the yield is certainly small, and decomposes rapidly. In addition to this natural paucity, the very low counts of pollen even after the advent of the tree may reflect the activities of man. As demonstrated by Troels-Smith's remarkable paper, the ash since early times has been second only to the elm as a valued fodder crop in central Europe, from Scandinavia to Switzerland. After its young shoots have been harvested, the ash cannot flower for two to four years, which of course seriously reduces the pollen evidence. The tree is sensitive to frost and cold, and hence did not appear in the general area until the "hazel time" of the early Atlantic, or even until the middle Atlantic.

A somewhat more special problem is the relation of the common ash to the so-called mountain ash. The European mountain ash or Rowan tree (*Sorbus aucuparia*) is attested far more widely in the pollen than is the ash proper, as Frenzel and others have shown; remarkably cold-resistant, it appears to have diffused shortly after the glaciers, if not actually during the glaciers (Firbas 1949, pp. 188–99), and today extends north of the tree line in Scandinavia. The mountain ash is a member of the rose family in the taxonomy of contemporary botanists, but is called "ash" in so many folk taxonomies such as those of English and German because it does resemble the "true" ashes of the *Fraxinus* genus in leaf pattern, hardness of wood, and other conspicuous traits. I think it quite possible that the PIE speakers labeled both trees by the single term, **os-*, plus appropriate differentiating modifiers; the descendents of **os-* then came to be limited to the common ash in seven stocks, and to the mountain ash in the *ornus* of Classical Latin, where, as already stated, the common ash is named with a reflex of the PIE birch term (*Fraxinus*, from *bherVǵos*).

The common ash and the mountain ash may have been grouped together on the basis of a *tertium comparationis*—the flowering ash, which displays many properties typical of both trees. In fact, in some languages such as German the same term

(*Bergesche*) may in some dialects be used for either the flowering ash or the mountain ash, or it may be used in a way that indicates that some native speakers (including the authors of some Modern German dictionaries) confuse the referent. In Classical Latin, *ornus* denoted the mountain ash, as already stated but was selected by nineteenth-century botanists to designate the flowering ash (*Fraxinus ornus*), whereas at the same time the mountain ash was botanically designated by yet another term: *Sorbus aucuparia*. All this taxonomic shuffling implies that the trees are perceived as similar.

Today the common ash enjoys a wide distribution—from Ireland through western and central Europe (from southern Scandinavia all through mainland Italy), and eastward well into northern Middle Russia, northern Turkey, and the Caucasus. The tree is generally a minority member of hardwood communities, but stands and forests of ash also occur. The flowering ash is found in the north Mediterranean area from the Catalan coast through Italy and the Balkans to western Turkey. Yet another species, the *Fraxinus oxycarpa*, has about the same spread except that it includes all of Spain and most of western North Africa and, in the east, all of Turkey, northern Iraq, the Caucasus, and the Cossak and Kalmyk steppe from the southern Don to the Caspian Sea (Walter 1954, p. 161); the prominence of *oxycarpa* in part of the PIE homeland opens the possibility that this species, and neither *excelsa* nor *ornus* nor *Sorbus*, was the original referent of PIE *os-.

On the basis of the combined philological and botanical evidence, I would conclude as follows: (1) one or more species of the botanical ash were originally denoted by the PIE *os- (with long or short vowel alternates, and considerable dialectal variation in the consonantal extensions); (2) the reflexes of *os- shifted their denotation in three stocks: Latin (to mountain ash), and Albanian and (post-) Homeric Greek (to beech); (3) ashwood was used for spears, and PIE *os- probably denoted or connoted spear (one cannot reconstruct which kind of meaning the PIE was); (4) *os- probably denoted the common ash, but may have referred to some combination of the common, flowering, mountain, and oxycarpal ashes. I would conclude with Kluge (1963, p. 174) that, "Die Esche ist ein Charakterbaum der Urheimat gewesen."

14. *The Hornbeam: *grōbh-*

The hornbeam, like the cornel cherry, is so little known to American linguists that a brief characterization is in order. Although it is often stumpy, it can grow to sixty or seventy feet, and produces valuable harvests of nuts every two years. The leaves are sharply serrated and beechlike, and the bark, when young, is gray with pale striping. Above all, this tree (genus *Carpinus*) is marked by heavy, hard, elastic wood that is difficult to work but is ideal for tools, weapons, and armor; the American hornbeam or "blue beech" or "ironwood" (*C. carolina*) was used for "Old Ironsides." Because of the wood there is often confusion or identification with the species of an entirely different genus (*Euonymus europea*), variously labeled as the spindle-, skewer-, witch-, or hardwood.

The hornbeam has many species and is found in most of Europe, although there is a definite concentration in the central, southeastern, and eastern areas (particularly in the Carpathians). The tree is absent from some peripheries—Spain, Ireland, and Norway—and is not hardy in northern Russia, and east of a line somewhat east of the middle and northern Dnieper. Only the common hornbeam or so-called white beech (*Carpinus betulus*) is found in Germay (*Weiss-*, *Hain-*, or *Hagebuche*), and this is also the dominant species in the USSR, with extensive growths and even climax forests in the Ukraine (in an area north of the Sea of Azov, and west of the Donets), where it is outnumbered only by the pine and the oak. The tree abounds in both Cis- and Transcaucasia, extending north into the steppe, and growing at an altitude of over two thousand feet; the Caucasian species include the common hornbeam, the eastern hornbeam (*C. orientalis*), the Caucasian hornbeam (*C. caucasica*), and *Carpinus schuschaensis*. Today the greatest concentrations are in the USSR.

The hornbeam yields medium amounts of pollen, which keeps well and permits the expert to distinguish between the eastern and the common species; it is resistant to cold but, like the beech, very sensitive to summer droughts and surface dryness. During the Boreal the tree was practically absent from European Russia (except for the southern Bug area), but in the Caucasus all four species mentioned above had probably attained their

99

present distributions (Nejshtadt 1957, p. 269). During the early Atlantic there was a rapid spread northward from the Caucasus and northward and eastward from the Carpathians, probably because of increased moisture. For the Atlantic, pollen of the hornbeam has been found all through the Caucasus, and along the southern Volga (Frenzel 1960, pp. 395, 393). By the late Holocene there may have been a continuous belt of hornbeam growth between European Russia and the Caucasus. Higher distributions and frequencies were being attained—usually 6 to 14 percent, but also going as high as 38 percent of the pollen spectra. In central and western Europe the tree multiplied during the first half of the second millennium (Kubitski 1960, p. 140), and flourished as an understory beneath the beech (Straka 1960, p. 317)—a preferred ecological niche for this moisture-loving, shade-tolerant genus.

Turning to linguistics, the hornbeam is most widely attested in Slavic, where it occurs in several languages of each stock— e.g., Ukrainian *hrab*, Serbocroatian *grȁb*, *grabar*, usually with the denotation of common hornbeam (*Carpinus betulus*). In Poland and adjacent territories the root shows up in place names such as *Grabowo*.

Three Baltic words may be cognate: Old Prussian *wosigrabis*, Lithuanian *skrúoblas*, and a Latvian place name, *Gruõbina*. The root vocalism of the latter may be the oldest, and go back to a Proto-Baltic *ō*, which would correspond to one of the possible sources of the many Slavic reflexes with *a* (from *ā* or *ō*). The Old Prussian denotation of "spindle-tree" probably represents a shift based on the hardness of the wood, whereas the Latvian place name may reflect either the northward migration of the Balts or the southern withdrawal of the hornbeam (Nejshtadt 1957, p. 273). An original Baltic **grōb-* cannot be excluded (presumably from PIE **grōbh-*).

Jokl, in four pages of interesting etymologizing (1929, pp. 71–75), proposed that the Lithuanian *skrúoblas*, "hornbeam," and *skir̃pstas*, "elm" (but also "beech" or "hornbeam" dialectally), might go back to a Proto-Baltic **skrēbr*, presumably denoting the hornbeam or similar trees. Albanian *shkozë*, "hornbeam, beech, or live oak," may consist of a root **shko-* (related to *shkror*, *shkrēbr*), plus a diminutive or collective suffix, but this is extremely speculative. The forms in both

Albanian and Baltic may go back to a dialectal form shared
when the two tribes adjoined each other somewhere in the
Ukraine west of what was then the hornbeam line.

That the Slavs, Teutons, and Balts tend to perceive the hornbeam and beech as similar is reflected taxonomically in the use
in some dialects of Slavic *grab*, "hornbeam," for the beech, and
of German *Buche* and some cognates for the hornbeam, and of
the just mentioned Lithuanian *skirpstas* for either. Both of these
trees may have been denoted by single forms in Proto-Germanic
and Proto-Balto-Slavic.

The Greek evidence is variegated. First, the Macedonian (or
Illyrian) is *grábion*, "torch, the wood of a kind of oak" (Polomé
1966, p. 61); at least one of these voiced stops might be the reflex of an antecedent aspirate. Second, Frisk (1954, p. 323)
thinks that the Greek γράβιον, "the wood of a kind of oak," came
from an Illyrian *grabu*, "hornbeam, or oak," and says that it
has survived as Modern (Arcadian) Greek γάβρος, and (Epirote)
γράβος, "a kind of oak." Third, *graboúna*, "large hornbeam,"
may be native Greek; the mere suggestion of a borrowing from
Slavic is forcefully rejected by Georgakas (1941, 361–62).
Fourth, γραφίοις has one locus in Sophocles (Ἑλένης Ἀπαίτησις
179), with a substitution of a voiceless spirant that is assumed
to be an esthetic or expressive literary embellishment, but which
might also be a clue to dialectal variation in the vernacular.

The Greek evidence suggests that a PIE form (*grābh-?*) for a
beechlike tree (the hornbeam?) had shifted to denote a kind of
oak. This hypothesis fits with the rarity of both beech and hornbeam in southern Greece, and with the numerous physical similarities (particularly the hardness) of the hornbeam and the
brown and holly oaks. The parallel shifts may be summed up
as follows:

1. PIE *grā/ōb(h)-*, "white beech" shifted to Greek *grab-*,
"type of oak."[19]
2. PIE *bhāĝo-*, "beech" shifted to Greek φᾱγός, φηγός, "oak."

Possible reflexes of a PIE term for the hornbeam have been
found in other Balkan languages; for example, the name of the
Illyrian king *Grābos*, and the Venetic place name *Grēbia* (Po-

---

[19] Meillet's assertion that "Il n'y a pas de racine qui commence et
finisse par une occlusive sonore non aspirée" (1937, pp. 173–74), would
if accepted, be an argument in favor of *grābh-* or *grōbh-*, as against *grāb-*.

korny 1959, 1:404). But none of these alleged cognates is known to have meant hornbeam, or even tree, and I perceive no need or advantage in following what appears to be the consensus that these represent an "Illyrian loan" (e.g., Porzig 1954, p. 148). If *grābh-* or *grōbh-* was borrowed into Greek, as *grab*, and many scholars feel it was, a more cogent provenience would be the South Slavic dialects where it is so ubiquitously attested.

Most fascinating is the data from the Italic peninsula. The Latin form *carpinus* could not be a cognate by the usual rules whereby *k, p* are reflexes of the PIE voiceless stops; on the other hand, the obvious phonetic similarity between *grab-* and *carp-* suggests that there may have been a restructuring of the former on the model of the verb *carpo*, "to reap, harvest" (implicitly, "to cut"); as already noted, both the hornbeam and the spindle-tree tend to be renamed after the properties and functions of their wood. Indo-Europeanists are divided as to the voicing of the stops, and have posited original verbs meaning "to cut, carve" that include both *gerebh-* (Pokorny 1959, 1:404), and *(s)qerep-* (Walde and Hofmann 1938, 1:71). According to Jokl, the Baltic forms go back to a verbal root *sqerebh-*, whereas the Slavic forms go back to *qerebh-*, both meaning "to cut, to carve." In sum, an etymological relation between the verb and the tree name seems possible, but has not yet been demonstrated.[20]

A similar formal problem involving the consonants arises in a second Italic language, early Umbrian, with *krapuvi*, *crabouie*, and *grabovius*. The latter form, which occurs in an overwhelming majority in the Iguvine Tables, is a Latinization made up to gloss the Umbrian. Its precise referent will probably never be settled because of the fact that written Umbrian did not indicate the voiced-voiceless contrast for the velars.

As for the Umbrian meaning, in the first Iguvine Table *grabovius* follows directly after the name of Iovis, Mars, and a third god called Vofionus (perhaps "God of Praise"). Elsewhere it is particularly frequent as an epithet of Iovis (Iupiter)—occurring eleven times in as many lines at one point in the text (Blumenthal 1934, p. 19). The following passage in Latin translation is

---

[20] The arboreal status of the Latin *carpinus* is enhanced by the final *-inus*, an adjectival ending found in other tree names (*sap(p)īnus*, *fraxinus*)—all cases where a modifier has come to be used substantivally for the material to which it refers.

illustrative:

> Sancte, te invoco invocationes Iovem Grabovium, sanct
> fiducia te invoco invocationes Iovem Grabovium. Iuppiter
> Grabovi, te hoc bove opimo piaculo pro arce Fissia.

Kretschmer, in an interesting, if inconclusive, article (1921), pointed out the correspondence of form between the *-ov-* of Umbrian and Slavic; both, like Latin *-inus*, are used to derive adjectives, and arboreal ones in particular. He also argued that *grabovius* was an epithet meaning "oaken, oak god," and the like. Such an Umbrian shift of denotation from hornbeam to oak would parallel the Greek history discussed above, and presumably be motivated by similar causes. On the other hand, the two stocks might contain the surviving vestiges of the original PIE meaning: not hornbeam, but oak.

The Umbrian form with its religious associations also may have been borrowed into another Italic language whose linguistic affinities are still debated. Regarding the longest extant text of the "mysterious Etruscans," Pallottino (1955, p. 273) writes: "The most remarkable section of the text . . . on the mummy wrapping . . . consists of a liturgical sequence, repeated, with small variants, at least four times, in honor of the 'gods' . . . of a god *in crapśti*, and of Neptune." (I am grateful to M. Van Loon for bringing this interesting data to my attention.)

Having reviewed the evidence on the hornbeam, one is left with a sense of enigma, and at least two alternative hypotheses. First, a PIE *grōbh-* could be said to be attested in five stocks: Slavic, Greek, Baltic, Albanian, and Italic (more or less in that order of validity)—perhaps there are even historical connections in Etruscan. This relatively permissive hypothesis leaves many unresolved and perhaps unresolvable complications. Second, the problematical character of the reflexes everywhere else contrasts with the extent and regularity of the phonological and semantic correspondences throughout Slavic; *grōb-* or *grab-* may have been limited to Proto-Slavic, from whence it passed into neighboring dialects such as Baltic and Greek. Such a Slavic priority would correlate with the physical prominence of the tree in the Carpathians, the Ukraine, and the Caucasus. Both the alternatives—the narrow Slavic and the broad "central dialectal"—leave the hornbeam decidedly marginal within the arboreal

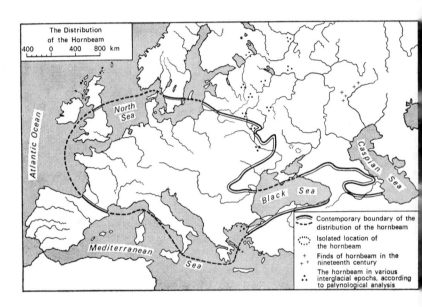

Map 14. Contemporary distribution of *Carpinus* (from the *Bol'shaja Sovetskaja*

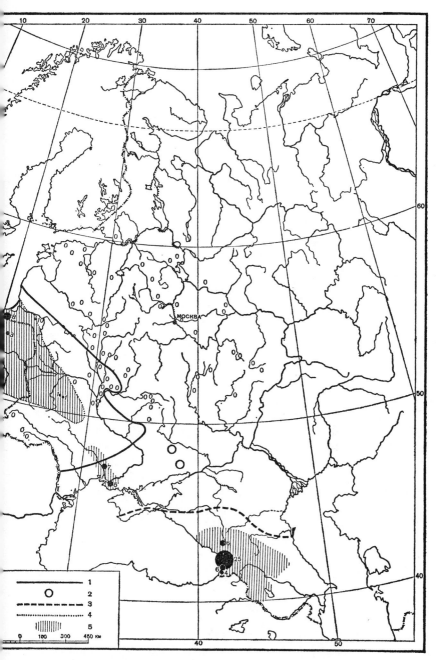

MAP 15. Distribution of *Carpinus betulus* in the first half of the middle Holocene (from Nejshtadt).

105

inventory—approximately of the order of the cherry, the apple, and the juniper-cedar.

15. *The Beech: *bhā:ǵo-*

The beech has been much debated in the past by various specialists, most memorably Schrader (1919–29) and Bartholomae (1918). The botanical "beech line," partly because it has been so often misused, has guaranteed this tree a sure place in all discussions of the PIE homeland (e.g., Thieme 1953). The phonologically perfect correspondences between some Germanic forms, and those in the classical languages, have made it a standard item in theoretical discussions of PIE phonology and morphology. Since the recent articles by Wissmann (1952), Krogmann (1955, 1957), Eilers and Mayrhofer (1962), and Lane (1967), the beech stands alone as the only tree with a name that has been subjected to a thorough and modern etymological review; I refer the reader to the totality of these articles, the dictionary entries, and the present discussion, as an illuminating instance of how much data and how many interpretations can exist about one tree name. Let us now consider in relatively cursory fashion the phonological evidence, and then take up several semantic components of *"die Buchenfrage."*

The phonological problem consists of two related facts. First, the adduced reflexes vary greatly in their root vocalism. Second, authoritative Indo-Europeanists have at various times reconstructed at least five divergent PIE vocalisms, and several, beginning with Osthoff, have included as alternates forms with a long diphthong, a long semivowel, a short semivowel, and a long vowel. Pokorny (1959, p. 108) dubbed this "ein indogermanisches Nebeneinander," and Lane is scarcely less critical.

The long diphthong form (*bhāwǵo-*) is allegedly attested by Modern Icelandic *baukr*, "mug, box," and *beyki*, "beech forest," and by Old and Middle High German *buohha*, "beech woods," and Modern English "beech," and perhaps "buck." Yet some of these are obviously contradictory in the protoform implied, and others are of dubious ancestry; Lane (1967, pp. 202–5), largely on semantic grounds, has practically invalidated both *baukr* and *beyki* (although others have cited them in support of a short diphthongal *bhǝwǵo-*).

A second alternate, with a long semivowel, *bhūǵo-*, may be

reflected in a few Slavic forms, such as Ukrainian *byźe*—but these are in a distinct minority, compared with the *buziná*-set to be discussed below. The main Germanic form is Middle High German *būchen*, "to wash or soak in hot lye or buck" (Old English *būk*, "buckets," is probably not cognate). The long semivowel may also be supported by the Thraco-Illyrian forms *mūgo* and *mūso*, attested in Strabo and Hesychius; there appear to be parallels in this "stock" for a shift from PIE *bh-* to *m-*. Finally, Lydian (or Mysian) *mūsós*, "beech," and *moesia*, "beech forest," also have been adduced, although the arguments against them are powerful. The Anatolian and Thraco-Illyrian forms have even been lumped with the Icelandic *baukr* as reflexes of a PIE *bhewaǵo-*, which again illustrates the serious formal contradictions implied by many of the beech reflexes.

The alternate with the long semivowel was for decades thought to be supported by Kurdish *būz*, but Eilers and Mayrhofer have proved that this is simply a dialectal variant of *vīz*, "elm." The same Iranian dialects show parallel shifts and alternations in the initial and medial segments; moreover, the referent of the Iranian *būz* (the old beech cognate) actually is "elm"—exactly the same as that of *vīz*. Both of the Iranian forms thus belong with Russian *vjaz* and the other Slavic "elm" cognates, and go back to one of the PIE "elm" morphemes that I have already discussed. The paring away of the Iranian cognate by Eilers and Mayrhofer, and of many Germanic cognates by George S. Lane is a good illustration of Malkiel's contention that the "uniqueness" of etymological solutions can be increased by applying varied analytical tools to eliminate false hypotheses and spurious data.

The third alternate vocalism, that with the short semivowel (*bhwǵo-*), is supported by some important Slavic forms such as Russian *bъzъ*. Many others, however, support a short *u* (Russian *boz*) or a short *u*-diphthong (Russian *buziná*); the range of variation in the attesting forms of eleven languages in this stock, surpasses that of Germanic, and includes Serbocroatian *bâs*, m., and *bäza*, f., "elder," and Czech *bez*, "elder," *bzína*, "elderberries," and *bzóvina*, "elder leaves." The Slavic forms without exception denote not beech, but elder.

Albanian *bunge* (the *ng* is phonetically ŋ), is cited by Krogmann (1956, p. 18) as meaning *Quercus esculentis*, and could stem
from an earlier **bhāg-* (Eric Hamp, personal communication).

Against the partly contradictory and partly precarious forms
discussed above, there stand a set of reflexes in several stocks
that are in essential conformity to "sound law." The *ā* of Latin
fāgus is the usual reflex of PIE **ā*, just as *f-* is of **bh-*; the Latin
word was borrowed into Irish as *faighe*, and appears in Gaulish
bāgos, and Celtic place names such as *Bāgācon*; on the other
hand, these Celtic forms may not reflect borrowing, but may go
back to an earlier Celtic **bāgo-*. The Germanic *ō* of Old High
German and Old Norse *bōk* is the regular reflex of PIE **ā*. The
Greek forms such as Doric φᾱγós and Attic φηγós also correspond point for point. Probably Germanic, and not Celtic, is the
name of the forest where the doughty Suēbi resolved to await
the onslaught of Caesar's legions (*De bello Gallico* 6.10) "Esse
siluam ibi infinitae magnitudinis, quae appellatur Bacēnis."

I have concluded that a PIE and possibly a pre-PIE form for
the beech began with a labial aspirate *bh-*.[21] The final segment
may have been a simple *g*, but the many Slavic cognates make
a palatal *ǵ* virtually certain. The strongest evidence on the root
vocalism is for a lengthened *ā*. The variously attested and
posited ablauts are diverse, it is true, but I would interpret this
as a result of the wide distribution of the cognates, and as evidence for the antiquity of the PIE term. I do not think it justi-
fies rejecting *all* the cognates which do not mean "beech" and
support a long vowel; as Meillet has pointed out, the tree names
tend to display phonological irregularities. As for gender, the
reflexes are feminine in Greek and Germanic, and Latin *fāgus* is
one of a set of feminine second declension nouns denoting plants.
The Slavic masculine forms represent a type of regular transfor-
mation from a PIE feminine *o*-stem. In sum: a PIE feminine
o-stem with the shape **bhāǵ-o-*, which Meillet, Specht, and
Wissmann thought belonged to an archaic stratum.

---

[21] It has been suggested that the forms with *f* and *b* represent consonantal simplifications from *fw-* and *bw-*, for which there are parallels.
By this scheme, **bhāǵo-* would go back to a **bhweHǵo-* (Maurits Van
Loon, personal communication). I am indebted to George S. Lane for
his discussion of the beech name.

Let us now review the semantic associations of the beech name. The Doric and Attic Greek and Albanian denotation of *Quercus esculentis*—a species of oak with edible acorns—may denote a shift motivated by the religious oak orientation of the speakers of these dialects. Either religious fear caused a taboo to be placed on the original oak term or a positive preoccupation with the oak induced a maximal terminological differentiation of its many varieties; in either case, the beech term might have shifted "to fill a gap."

A more immediate and likely *tertium comparationis*, and a basis for the Greek shift from beech to oak, would have been the edibility of both *Aesculus* acorns and beechnuts—the latter are three-sided nuts about half an inch long that occur in pairs inside a petite, four-sided burr. They may be rendered into soap and, because they are sweet and tasty, into oils for cooking, as is in fact done in France and the western Caucasian state of Dhagestan. Bender (1922, p. 30) has suggested that the Greek shift took place in two stages, first from the beech to the "native sweet chestnut that is still so characteristic of northwestern Greece," and then to the oak. "In any case, all three trees, beech, oak, and sweet chestnut, bear edible nuts, and belong to the same family, *Fagaceae*"; at some prehistoric time a Greek reflex of PIE *bhāǵo-* may have referred to some combination of two of these possible referents.

Various scholars have tried to derive *bhāǵo-* from various verbal roots. Some have suggested a relation to Greek φάγειν, "to eat," and Armenian *bucanem*, "nourishes," and the like, beech thus denoting "tree with edible fruit." The "beech" and "eat-nourish" forms have also been linked with Indic, Iranian, and Slavic: e.g., Indic *bhaga-*, "property, luck," and Slavic *bogat-*, "rich" and even *bogъ*, "god," the entire lot supposedly stemming from a distinct verbal root meaning "to apportion." I would agree with Krogmann that the short vowel, the simple velar, and the devious semantic shifts combine to militate against these forms as cognates—although the deviation is not greater than that discussed much more seriously below under *dorw-*. On the other hand, I cannot agree with the same philologist's derivation of *bhāǵos* from a PIE verbal root *bhā-*, "to shine, gleam" (allegedly paralleling the "birch-bright" equation analyzed—and rejected—in an earlier section).

Another interesting hypothetical relation of PIE *bhāgos* is to notions of writing, and the therewith connected religious ritual. The PIE tended to associate tree names with the names of artifacts into which the wood was converted. Some of the early tribes may have utilized the smooth, gray bark of the beech for inscribing symbols—perhaps connected with some early game of chance, or occult sooth saying activity. Scattered but direct statements show that the beech did have religious connotations: on the Alban Hills were sacred beech groves dedicated to Diana, and on the Esquiline Mountain stood a similar sanctuary with beeches (*arbor quae Iouis sacra habebatur*). Meillet (in Ernout and Meillet 1951) noted that the reflex had survived in Italy, although the beech prospers only at high altitudes. "Le caractère réligieux de l'arbre a pu aider à la conservation. Car ce n'est pas un accident que le mot subsiste aussi en Grèce, où l'arbre n'existe pas, et où φᾱγός a dû être appliqué à un autre arbre, ainsi E 693: "... 'ὑπ' αἰγιόχοιο Διὸς περικαλλέϊ φηγῷ."

Intimations of writing, some of it certainly sacred, are strongest in Germanic, where at least some of the early reflexes, such as Old Norse *bok*, meant "letter, little stick for writing," and probably earlier meant "Tafel aus Buchenholz zum Beschreiben" (Feist 1939, p. 102). Another source has it that the ancient runic tablets were made from slabs of beechwood. At a later stage, Old High German *buohstap* "book-staff") had come to mean "letter," as does its modern descendent. By a similar route, Old English *bōc*, "beech," led to our modern "book." Both of the Germanic meanings of "letter" and "book" passed into Slavic during the first millennium A.D.

Having reviewed the edibility of beechnuts, the religious connotations, and the use of beech bark for writing, let us now ask about the tree actually referred to in the texts. The Greek forms are variously glossed as "oak, oak of Dodona, *Quercus aigilops*," and so forth. The Latin forms—and the Irish borrowings of them—are generally translated as "beech" and identified as the botanical *Fagus*; for example, translators concur that Caesar was talking about beeches when he declared (erroneously) that there were none in England: "Est materia cuiusque generis, ut in Gallia, praeter fagum atque abietem" (*De bello Gallico* 5.12). The other cognates in Germanic, and Celtic, are often taken to denote *Fagus*. If the translators and lexicographers, particularly of Latin and Germanic, are correct, then there was substantial agreement about the referent within a large area. However, the meaning was probably not Copper Beech (*Fagus silvatica atropurpurea*, the German *Blutbuche*), but the far more widespread common beech (*Fagus silvatica Linnaeus*, the German *Rotbuche*).

As was already noted, all the Slavic reflexes of PIE *bhāǵos* shifted their referent to various kinds of elder; Ushakov, for example, mentions *Sambucus nigra* (Russian *chërnaja*), *racemosa* (Russian *krásnaja*), and *ebulus* (Russian *díkaja*). These shifts presumably were caused or at least facilitated by features which are shared by the elder and the beech, such as their smooth, light bark, their bright green, oblong leaves, and the large, round-headed, and spreading form. Coordinate with these shifts, the Slavic languages borrowed from Medieval Germanic their forms for the beech tree, as reflected today in Russian and White Russian *buk*. As for the Baltic words such as Lithuanian *bū̃kas* or *bùkas*, Mayrhofer and Senn think they are eighteenth-century loans from learned Latin *sambucus*, with loss of the unstressed initial syllable, whereas Fraenkel and others (including myself) are of the opinion that they were borrowed from Slavic, probably White Russian or Polish. But the important point is that, *whether or not they come from Latin or from Slavic*, the Lithuanian forms today *do* mean *either* beech, *or* elder (Fraenkel 1962, p. 63; the Lithuanian Academy Dictionary of 1941, p. 930, cites only the common beech). Lithuanian thus provides a sort of taxonomic missing link and demonstrates beyond cavil that Indo-European speakers in these regions can and do treat the two genera (*Fagus* and *Sambucus*) as alternate referents of a single term. (Latin *sambucus* may itself derive from PIE *bhāǵos*, although I would follow Osthoff in denying this connection). I would posit that PIE *bhāǵos*, "beech," shifted to include both "(1) beech and (2) elder" in Proto-Balto-Slavic, and then was dropped altogether in Proto-Baltic but contracted to "elder" in Proto-Slavic. This last change took place either after the Balts and Slavs moved north from their homeland or after the beech itself moved westward during the aridity and cold of the Subboreal; both processes may have been involved.

The beech does not flower annually. Its pollen is not produced copiously, does not carry far, and cannot be used to distinguish species. However, botanists concur that for prehistoric times two

111

species were primarily involved: the common or European beech, and the eastern or Caucasian beech.

The eastern beech (*Fagus orientalis*) is one of the basic arboreal components of the Caucasus, where it has been present since the Tertiary, and ascended to maxima of 20 to 40 percent in the pollen spectra during the Atlantic, when it also extended northward into the Cossak steppe. Today it constitutes about one-quarter of the Caucasian tree population, doing particularly well at altitudes of two to three thousand feet. As those persons with a penchant for "beech line" arguments have chosen to ignore, this eastern beech differs very little from the common beech.

The common beech (*Fagus silvatica* Linnaeus) is a sensitive tree, limited in its distribution by a subtle combination of surface dryness, late frosts, long winter cold, and continental summer drought. By the Preboreal it was present on the lower Bug River and in the Carpathian area, and during the late Boreal and early Atlantic expanded slightly into western Europe and eastward into what is now White Russia and western European Russia (Nejshtadt 1957, pp. 305–11). During the subsequent cold and aridity of the Subboreal in European Russia the beech held its own, according to Szafer (1935, 1954), but retreated westward according to more recent judgments. It certainly continued to flourish in the Carpathians. In western continental Europe the beech spread sensationally and formed extensive climax forests—presumably because of the increased warmth and moisture. Often this spread was together with its typical understory, the hornbeam, and with the spruce, and was at the expense of the mixed forests of oak, elm, linden, ash, and hazel. By the middle of the Subboreal (about 1500 B.C.), the common beech was dominant or at least frequent in many areas from France to the Carpathians and formed, together with the oak, the vast primeval forests of prehistoric Gaul and Germania. Today, however, it is clearly restricted to an area west of a boundary from about eastern Prussia to Odessa (see maps 16 and 17).

Taken all together, the botany of the common beech and of the eastern beech assures us that many early IE tribes, especially those adjacent to the southern Bug, the Carpathians, and the Caucasus, must have been essentially familiar with the genus—indeed, for some of them it may have been a conspicuous

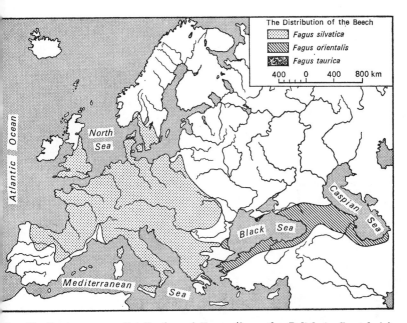

MAP 16. Contemporary distribution of *Fagus* (from the *Bol'shaja Sovetskaja*).

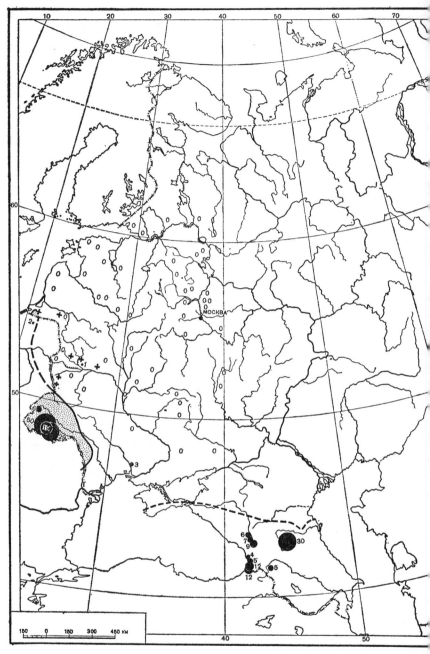

Map 17. Distribution of *Fagus silvatica* and *F. orientalis* in the late Holocene (from Nejshtadt).

114

and highly valued tree. Its westward migration and climax during the Subboreal roughly coincides with the westward movement of the Italic and Germanic speakers—precisely the two dialects which preserved *both* the presumed original denotation and the phonologically regular form. On the other hand, the millennial scarcity or absence of beeches from the east Baltic area correlates neatly with the absence of a reflex of **bhāǵos* in the Baltic languages. Such inferences and hypotheses strike me as the valid use of the "beech line."[22]

16. *The Cherry:* *K(e)r-n- (?)

The paleobotanical evidence on the cherry in the fourth millennium of Eastern Europe is virtually nil, and the linguistic evidence is largely speculative, improbable, or fragmentary. Nevertheless, three considerations—the ubiquity and economic importance of the "cherry" today, the probable presence of the wild cherry in the PIE homeland, and the complexity and semantic interest of the philological materials—have encouraged me to attempt a comprehensive hypothesis. I will review the cognates in four parts, moving from the sure correspondences in Latin and Greek to two highly controversial possibilities in Baltic and Slavic, then to an unlikely cognate in Albanian, then to a distantly related Greek form that may have been borrowed from an "Asiatic language." Perhaps this detailed reevaluation of the evidence will lead eventually to a more satisfactory theory.

The only sure cognates are found in the contiguous Latin and Greek. In the latter the "cornel cherry" was denoted by κράνον (or κράνος), with the Homeric variant κρανεία, which occurs in an unforgettable scene in the *Odyssey* (10):

> So they were penned there weeping, and before them Circe flung mast and acorns, and the fruit of the cornel tree, to eat, such things as wallowing swine are wont to feed upon.

The Greek forms are matched by Latin *cornus* or *cornum*, with

---

[22] A beech line in the United States begins to run south at the Indiana Dunes on southern Lake Michigan (although the beech does occur in eastern Wisconsin); compare, for example, the woods of western Michigan and those of Minnesota, or the splendid stands between Philadelphia and Swarthmore with the absence in Iowa.

the same denotation. One might posit an Italo-Greek dialectal **krnom*, **krnos*, but Meillet (Ernout and Meillet 1951, p. 257) decided that "on a peine à croire que *cornus* et son synonyme grec κράνος ne vienne pas d'un language méditerrannéen."

The forms in both stocks were probably linked by connotation and folk etymology to the words for horn (κέρας, *cornu*), since the wood of the "cornel cherry" is quite hard, and suitable for spears; in Latin, one variety of the cornel is called the "oak cornel" (*Cornus cerrus*; cerrus is a kind of oak). On the other hand, Boisacq (1938, p. 90) rejected any etymological connection on the grounds that the words for horn go back to a PIE palatovelar, as against the simple velar indicated by the correspondences for cornel cherry.

A serious Baltic cognate was proposed originally in Schrader's *Reallexicon*, and advanced by Niedermann (1902, p. 97). In brief, there is a Lithuanian "patron god of cherries" called *Kìrnis*, whose name supposedly goes back to an earlier **kirnis*, "cherry." Phonologically, this candidate matches the Greek and Latin forms perfectly, not only in the consonants but also in the sonantal nucleus: Greek *ra*, Latin *or*, and Lithuanian *ir* are the regular reflexes of the PIE syllabic liquid *r*. By accepting *Kìrnis* one attains a general PIE arboreal root, **krn-*, reflected in three stocks, one of them not contiguous with the other two.

A scatter of possible cognates in Baltic includes Old Prussian *kirno*, "bush," and Lithuanian *kìrna*, "the pointed end of a stem, a low bush," and the like. Two Baltic words for "swamp," Lithuanian *kìrno* and Latvian *kirba*, may be related on the grounds of the alleged preference of the cornel cherry for moist soil; possibly there was a shift from a swamp-loving bush to "swamp" after the Balts moved into an area where the cornel cherry has in fact never been active. Balticists such as Fraenkel, however, prefer to relate these forms for swamp and bush to other Baltic roots meaning "bunch, bush, root," and the like.

Indo-Europaenists, and authoritative Balticists in particular, dislike the Baltic cherry god, for reasons that are generally cogent. For example, *Kìrnis* actually was not attested until the seventeenth century, and then by Jean Lasicki, who, although writing about Lithuanian gods, did not actually know the language (Alfred Senn, personal communication). Other arguments, like those against the "hazel spear," are less conclusive.

The Cherry: *K(e)r-n-* (?)

Meillet (Ernout and Meillet 1951, p. 257) argued that "Malgré lit. *kirnis*, dieu protecteur des cerisiers, dont le nom doit venir de quelque adaptation d'un mot indigène." This would seem to illustrate the widespread practice of disposing of somehow problematical forms by calling them "loans" from a foreign language the patterns of which, even the name of which, often remain shrouded in mystery.

By a second and also highly speculative hypothesis, the potential Indo-European cherry word may be supported by a set of forms from the Slavic stock. It should be manifested at the outset that most Slavists would probably derive Russian *cherëmukha*, and its cognates, such as Slovenian *črệmha* from a root for "red, black" (*chern-*), after the color of the berries. But the same form can be carried back through time to a PIE root for "cherry, bird cherry." The *-ukha* of Russian *cherëmukha* is a diminutive suffix, possibly a recent formation, but more possibly a heritage from Common Slavic, since there are correspondences in Serbocroatian, Czech, Slovenian, Ukrainian, Polish, etc. Second, *cherëm-* must be a reflex of a prior **cherem-*, since during Middle Russian (roughly the thirteenth and fourteenth centuries), the *e*, which is automatically preceded by a soft consonant, shifted to *ë* when occurring before a hard consonant and under stress. Third, **cherem* would be a regular reflex of an earlier **cherm-*, following the "pleophonic shift" between Common Slavic and Common East Slavic of any *CerC* to *CereC*. Fourth, the *er* of Common Slavic **cherm-* goes back to a PIE *e*-grade, or at least a very early *e*-grade. Fifth, at some time in late PIE there may have been dialectal variants with two different nasals—a not unprecedented situation (compare, for example, the apparent reflexes of the kinship term for "daughter's or sister's husband"—Avestan *zāmaoya*, Latin (e.g., Plautinian) *gener*, etc. (Friedrich 1966, p. 14)—the Avestan reflex actually means "son-in-law's brother"). Eventually the form with *m* was established in Slavic, and the *n*-form elsewhere. Finally, the initial *ch-* of Slavic would be the regular reflex, following the "first palatalization," of a Balto-Slavic *k-*, and so go back to a PIE *k-* or *kʷ* (before the merging of the velars and labiovelars in pre-Balto-Slavic). The six steps just described take us back from Modern Russian *cherëmukha*, "bird cherry," to a PIE **kʷern-*, or more probably **kern-* (because of the Latin and

117

Greek cognates), meaning "bird cherry." This derivation is not found in Vasmer or any other etymological dictionary or historical grammar that I have encountered, and is presented here as a hypothesis for the professional Slavist.[23]

Albanian θαnε, meaning "cornel cherry," may represent a very early borrowing from a Greek or Thraco-Phrygian dialect. Or it may descend internally from an earlier *Kern-*, with an initial velar stop that we leave unspecified. Or finally, we may take it back to an ancestral *k̑ern-*, on the basis of an unsure rule that derives the voiceless spirant from a palatovelar *k̑*, which of course contradicts the simple dorsovelar that is indicated by Latin and Greek (G. Meyer 1891: 88).

Let us turn to the last bit of evidence. English "cherry," Spanish *cerezo*, and so forth, all go back by borrowing to Latin *cerasus*, which goes back to Greek κέρασος, still meaning "cherry," which could go back to a PIE *ker-*. According to the authoritative Frisk (1954, 2: 7), the relation of this κέρασος to κράνος "bleibt often," but regarding the former he says, "Da der veredelte Süsskirschbaum aus dem Pontos gebiet stammt (daher κερασοῦς Stadt am Pontos, 'die Kirschenreiche'), ist gewiss der Name kleinasiatisch. Herkunft sonst unbekannt." Meillet also mentions "an Asiatic language". However, the Asiatic language may have been the Indo-European Thraco-Phrygian; the *-assas-* suffix is characteristic of the contiguous, and likewise Indo-European, Luwian language of Anatolia.

---

[23] Some additional points are as follows. In Baltic and Slavic there is a large family of similar forms denoting "handle" (Russian *cherenók*) or shrub, or bush; Miklosich tried in his etymological dictionary to link these to Baltic *kirnas*, but Berneker (1908–13, 1: 146) thought "sicherlich mit Unrecht." In the second place, Moszyński has pointed out that the Slavic *chermъkha*, "bird cherry," may be compared with the Baltic sorb or service tree, *jarzebina*. The bird cherry emits a strong and unpleasant odor when in bloom (hence Old Prussian *smorde*, "stink [tree]"), and the sorb smells "completely unbearable" during its blossoming season (Ukrainian *smerdák*, "stinker"). These Proto-Slavic and Proto-Baltic names for the bird cherry and sorb tree are formally and semantically similar to yet another very old Indo-European name, that of the strong-smelling, acrid-tasting wild garlic (*Allium ursinum*): Proto-Slavic *chermъsha*, "wild garlic," Greek κρέμυον, "species of onion," and Sanskrit *kramukah*, "betel pepper." Georgiev (1958) has recently derived Proto-Slavic *čeršja* and Greek κέρασος from *k^weros-*, "black-dark" (1958: 25–26; reported in Hamp 1964, p. 298).

Let us draw together these etymological components. Greek and Latin descend from a two-stock dialectal **krnom*. Linked to this may be the Baltic cherry god, *Kìrnis*, and all three may go back to a PIE *krn-*, with a zero grade attested by the most solid cognates, and perfect agreement on the simple character of the initial velar. The Albanian word for cherry may go back to a PIE *k̑ern-*, and Slavic forms for cherry and bird cherry may go back to *k͑ʷern-* or *k̑ern-*; clearly there is contradiction regarding the initial segments of the five stocks. Finally, all these forms may be historically or genetically related to the Greek or Thraco-Phrygian *ker-*, also "cherry." In sum, a number of morphs in half a dozen stocks are identical or close in meaning, and partly correspond in form. They may go back to a pre-PIE morpheme, with the shape *K(e)rn-*, and referring to several "cherries," to the botanical nature of which we now turn.

Involved are two genera: the "cherries" (genus *Prunus*), and the "dogwoods" (genus *Cornus*). Leaving aside the "American dogwood," the two relevant species of *Cornus* are the European or red dogwood, and the so-called cornel cherry. The cornel cherry is labeled as "manly, vigorous" in the botanical nomenclature (*Cornus mas*), partly because it attains the greatest height—twenty to thirty meters. The cornel cherry is found extensively in wild form in central and southern Europe, the southwestern USSR, the Crimea, and the Caucasus (the Russian name is *kizíl*). Its berries, red, succulent, and sweet-sour, may be prepared in a number of ways or eaten plain. Pollen is rare for the Atlantic period, but has been reported for the southern Volga (Frenzel 1960, p. 392).

Let us turn to the second genus, *Prunus*, of which at least four species are relevant. The first is the bird cherry (*P. padus*), which attains heights of seventy feet but normally grows to only twenty-five or thirty. The bird cherry is hardy on rocky mountain slopes, but prefers moist valleys. It may have come in shortly after the pine, but the pollen is spread by insects and consequently does not show up in the records. That the black and shiny berries were gathered by man is indicated by the evidence from early Mesolithic sites. Today there are seven subspecies in the USSR alone, some of which extend to the northern tree line, and others—be it noted—occur throughout the Baltic area (Firbas 1949, p. 187).

Of the remaining species, the cherry proper may have entered the regions north of the Alps during the Atlantic, although this is largely conjecture; it grows to forty feet, prefers warm, sunny situations, and often coexists with the oak. A second species, the sour cherry, normally reaches thirty feet and, being highly cold-resistant, extends almost to the Arctic Circle. Finally, from Moldavia to the Crimea and the western Caucasus and beyond there flourishes yet another species, *Prunus mahaleb*. At least some of the four species of "cherry" may have formed part of the PIE environment during the Atlantic. There probably was a PIE name for trees of this type.[24]

The linguistic and botanical evidence has been reviewed, bringing us to two cultural factors. The first concerns folk taxonomy. Contemporary Indo-European languages show that the cornel cherry—because of its edible red berries, and possibly because of its height, is often classified with the cherries rather than the dogwoods. It is reasonable to assume that a PIE term originally comprised both the cherries and the cornel cherry, and then underwent a semantic split, contracting to the latter denotation in Greek and Latin, and to the former in Albanian, Baltic, Slavic, and Thraco-Phrygian.

The second factor is that the names for cherry, apple, and other fruits and fruit trees are especially subject to distortion, as is demonstrated by known histories. Very often the name of a fruit (tree) that has long been cultivated will be replaced by a more prestigious label, possibly together with a new cultigen from a higher culture. For example, the pear was cultivated in Switzerland before the Romans, but the German *Birne* represents a borrowing from Romance in the eighth and ninth centuries (Moszyński 1957). By the same token we may expect that genetically related names for the cherry were often borrowed in early times in the zones where the Albanians, Balts, Slavs, Greeks, and Thraco-Phrygians came into contact in the marketplaces and during ritual exchange. The probability of such bilingual interference may be connected with the irregularity of the correspondences (i.e., in the initial velar stop). The

[24] I shall not review or attempt to disentangle here the confusion and cross-referencing of names for the cherry in both natural languages and the nomenclature of the botanists of various regions.

same generalizations about fruit names presumably apply to the apple names (*ăbVl-, *maHlo-), discussed above.

17. The Yews: *eywo-, *tVk̂so-

Eight stocks contain potential cognates of the first yew term that correspond in form—sometimes very closely. A great divergence in meaning, on the other hand, reduces the validity of this arboreal morpheme, and raises perhaps unsolvable questions about the PIE perception and classification of trees.

The first three stocks are Latin, Greek, and Armenian. In Latin, "grape, bunch of grapes," and "laurel berry," were denoted by ūua, which may go back to *oywa- (just as ūnus, "one," and Greek oἴνη, go back to a PIE oy-diphthong). Others have tried to take Latin ūua, Slavic jagoda, and so forth, back to a different PIE root.

Armenian oigi or aigi (genitive aigvoy) meant "grapevine," and has been traced back to *oywā- or *oyyā- by Lidén (1905–6, p. 500), but neither Hübschmann nor Solta mentions it.

To these very problematical Latin and Greek forms have been joined the Greek words denoting "service tree" or "bird cherry," both of which, like the grapevine, have dark, edible berries. Greek ὄα, oἴη would go back to *oywa- or *oywā.

Thus in a chain of southern stocks an ancestral form *oywa- may have meant grape(vine), or certain berry bushes.

All the possible cognates in Baltic also denote low trees with berries: Lithuanian ievà, "black alder," Latvian iêva, "bird cherry," and Old Prussian iuwis (īwis), "yew" (Fraenkel 1962, p. 183). In Slavic, Czech jiva denotes "yew," but Kluge claims that this reflects the influence of the German speech community. The great majority of the Slavic forms denote "willow" (e.g., Serbocroation iva), which may bespeak an ancient shift by speakers living in eastern zones, from which the yew has withdrawn; fossil remains indicate that the yew was more widely distributed in prehistoric times. Both Vasmer and Fraenkel think that in Baltic and Slavic the red wood—especially the red heartwood— may have provided an adequate *tertium comparationis* for grouping trees as diverse as the ones just cited, or for shifting from one denotation to another. This seems unlikely.

In only two stocks do the reflexes denote nothing but the yew. Half a dozen Germanic languages have cognate forms such as

German *Eibe*, Old English *īw*, and Old High German *īwa* and *īha*. The Celtic cognates include Breton *ivin*, Gaulish *ivo-*, Middle Welsh *yw-en*, and Old Irish *ēó*, *ì* (from **iwo-*, according to Pedersen). Within both these stocks, some languages indicate a shift from yew to the hypertypical yew product, the bow (both Old Norse *ýr* and Old Irish *ibhar* can mean either the tree or the weapon).

On the precarious assumption that the above forms can be treated as a set, the phonological congruities are impressive. Slavic *i*, Old High German long *ī*, Lithuanian *ie*, and possibly Irish *e(y)*, all point to a PIE short diphthong, *ey*. The same four stocks indicate that this was followed by a *w*-sonant. The other vocalic correspondences are contradictory, however: the Slavic is ambiguous, the Irish and German indicate *o*, and the Lithuanian *a* reflects a PIE *a*, according to Mikkola, Meillet (1937, p. 100), and others. The reflexes are feminine in all stocks but Armenian, which lacks grammatical gender. I would tentatively posit a PIE *o*-stem, **eywo-*, and follow Meillet in assigning it feminine gender. Though lacking Indo-Iranian cognates, the *form* is attested widely enough—from Old Irish to Armenian—to be attributed to the period of PIE unity, *if* one's only criteria were phonological.

Let us address ourselves to the semantic questions. The first possibility is that the referents in the later stages of the seven daughter stocks reflect diverse contractions from what was originally a cover term for any red-wooded, berry-yielding plant. But these two dimensions seem inadequate for grouping such disparate phenomena—which range from vine to bush to tree. Also, the willow, denoted by most Slavic forms, lacks berries. A second possibility is that the members of this set derive from a PIE root for "colored, red" (**ei-*; Sanskrit *ei-to-*, "colored"; Pokorny 1959, 1: 297). A third possibility is that *PIE *eywo-* originally denoted one clear-cut class, most probably the yew, which is the only referent in Celtic and Germanic, and the referent of at least one language in Baltic and Slavic (Old Prussian and Czech). From this it shifted to willow, bird cherry, and so forth, on the basis of shared properties.

As for its botany, the yew corresponds to the genus *Taxus*, which includes bushy varieties, and trees fifty feet or more in height and of fabulous longevity (up to over three thousand

years). Because of the perishability of the pollen, the prehistory
of the yew remains practically unknown, although an educated
guess is that it entered the German area during the middle
Atlantic (Firbas 1949, p. 270). By the first millennium B.C. and
for many subsequent centuries, what is now France and Germany was notable for the abundance of yew, whose frequency
impressed Caesar; writing of Catuvolcus's suicide by yew-leaf
poison, he spoke of the "taxo, cuius magna in Gallia Germania-
que copia est" (*De bello Gallico* 6.31). The wood of the "English
yew" (*Taxus baccata*) was exploited for bows by the early Celts
and Teutons, and it was mainly because of such extensive exploitation that most of the European stands were eventually de-
pleted or destroyed during the Middle Ages; today many have
come to think of the yew as an exclusively ornamental or arti-
fically propagated shrub or tree. Almost in the same way as the
beech, the yew is not hardy east of a line from the Åland Islands
to the mouth of the Danube, but does grow in parts of the
Balkans (including Greece) and in northern Anatolia, and the
northern Caucasus, never in pure stands, but together with the
spruce, the beech, and so forth. Today its wood is exported from
the Caucasus to many parts of Europe.

This leads us to the evidence in an eighth stock: Hittite. A
Hittite form *eyan* appears preceded by the Sumerian logographi-
cal determinative used before trees and fruits (and an odd assort-
ment of other objects). *Eyan* is found in legal texts such as the
following (Pritchard 1955, p. 191):

> 50. The people who live in [three towns] and the priests in
> every town (shall be) exempt. But their associates shall
> render the services. The house of a man who stops in Arinna
> 11 months, and he at whose gate an *eyan* tree is erected
> (shall be free).

And in the texts of rituals, such as those employed to get the
help of protective demons (Pritchard 1955, p. 348):

> Tarpatassis! Accept this *eyan* tree from me and set me free!
> Let not (evil) sickness get me! Stand by the side of my
> wife, my children, and my children's children.

> Just as the *eyan* tree is everlasting (*cultiviert, angebaut,
> grünend*) and does not shed its leaves, so let the king and

queen thrive, and let their words be everlasting [Ehelolf 1938, column 4, lines 17–21].

On the basis of such texts the Hittitologist, J. Friedrich, stated what is now the established definition as "as evergreen tree that was planted or set as a post before a house as a sign of tax exemption (*Lastenfreiheit*)." *Eyan* was a cultivated evergreen, and a symbol in legal and religious ritual.

Assuming that Hittite *eyan* meant "yew," how are its form and meaning concatenated with other Hittite and Indo-European evidence? First, as already indicated, the yew and grape are physically similar in important ways; within Hittite, a phonetically unrelated form, *maḫluš*, meaning "grapevine," also occurs in comparisons with royal persons, as follows:

> Just as the ᴳᴵˢ *geštin* sends out shoots downwards and the grapevine upwards, so let the king and queen send out roots and (grape)vines. [*maḫluš* is listed under *maḫlaš* in J. Friedrich].

In other words, within Hittite the yew and the grape shared certain ritual and formulaic connotations.

Hittite *eyan* is close in form and meaning to IE **eywo-*, "yew." Outside the Anatolian area, and particularly among Germanic peoples, the yew (*íwa*, *Eibe*, etc.) also figured in legal symbolism, such as the judge's staff, and in ceremonies involving the supernatural—the yew was planted in graveyards and used for protection against witchcraft. One alleged reflex of PIE **eywo-* was Latin *ūua*, "grape," which, like the yew in Germanic and Hittite, connotes sacred ritual (e.g., libations of various kinds). And as has already been discussed, in both Italic and Germanic the apple had certain ritualistic connotations. To complete the circle, a single Hittite term may have denoted either the grape(vine) or the apple(tree). The various similarities, parallels and associations can be summed up in a paradigm (chart 3).

I would conclude that the Hittite *eyan* denoted not "tree" but "yew," and specifically the brilliantly dark green "English yew" (*Taxus baccata*), which, as already noted, is hardy in the northern Caucasus. Hittite *eyan* goes back to an early Proto-

Linguistic Group	Denotation	Connotation	Form
1. a. Hittite	evergreen tree	legal sign, formula ref. royalty	eyan
b. Germanic	yew	legal symbolism, graves, witch-craft, etc.	*īwa
2. Latin	grape	sacred and legal ritual	ūua
3. Northern IE	apple	ritual associations	ăbVl-
4. Hittite	apple (tree) or grape (vine)	legal ritual, formula ref. royalty	maḫlas

*The bracket diagram to the right groups: yew (eyan, *īwa) and ūua under *eywo-; apple (ăbVl-) and maḫlas under apple; "yew"+"*eywo-" labeled "legal and ritual symbolism"; apple labeled "fruit"; overall "legal and ritual symbolism fruit".*

CHART 3. Ritual associations

Indo-European morpheme with the shape *eywo-, denoting *Taxus baccata*, and figuring in formulas and ritual life.[25]

The Second Yew Word

The second word for the yew is attested unambiguously in only two stocks. The name in all stages of Latin was *taxus* (f.); Meillet actually has an occurrence where Latin *taxus* is identified with a reflex of the first yew name: taxus arbor quam uulgus iuum uocat.

Latin *taxus* was matched by the Proto-Slavic (m.) *tisō-, as reflected in Serbocroatian *tȉs,* "yew, larch," and Russian *tis,* "English yew"; the reflexes in nine other Slavic languages also denote this species of the tree, except for Old Russian, where Sreznevsky's glosses are "cedar, fir" (1958, 3: 959).

The noncontiguous Slavic and Italic forms correspond regularly in their consonants, since PIE *ḱs* normally evolves into Slavic *s* (as also in *loso-* from *laḱso-,* "salmon"). I would posit an *o*-stem, *tV́ḱso-, and leave the gender and root vocalism as open questions. Specht thought that the indeterminate vocalism

---

[25] For help with the data I am indebted to Hans Güterbock and Maurits Van Loon. Among several parallels for the -*yw*- sequence might be cited PIE *ayw-, "age, eternity," as in Homeric *aieí,* "ever," Gothic *aiw,* "ever," *aiws,* "age, eternity." Someone has suggested a connection between these meanings and the evergreenness or fabulous longevity of the yew.

125

and the so-called s-extension indicated great antiquity, but this is questionable. The second yew name is so well attested in two noncontiguous stocks that one is obligated to carefully scrutinize and not lightly reject other potential cognates.

The Iranian evidence is somewhat more problematical. There are several Scythian place names such as *Taksakis* and *Toksaris*. More convincing is the Iranian form for "bow," **taxša*, with a Medieval Persian reflex that has been preserved felicitously in Firdausi:

> Those are slaves before my horse (*RaXš*)
> Their heart broken by my sword and bow (*taXš*)

Hoffmann said of the supposedly "Scythian" form, "dieses **taXša*- kann mit lat. *taxus* f. Eibe (vgl. spätai. *takṣaka*- ein Baumname) identisch sein." Benveniste, with the benefit of his extraordinary control of Iranian, said, "il n'est impossible non plus qu'il soit en iranien le correspondant de lat. *taxus*." In fact, the history of other tree names, such as the ash, shows that a PIE form may show up in a daughter language as meaning the original tree, or a product for which its wood is typically used, or both. And Iranian **taxša*- corresponds well phonologically; in addition to the agreement of the initial stop with Latin and Slavic, and the agreement of *a* with Latin *a*, the cluster *xš* follows the rule whereby PIE *s* goes to *š* in Iranian after *k*, *r*, *y*, *w*, and *k* goes to *x* before *š*, as when the PIE future **-sya-* appears in the Gâtha form *vaxšyā*, "I will speak" with *x* from an antecedent *k* "I will speak" (Meillet 1937, p. 96). On the other hand, Benveniste, in the same guarded sentence just quoted, attaches a condition: "si l'on peut y comparer le mot tardif *takṣaka-* (lex.)," which he describes as the name of "un arbre à vrai dire indéterminé" (1937, p. 41), and which Mayrhofer characterizes as a "philological abstraction." Both Mayrhofer and Vasmer assert that Firdausi's *taXš* and its cognates are derived as agentive nouns from the verb for "to shoot" (*takti*). In sum, despite the regularity of the phonological and semantic correspondence, Iranian **taxša*- is seriously questioned by various scholars.

The possibly cognate forms in Greek were long accepted in certain quarters, but widely denied in others: for example, Chantraine (1933, p. 378) described Greek τόξον as "doubtlessly borrowed" (without explaining why); Liddell and Scott (1961, p. 1805) simply refer to the bow as "an oriental weapon"; and Meillet, in Ernout and Meillet, says of *taxus*, "sans corre-spondant clair." The entire problem was rendered acute by Benveniste (1937, pp. 37–41) who argued that Greek τόξον was a Scythian loan, on the grounds that the Homeric and post-Homeric Greeks did not know how to use the bow and had, as it were, forgotten the weapon. I shall try to render Benveniste's position untenable by a scrutiny of the Homeric texts, by certain facts of prehistory and history, and by one theoretical considera-tion.

Turning to Homer, Greek τόξον occurs about twenty-five times with the meaning of bow—about a dozen times each in the singular and plural—twice in the plural with the meaning of arrows and of archery equipment, and finally, in several deriva-tions such as τοξάζομαι, "I shoot" (with a bow) (Cunliffe 1963, p. 387). Second, the Homeric τόξον does not appear to have de-noted or connoted the yew or any other tree; on the contrary, it contrasts both with a specific word for the yew σμῖλαξ, which lacks an Indo-European etymology, and also with a poetic form for the bow βιός that goes back to a PIE form for the bowstring that is reflected in Vedic *jiyā́*, Lithuanian *gija*, and so forth. Third, it is true that all but one of the Iliadic bow references are to the Trojans—as in the famous scenes involving Pandarus and Paris, and that the sole Danaian chief described as "well-skilled in archery" (2.718) is actually from the relatively peripheral and northern region of Thessaly. On the other hand, the bow figures in the mythical and heroic past as diagnostic of "the mightiest of men" (*Iliad* 9.559), and does emerge as a primeval symbol of masculinity at the climax of the tale of Odysseus—who was no Trojan. All in all, the texts indicate that τόξον meant bow and never yew, and that the Homeric heroes rarely used the bow.[26]

[26] Benveniste is correct that the bow is saliently associated with Apollo, but the question of the latter's "oriental provenience" is moot. Grégoire, Goossens, and Mathieu (1949) have discussed the following tightly-knit paradigm:

Homeric Greek	*Vedic Sanskrit*
A.1. Apollo-sun-god, archer, strong, virile, curer, dis-ease-sender, and *the rat god*	B.1. Rudra-Indra—sun-god, archer, strong and virile, curer, his *vehicle the mole*

Let us turn now to the prehistory and history, both the basic, general facts, and the specific results of recent research. First, the bow and arrow have been known and used throughout most of Europe since the Mesolithic. Second, archery was a favored sport and hunting form among many early Indo-European aristocracies—notably the Hittites, the Vedic Aryans, the Old Persians, and the Mycenaean Greeks. Bows are depicted in two hunting scenes on Mycenaean monuments, on a gold ring from the Shaft Graves, and on one Lion-hunt dagger blade (Lorimer 1950, pp. 276–305). Projectile points believed to be arrowheads have been found in the palace of Pylos (Vermeule 1904, p. 166). A Linear B tablet from the same place lists personnel, including the following tradesman: *to-ko-so-wo-ko* (= *toxoworgoi* = "bow-makers"); in short, *tokso-* is attested as "bow." The same palace contained the charred remains of two wooden boxes in which were found arrowheads and carbonized arrow shafts; the sealing *pa-ta-ja* assuredly meant "arrow." Mycenaen *pataja* (*paltaia*) is probably related to the later *paltón* of Aristophanes' time, meaning "anything brandished or thrown, dart, javelin" (Liddell and Scott 1963, p. 515). Elsewhere the arrow ideogram is followed by high numbers (for these various points see Ventris and Chadwick 1959, pp. 356, 361, 404). It is true that archaeological evidence for the bow is virtually absent for the twelfth to eighth centuries, but our evidence is largely from graves rather than town sites (where one would expect the bow if indeed it was a less prestigious weapon), and bows are well attested for Crete for these same centuries (Snodgrass 1964, pp. 142, 144).[27]

This brings us to the Scythians. The Scythians in the Cis-Caspian steppes, like the pre-Roman Irish in their insular seclusion, appear to have retained many aboriginal PIE patterns of

Homeric Greek	*Vedic Sanskrit*
A.2. Asklepios—son of Apollo, benevolent curer, his *vehicle the mole*	B.2. Ganapati—son of Rudra-Indra, benevolent curer, his *vehicle the rat*

On the basis of these remarkably detailed parallelisms, I would posit for PIE times an Apollo-Rudra figure—sun-god, archer, curer, and so forth. Particularly interesting is the crisscrossing of vehicles between Greek and Sanskrit.

[27] I am indebted to Nancy Spencer for several valuable points regarding the Greek evidence.

warfare. Archery was a quintessential skill of the Scythian aris-
tocracy, as it was later of the Iranian Parthians and Sogdians.
But the Scythians did not move from the eastern marches into
the Don Cossak steppe and the southern Ukraine until about
800–700 B.C.—well after a late date for the composition of the
Iliad, or even the existence of the Homeric Greeks; in other
words, the Homeric Greeks could not have borrowed some
tókson-like form from the Scythians, because they were not yet
in contact. During and after the eighth century the Greeks
hired as archers an ever increasing number of Scythians, who
continued to adhere to the archaic bow long after their western
employers had shifted to other weapons. But—and this is my
theoretical objection—can we assume that the physical disuse
or infrequency of an artifact as elementary as the bow and
arrow will necessarily lead to a loss of the corresponding term,
especially when the artifact is being wielded by one's foes and
mercenaries with lethal effect, and when the term is embedded
in the oral traditions of one's language?

One may conclude that in pre- or Proto-Greek the reflex of
PIE **tVḱso-* still denoted "yew"—probably the English yew,
best suited for bows, but that well before the Mycenaean period
this shifted to the typical yew-wood weapon, the bow. About the
same time, a borrowed word for the yew was combined with a
"popular" suffix to produce σμῖλαξ, "yew" (Chantraine 1933, p.
378). The subsequent Mycenaean *to-ko-so-* and Homeric τόξον
denoted the bow, which was then replaced by other weapons.

One subsidiary problem must be mentioned. An originally
Greek word for arrow poison appears as a Latin borrowing,
toxicum, and may be related etymologically to the adjective for
yew, *taxicus*; several Latin authors such as Virgil mention yew
foliage as poisonous to cattle, and Caesar, as already noted, describes yew-leaf poisons being used for man. Was there a genetic
connection in Proto-Greek between a word for (arrow) poison,
and the poisonous yew tree? If so, the arboreal meaning of
Greek τόξον would be significantly reinforced.

18. The Oaks
Botany

The oak looms relatively prominent in the paleobotanical
landscape, despite various gaps in the evidence. On the one

hand, oak pollen does not carry far, is produced in relatively small quantities, and cannot be used to distinguish species from each other. On the other hand, certain ecological criteria, the wide distribution of pollen sites, and a dose of botanist's intuition have led to the consensus that the brown or English oak (*Quercus robur*) came in not long after the glaciers, following which it remained a minority species for some five millennia. The winter oak entered much later. The oaks were first outnumbered by the elms and lindens, but by the middle Atlantic they abounded in the Ciscaucasus, and probably extended far north into the Cossak steppe; percentages of 20 to 30 percent had been reached in various parts of the Ukraine (Nejshtadt 1957, p. 302). Oaks flourished three hundred miles north of their present line. During these same centuries the English oak, often intermingled with the winter oak, became frequent or dominant in western Europe; percentages of over 50 had been attained in southwestern Germany by the middle Atlantic (Firbas 1949, p. 169). Mixed oak communities and climax forests of oak became typical. *Quercus* was the focal genus during the great hardwood efflorescence of the middle and late Atlantic. During the Subboreal the oak yielded somewhat to the fir and beech. Oaks were widely exploited by man; in one Lausitz site, 53 percent of the wood used in construction was oak (Firbas 1949, p. 169). Then, as today, the calories, sugar, and albumin of the acorns were important for pigs and game.

The contemporary distribution of oak species is relevant, partly because the paleobotanists' decisions have to some extent been based upon it. Today in western Europe there are two main kinds of oak: the winter oak (*Quercus sessiliflora*— the German *Stein-* or *Wintereiche*), and the brown or English oak (*Quercus robur*—the German *Stiel-* or *Sommereiche*); the latter species has alternate names in the botanical nomenclature: *Quercus robur*, because of its strength, and *Quercus pedunculata*, after the two small projections at the base of each leaf. The "line" of the English oak begins in Leningrad, runs to Vyatka in northern European Russia, on eastward to the Ural Mountains, then back to Saratov on the Volga, and along the ecological boundary between the forest-steppe zone and the steppe, and so on to southeast Europe and the Balkans. West of this zigzag line the oak is hardy.

130

In the separate Caucasus area there occur today at least seven species of oak: (1) the English oak; (2) the Caucasian oak (*Q. iberica*), which is practically ubiquitous, either in pure stands or mixed with the hornbeam; (3) the Armenian oak, both of the Cis- and Transcaucasus; (4) the chestnut oak of the eastern Caucasus; (5) the sessile oak (*Quercus petraea*), also in the east; (6) *Quercus macranthera*, in the southern and eastern highland zones; and (7) the Turkey oak (*Q. cerris*). (There is great variation in the application of the term *Q. esculentis*, which is used, among other things, for *Q. robur* and *Q. cerris*.) Soviet authorities list other, less important species. The subgeneric differentiation of the oak in the contemporary and, it is believed, prehistoric Caucasus suggests that this is the area where the genus has flourished the longest, and where it has longest impinged on man and his economy. Let us now turn to the concatenated philological evidence.

The Acorn: *g^welH-*

The morph for "acorn" is widely reflected and almost universally accepted by Indo-Europeanists; it is characteristically cited in discussions of the voiced labiovelar g^w. The reflexes include Armenian *kałin* and Greek *βάλανος*. Latin *glans* meant "acorn, object in the form of an acorn" (including the glans of the penis). Rarely cited but critical would appear to be the Sanskrit *gulaḥ*, "acorn, penis, clitoris," which may in turn be related to a set of words for "ball, pill," and the like (Mayrhofer 1956, 1: 341). The Slavic forms include Old Slavic *zhelǫdъ* and Serbocroatian *žêlûd*. The Baltic cognates include Lithuanian *gìlė* and Latvian *zīle*. Albanian *lëndë* (*l'ëndë*) has been adduced and does mean "acorn," but raises grave phonological difficulties; since *lëndë* is also glossed as "wood, material," I have included it above as one of the possible cognates of the "linden" term, *lenTā-*. Except for the Baltic forms, all these diverse reflexes show dental extensions—specifically *n* in Greek and Armenian, and *d* in Slavic. Various ancestral forms have been posited, including *g^welH-*, to which I subscribe.

The semantics of the acorn name implies much about the cultural significance of the oak. I would agree with Hirt (1892) that "acorns were very important in ancient times for the raising of pigs, but often also served man as a foodstuff." To this evaluation can now be added the results of a brilliant exercise in diachronic semantics in which the great Benveniste demonstrated that the two Indo-European words for pig (*sū* and *porko-*) probably denoted the adult (sow) as against the porker or piglet. "Both [words], carrying back to the proto-language [*la langue commune*], prove that—contrary to the general opinion— the raising of pigs had been in use since the period of the common speech community [*la communauté*], well before its establishment in Europe, and therefore already under the material conditions of sedentary life" (1949, p. 89).[28] The validity of this philologically deduced hog-raising may be connected with the phonological validity of the acorn morph; both imply the early importance of the oak.

In addition to its economic role, the acorn was part of the oak complex of the pan-Celtic Druids, who ate acorns "in order to acquire powers of divination" (Hubert 1932, p. 280). The attitudes underlying these arcane rituals may be connected in some Humboldtian fashion with a grammatical fact that has been independently noted by Meillet: "This name of a fruit is of animate gender, in contrast with the names of other edible fruits."

The First Oak Name: *ayg-

The first oak name is reflected in only three stocks, and was probably limited to a few early dialects. First, Proto-Germanic *aiks* (Kluge 1963, p. 154) is widely reflected, as in Old Norse *eik*, "oak, ship (poetic)", and Old English *āk*, "oak, ship out of oakwood"; in these cases, the primary denotation is "oak," and the secondary, metonymical extension is "ship" (see de Vries 1961, p. 96); for ship construction the oak is obviously ideal, particularly the harder species of it. Forms such as *eik* and *āk* have also been linked to a second set in the Germanic languages such as Old Norse *akarn*, "fruit of a wild tree," and Old English *æcern*, "nut, acorn, although this is not generally accepted.

The second stock with supposed cognates is Greek, notably in in κράταιγος, "white thorn tree" (*Crataegus oxyacantha*, cited

[28] "Reportés l'un et l'autre à la langue commune, ils donne la preuve que, contrairement à l'opinion générale, l'élevage du porc était en usage dès la période de communauté, bien avant l'établissement en Europe, donc déjà dans les conditions matérielles de sédentarité."

in Theophrastos, and of which Hofmann (1950, p. 158) says "wohl χρατύς hart + αἰγ-). Another possible cognate occurs in αἰγίλωψ, which denotes an oak with edible acorns, *Q. aigilops*, that is native to the eastern Mediterranean; the form consists of αἰγί- plus λώπη, "bark." (The derived Latin form, *crataegus*, has become the standard botanical taxon for a genus of thorn trees, of which the American hawthorns are species.) The same Greek root, αἰγί, may occur in two words for weapons: αἰγανέη, "spear," and αἰγίς, which Hirt (1892, p. 482) interpreted as "oak shield of the oak god"; again, the oak is obviously suited for such artifacts—although most classicists would take issue with this particular deduction. The Greek form αἴγειρος, "black poplar," has been aligned with this set.

The possibly cognate Latin *aesculus* (from **aeg-s-colo-*) presents a confusing history. In the classical language the word denoted the mountain or the evergreen oak, according to some, but an oak with edible acorns, according to others such as Meillet (Ernout and Meillet 1959, p. 13)—presumably *Q. esculentis* or *Farnetto*. Later the term came to mean "horse chestnut," and was borrowed as such into the technical vocabulary of botany (botanical *Aesculus* now also includes the American buckeye); there is no evidence of horse chestnuts in the PIE homeland.

I have concluded that a PIE **ayg-* was applied to one species of oak—primitive peoples not infrequently differentiate six or more species of this genus.[29]

*The Second Oak Name: *perkʷ-*

The second name for "oak" involves much intriguing evidence and many conflicting interpretations, and no little insight into the possible cultural implications of a tree. The following abbre-

---

[29] Among the Sierra Tarascans, for example, the number of oak species differentiated by distinct roots runs to six. In all, a total of six PIE roots have at some time been glossed as "oak": **ayg-*, **perkʷ-*, **dorw-* ("tree" or "oak" below), **bhāǵo-* ("beech" above), **grōbh-* ("hornbeam" above), and **gʷelH-* ("acorn" above); see Krogmann for the references. Thus one could construct a case for six oak terms somehow corresponding to the seven or more oak species in the Caucasus. This would be erroneous in terms of the semantic structural theory being used here—among other things, because it would leave two major tree types unnamed for the sake of an exceptionally fine differentiation of the oaks.

viated review has profited greatly from the articles by A. Meyer and by V. V. Ivanov (the latter being particularly valuable for Baltic data and for the scholarship in Baltic languages on this problem).

Let us begin with the weakest evidence. Two stocks, Iranian and Tocharian, provide no evidence. Armenian *orot*, "thunder," has nothing to recommend it beside the medial liquid, and neither Solta nor Hübschmann admits it. Only somewhat less tenuous is the Albanian Perëndija (Lambertz 1954; p. 149), or *persndi*, both meaning "god." Greek κεραυνός, has been proposed; its primary denotation was "lightning," but it was also used as the name of a god, and would reflect the heteroclitic *wer/wen* type of nominal (Benveniste 1935, p. 112). Finally, A. Meyer has argued cogently and eruditely that the island name Κέρκυρα (today's Korfu) contains the Illyrian cognate of PIE **perkʷ-*, and that the Venedic tribal name, *Quarqueni*, should be glossed as "oak men"; both the Illyrian and the Venedic forms show an Italic assimilation of initial *p-* to *kʷ-* before a following *kʷ*.

The Hittite word for "cliff," *perunaš*, from *pirу̯a-, perу̯a-*, has been cited as a cognate of this oak set (J. Friedrich 1952; p. 168), as is quite reasonable both phonologically and morphologically; *perunaš* could have been formed from *per-* plus *un-o*, paralleling Old Russian *perъnъ*. Semantically, many of the **perkʷ-* reflexes in other languages refer to mountains or rock-topped heights. As pointed out by Ivanov, in the Hittite myth of Ullikummi, the great cliff, *šal-li-iš, pi-ru-na-aš* gives birth to a lithic monster who is obliged to kill the enemy of his father. This father bears an epithet, Kunkunnuzi, which is apparently a reduplicated formation from *kу̯en-*, itself deriving from **gʷhen-*, "to strike." A similar structure of elements appears in Old Norse mythology, where *Fjǫrgyn* (whose name is a reflex of **perkʷ-*) gives birth to Thor, who is called upon to slay his father's enemies with a stone hammer.

The Indic evidence includes Vedic Parjányaḥ, "raincloud, god of storm," who impregnates the earth with rain. This Parjányaḥ was related to Punjabi *pargāi* by both Hirt and Brugmann, but the connection has since been denied by Mayrhofer (1956, 2: 221). Similarly, Wackernagel (1896, 1: 57, 117) relates the same Parjányaḥ to *pārījāta*, "paradise tree" (*Quercētum*).

More recently, Turner (1965, #9022) has connected Sanskrit *plakṣá-* and Late Sanskrit *parkaṭī*, both "sacred fig tree," to an earlier **prakṣá-*, the cognate of the European *quercus-faírguni* set. Sanskrit *parvata-*, "mountain" (from **par-ṵn-t-*) has been linked with the *parkati* just mentioned above, and with Hittite *perunaš*, "cliff." In sum, Indic appears to have cognates of the second oak name, and several major Indologists and Indo-Europeanists have adduced and interrelated several problematical Indic forms in a way that somewhat enhances the putative link between the oak and the sacred.

The "thunder god," Perunъ, was the principal deity among many Slavic tribes. There is considerable evidence from South Slavic of a Perunъ cult, connected with hills and mountains. In the west, Polabian *Peräunedan*, "Thursday," is a translation from Germanic *Donnerstag*. As late as 1156, a bishop visiting Lübeck saw "a grove in which was an oak tree enclosed by a court and a fence of stakes, and dedicated to the god of the land, Proven, of whom there was no idol present" (Gimbutas 1967; p. 741). There is some evidence of influence from Germanic on the west Slavic area, and of Scandinavian influence in the north, but Perunъ itself was surely not a borrowing from Gothic Faírhūns (Vasmer 1950–58, 2: 345), or from Illyrian, as some authors have proposed.

The strongest evidence of a Perunъ cult is among the East Slavs. Long after the Christianization of Kiev, Perunъ continued to be worshiped in north Russia, often on heights and, probably, in connection with Perun or oaks. The earlier record of the Russian Primary Chronicle reports that "[Vladimir] set up idols on the hill outside of the towered court: a wooden Perunъ, with silver head and golden lips, and a Khъrsa, and a Dazhъbog, and a Stribog" (Sreznevsky 1958, 2: 919). The various Old Russian verbal forms include not only Perun-, but Perъin-, and Pregъiin-; those with ъi are, of course, very close to Celtic Hercynia and Lithuanian Perkūnija, since all stem from an original with *-ūni*, whereas those with *gъin* are close to Indic forms such as Parjányaḥ, the god of storm and rain. These Slavic forms link eastward to Indic and westward to Celtic and Baltic, and presumably descend from a very early Indo-European formation.

Meillet, writing in 1926 (p. 171), linked Baltic Perkūnas,

Slavic Perunъ, and Vedic Parjányaḥ as evidence that "at a very early date the religious terms of the Slavs and their Aryan neighbors were almost the same." In fact, a Lithuanian god, Perkūnas, was widely worshiped in groves of sacred oaks, or in the shape of "the oak of Perkon" or "the oak of Perkunas." Perkon sites were often elevated, with prominent cliffs or stones (Ivanov 1958, pp. 108–9). Perkūnas is clearly related to Lithuanian *perkūnija*, "storm," and to Latvian *perkūns* and Old Prussian *percunis*, both meaning "thunder." There also is evidence in Baltic of an association between "sky" and "stone" (the "stone sky"), and of a cloud being perceived as a mountain or a cliff. In sum, the early Balts appear to have associated the ideas of thunder, storm, stone, hill, high god, and oak—the same concatenation in the semantic field that had been emerging from the foregoing discussion of other stocks.

Many Balticists and Slavists think that Perkūnas and Perunъ derive from a verbal root for "to strike," *per-*, (Lithuanian *pẽrti, periù*, etc.), which, of course, is cogent formally and congruous with the imagery of lightning bolts, stone hammers, and so forth. On the other hand, their polemical statements may reflect an overreaction to the paganological phantasmagorias of certain nineteenth-century German philologists. Even Jaskiewicz (1952, pp. 192–93), although adamantly rejecting the oak meanings as inventions of Simon Grunau, admits that "the earliest available text is 1261 . . . this deity is almost always mentioned as a god of thunder and lightning . . . the name Perkūnas in Old Prussian and Lettish sources does indicate the common Baltic character of the deity." Pokorny was probably right that these Baltic and Slavic forms were reshaped folk-etymologically on *per-*, *perō-*, "to strike," but go back to *perkʷ-*, "oak."

The Germanic reflexes are most diverse but, on the basis of their meaning, fall into five sets. First, some potential reflexes denote "pine" (Old English *furhwudu*, Old High German *for(a)ha*, Old Norse *fura*). Various kinds of oak are cited as glosses for Old High German *fereh-eih*, and Langobardian *fereh* (although A. Meyer says the latter meant *Aesculus*).[30] A third

[30] As with the conifers and *dorw-*, the shifts in meaning of *perkʷ-* to "pine" and "fir" may be connected with the northward movement of Germanic tribes, combined with a southward retreat of the oak in favor of the conifers—the latter fact has been well established for the Subboreal.

set is divergent enough to be rejected by some scholars, but is semantically plausible, and involves the well-documented shift from a tree name to the name of a forest or mountain where the tree predominates, and so on to "forest" or "mountain" in general, as in the Old English formations with *firgen* (*firgenholt* "mountain wood," *firgenstrēam*, "mountain stream"). This pattern of shift is illustrated by Modern German, as in *das Eich*, and in the Celtic of Julius Caesar's time, where the adjectival form *Hercynia*, from *Hercynia silua*, ended up being used for the forest in question. Similarly, Gothic *fairguni*, "mountain chain" (*Gebirge*), might go back to "oak forest," and then to "oak" (both *fairguni* and *Hercynia* contain adjectival, suffixal elements).

A fourth quite distinct subset among the Germanic reflexes of **perkʷ-*, includes members that correspond phonologically but have diverse, abstract meanings which can be accepted only by allowing two or three concatenated shifts; for example, Old English *feorh*, formally a cognate, meant not a tree but "life, soul, spirit," and the like. Similarly fascinating, and probably cognate, is the Old Norse set of *fjǫrr*, "tree, man," Fjǫrgynn, "thunder god," and *Fjǫrgyn*, "mother of Thor." Pokorny and others have admitted Gothic *fairhwus*, "world."

To generalize from this enumeration, a widespread spectrum of cognates have been advanced to support a Proto-Germanic **ferh-*, or **ferhw-*, going back to PIE **perkʷ-*. In their meanings, these potential cognates range from "pine" to "oak" to "oak forest" to "forested mountains" to "mountain (range)" to deities of oak and thunder, to abstract notions of "man, life, and the world." The proliferation strikingly resembles that to be discussed below under **dorw-*. The oak and its connotations motivated diverse extensions of meaning within the Germanic stock—as also among the Slavs—and seems to have been intimately reticulated with mythology and metaphysics.[31]

Perhaps the best known evidence for PIE **perkʷ-* is in Italic and Celtic. Latin *quercus*, "oak," shows an initial consonant shifted by assimilation; the first shift was of *p* . . . *kʷ* to *kʷ* . . . *kʷ*, then the second *kʷ* shifted to *kw*, eventually yielding *quercus*. The Celtic cognate of *quercus* is *Hercynia* in *Hercynia silua*

---

[31] A connection has been suggested between the Germanic forms and PIE **perkʷ-*, and also the PIE **porko-* set, with the oak as "pig-feeder" or the pig as "acorn-eater."

(from **Perkuniā*). *Hercynia silua* was the name for the great oak forests of the middle German Highlands (*das Deutsche Mittelgebirge*)—although the texts do not make necessary the inference that *Hercynia* referred to "oak." Several Germanic names for mountain formations were borrowed very early from Celtic, before the loss of the initial *p*- about 1800–1500 B.C., as in Old High German *Virgunnia* (Kluge 1963, p. 211). The second good Celtic cognate is *érkos* (ἔρκος), which has been transmitted in Greek sources and is glossed as "oak forest" (δρῦμός). Within Celtic, the sound shifts differed from Italic, beginning with that from *k*ʷ to *kw*, and then followed by the loss of initial *p*-, yielding **erkw-*, and eventually *Ercynia*, *Hercynia* (Watkins 1966, pp. 32–33). In short, the Celtic and Italic transformations of **perkʷ-* followed different rules and different orderings of rules. Ivanov (1958, p. 103), following Kuryłowicz (1935), has argued that the Italic labiovelar reflects the merger of earlier sounds under conditions that were lacking for the Celtic forms, *érkos* and *Hercynia*, both of which represent later developments. Last, several highly questionable Celtic cognates include Welsh *perth*, "bush, hedge," and Irish *ceirt*, "apple or fruit orchard."

Let us summarize this etymological panorama. Evidence for **perkʷ-* has been adduced from nine stocks (or eleven, if we admit Illyrian and Venedic), with particularly strong material from Baltic, Slavic, Indic, Germanic, and Italic. There seem to be several underlying forms: (1) **per-*, as in Hittite *perunaš*, (2) **per-kʷ-*, as in Lithuanian *Perkūnas*, and (3) **per-g-*, as in Vedic *Parjányaḥ*. The original root may be **per-*, followed by velar extensions and an *-ūn* suffix, or both. I would posit a middle PIE form, **perkʷ-*, with reflexes in at least four stocks: Celtic, Italic, Germanic, and Baltic. Among the many meanings and associations that have been discussed, I believe that of "oak" to be primary. The original shape and signification of this morpheme should be left as open questions, however.

This brings us to the anthropological and literary evidence. For many decades archaeologists have been unearthing statuettes in the Ukrainian area which are now dated at about the third millennium. Gimbutas identifies these statuettes as "thunder gods," and their sites as Kurgan—the archaeological culture believed to correspond to that of the PIE speech community. For at least five of the early PIE tribal divisions there is further evidence of the varied religious importance of the oak and associated concepts such as stone and lightning:

1. Among the Balts, with many sacred oak groves in the region, where oakwood fires burned to the primeval gods of thunder and to the high gods (particularly at the great religious center of Romove);

2. Among the Teutons, where sacred oakwood fires burned to *Donares eih*, the "thunder-god," and where anyone disfiguring certain living oaks was executed by fiendish tortures;

3. Among the Greeks, with their oracular oaks in the groves of Dodona, to which Odysseus is reported (falsely) to have gone "that he might hear the will of Zeus from the god's oak of lofty leafage." The Greeks prayed to the oak for rain, and oak brides of this high god were burned alive on Mount Kithairon (Cook 1940, 2: 977);

4. Among the Italics, with their perpetual oakwood fires of the Vestal Virgins and their high god, Jupiter, honored in the form of an old oak on the capital (Livy 1. 16). Of the religious status of the oak in later Latin times, Quintillian says (*Instituto oratoria* 10.1.88): "Ennium sicut sacros uetustate lucos adoremus, in quibus grandia et antiqua robora iam non tantem habent speciem, quantam religionem."

5. Among the Celts, the Druidic priests ate the acorns, worshiped in groves of oak, lighted the sacred oakwood fires by friction with oak sticks, and cultivated the mistletoe—the gold of Frazer's *Golden Bough*. The Celtic high god was personified in an oak tree. The Celtic Druids, with their vestigial oak cult, appear to have been the social structural cognates of the magi of Iran and the Brahmans of India where, because of cultural and ecological factors, the oaken aspects of religious ritual disappeared.

The five tribal divisions—Balts, Teutons, Greeks, Italics, and Celts—all strongly attest a connection between four complex symbolic clusters: tribal priests, thunder-lightning-sky, a high god or gods, and the oak tree alone or in groves. Both the wide diffusion and the emotional intensity of these ancient patterns of culture—not paralleled by those for any other tree—suggest that the oak was one of the underlying themes in PIE culture, a basic life symbol (Langer 1951, pp. 127–74), and a root of myth and of sacrament. The oak was a nexus of symbolic articulation between the semantic system of the tree names and the cultural system of religious beliefs and ritual concerning the supernatural.

The Third Oak Name:
*dorw-: "tree" (or "oak"?)

Of all the PIE tree names, *dorw- is the most solidly attested, although rivaled by *os- and *wyt-. Among the total of twelve supporting stocks, Germanic, in particular, shows dozens of cognates, with meanings that range from "tree" to "trim" to "tar." The many reflexes in the various IE languages also indicate the full play of ablaut variations in the vocalism of the root. For example, each of the following variants has two or more reflexes in two or more of the daughter stocks: (1) *derw-, as reflected in Russian *dérevo* and Middle Welsh *derw-en*; (2) *dorw-, as in Sanskrit *daru*, Greek δόρν; (3) *drw-, as in Greek Δρυ(ϝ)άs; (4) *drew-, as in Old English *trēo*; and (5) an additional *n* element is illustrated by forms from various stocks, including Albanian *drû, drûni*, "beam, piece of wood," and *dry, dryni*, "wooden peg, key to a sheepfold." At least three stocks—Greek, Celtic, and Slavic—illustrate all three vocalisms (e.g., Russian *dérevo, zdoróv, drová*). The formal variation of this richly attested, partly archaic paradigm is presumably connected with the extraordinary geographical distribution and semantic variation that will be outlined below. I have selected *dorw- as a convenient symbol for this entire cluster of forms.

The minor descendents of *dorw- fall into at least three groups. First, Latin *larix*, "larch," has been described as a loan from "an Indo-European Alpine dialect," with the initial segment reflecting the substitution of "a rustic Sabine *l*," and the meaning reflecting a displacement during or after the time when *quercus* became the word for oak. The similar shape of *larix* and *salix* may indicate some parallelism in the derivation (from *dorw-, and *soly- ?).[32] Second, an apparent reflex denoting "pine" occurs in Indic, sometimes alone, as in *dāru*, "species of pine, block, piece of wood." As the second element in a com-

---

[32] This has also been argued for the Latin *lēvir*, "husband's brother," from the PIE *daywer*. Latin shows the same replacement in *lingua/dingua, lacrima/dacruma*.

pound, it means "tree, wood," as in *dēva-dāru*, "godly tree"; the "pine' meaning is carried wholly or in part by the *pītā-* in *pītā-dāru*, "kind of pine tree." The shape of these compounds is paralelled in German *Fichtenbaum*, and the like. Last among the minor and miscellaneous problems are some Baltic derived forms with coniferous meanings, such as *dervà*, "tar," but also "log, piece of pine wood." These are greatly exceeded by the widespread reflexes in Germanic languages which indicate that the conifer-tar terminological association is very ancient in the stock. On the basis of the alleged reflexes in Italic, Indic, Baltic, and Germanic, Hirt and others have argued that the original meaning of **dorw-* and the like may have been a conifer of some kind.

This brings us to several sets of semantic correspondences. First, seven stocks have reflexes denoting products that are characteristically fashioned from wood: (1) spoons, in two stocks (e.g., Armenian *targal*); (2) troughs and the like, in four stocks (e.g., Old Irish *drochta*); and (3) bow or spear in three stocks, as in Modern Persian *darūna*, "rainbow," and Sanskrit *drŭṇam*, "bow." Since wood is hard, one could argue that this was an early connotation. In the second place, Osthoff claimed that the referent of early Indic *dāru* was a Himalayan spruce with particularly hard wood; the same form also meant bronze. Third, reflexes of **dorw-* meaning "hard, wooden," and the like, appear as the first element of compounds in several stocks; Δρυ-αχαρνῆς, for example, in the work of an unknown comedian (*Com. Adesp.* 75) has been translated as "the knotty ironwood-hard Acharnians." Last, the Greek combination, which may be translated as "neither oak nor rock" or "neither tree nor rock" appears several times in the ancient Greek literature, notably in Hector's famous speech to Achilles (*Iliad* 22. 126), where it "appears to be a quotation from an old folk-tale dealing with the origin of mankind from trees or stones" (Murray's *Iliad* 1. 462). In sum, evidence from three structural levels— lexical, morphological, and syntactic—supports the postulation of "hard, strong" and related connotations of PIE *dorw-*.

Physical hardness has psychological connotations. In no less than nine stocks reflexes of **dorw-* denote all or part of a conceptual complex that includes such qualities as "hard, hale, firm, strong, true, brave, and tough"; for example, Armenian *tram,* "firm, fixed," Welsh *drud,* "brave," Lithuanian *drútas,* "strong, stout," and Avestan *drvō,* "hale"; Latin *dūrus,* "hard" (*drūrus* belongs here, but *dūrāre* does not). Germanic, above all, shows a large set of semantically linked terms that mean: "true," as in Gothic *triggw-s;* "belief," as in Old Norse *trū,* and Old High German *trūen;* and finally, even notions of "loyalty, trust" and the connected meanings of "binding oaths," as in Gothic *triggwa,* "treaty, contract, agreement." This Germanic complex can be interpreted in three fundamentally distinct ways.

Osthoff (1901) thought *dorw-* meant "oak." In a long article entitled "Eiche und Treue" he pointed out the salience of such properties as "hardness, firmness. To the ambiguous Greek syntagma about "wood/oak and stone," mentioned above, he added others which definitely involved the oak, such as Latin *saxum aut robur,* and even German *Fels und Eiche.* From such physical qualities and lithic connotations the moral and psychological meanings followed by natural metaphors. Osthoff's position rests in part on premises about "primitive thought" moving from the concrete to the abstract, and his statement was blemished by an extraneous romanticism, with a last-page outburst devoted to lines from German folk songs about the oak, truth, steadfastness, and so forth.

Benveniste, in a contrasting and equally misguided position (1954, pp. 257–59), argued rationalistically that the notions of "hard, firm, steadfast," and so on were primary, and that from them are to be derived the secondary meaning not of oak, but of "tree." His alternative requires us to assume that the name for something as elementary in the environment and as clearly a semantic primitive as "stone, fish, or tree" is derived from the name of one of its several qualities. Should semantic inference depend on postulating a process that is typologically so exceptional?

As against Osthoff and Benveniste, a structural hypothesis has been advanced by Kuryłowicz (personal communication): the entire cluster of truth-belief-contract words are unconnected with the PIE *dorw-* constellation, and represent a purely Germanic development, since all of them are derived from a Primitive Germanic strong verb; in support, one can cite the vowel gradation, the gemmination of the consonants, and a meaning which some have felt to be "aberrant." This hypothesis, while certainly satisfying for Germanic, does not account for Old Prussian *druwi*, "belief," nor Latin *dūrus*, "hard" (either physically or physiologically), nor Greek δροόν ἰσχυρόν "firm, strong," nor the parallel between Old Icelandic *draustr*, "sureness, confidence," and the Iranian *durust*, "true." Such metaphorical extensions also are attested outside IE, as in Akkadian *kénu(m)*, "firm, true," and are in fact so widespread and "natural" that one cannot exclude them from PIE. In my opinion, the comparative method cannot yield a conclusive resolution to the romantic-concrete, rationalistic, and formalistic alternatives.

Having reviewed the secondary evidence and the secondary meanings, let us turn to what I think are the two major alternative hypotheses regarding the original denotation. The first is that **dorw-* meant "tree" or "wood." In ten out of twelve stocks at least one reflex does have this meaning, either exclusively or in part. The Germanic, Greek, and Baltic forms have already been cited. Early Slavic *drěvo* meant "tree." Tocharian AB *or* meant "wood." Avestan *draoš* meant "of the wood." Vedic *dāru* is frequent with the meaning of "wood," but also as "chariot pole, fuel, log," and so forth, while *druma* shows up as "tree" in later texts (Macdonell and Keith 1958, 1: 353, 384). Albanian *dru* is glossed as "wood, tree, post" (Tagliavini 1937, p. 109; *druvar*, "woodsman," comes from the stem **druva*, whereas *drushk*, "oak," is a later diminutive, according to Meyer (1891)). Hittite *taru* meant "wood," and almost always appears with the determinative for trees, wood, fruits, etc. (^{giš}, see J. Friedrich 1952, p. 274). Many other cognates could be cited from these and the remaining stocks to show that **dorw-* probably meant "tree" or "wood" or both ("tree-wood"), with the exact meaning determined by context. The peripheral dialects are notable in the way they support this gloss, and many of the secondary referents to tools and the like can be interpreted as naturally derived from "wood-tree." Benveniste and most Indo-Europeanists appear to agree that **dorw-* meant "tree" or "wood" or both. So much for the rule by majority— both of the semantic correspondences and of the opinions of the Indo-Europeanists.

Now let us turn to the evidence from Greek and Celtic.

The primary denotation of the *dorw-* reflex in Proto-Celtic was probably "oak," as preserved in Old Irish *derucc*, "acorn," and Old Irish *daur*, Cornish *dar*, and Middle Welsh *derwen*, all meaning "oak," as well as other cognates in the various Celtic languages. These inferences about denotation are congruous with the patterns of the Druidic cult; the Druids, or "wise men," are known to have cultivated the mistletoe and worshiped the oak as part of an oak cult with "a complete doctrine of morality and mythology." Hubert, the enthusiastic Celtologist, concludes that "Druidism belongs to the strictly Indo-European components . . . its origins go back to the most distant past of Indo-European societies'' (1932, pp. 282–83). But he avers that these Celtic patterns might also have been borrowed during a period of contact with the Dorian Greeks in central Europe.[33]

The richer evidence comes from Greek.

First, several reflexes are comparatively indirect. Δρυμά, "thicket, grove" (as on Circe's isle), is not specifically oaken, although δρύοχοι, "the stays or trestles for supporting a ship's keel under construction," might well have been so originally. In both Homer and Pindar the standard words for "tree"— δένδρον and δένδρεον—represent reduplications from some reflex of PIE *dorw-*; in other words, forms that clearly are secondary serve to denote "tree."

Let us turn to the more direct reflexes in Homer. The adjective δρυ(ϝ)ϊνος meant "oaken" or perhaps "wooden." The noun δόρυ meant "beam, wood, spear," with disambiguation by context. The main reflexes, δρῦς and δρυός, appear at least seventeen times in Homer, sometimes where the meaning certainly is "tree" and not "oak" (*Odyssey* 6. 167), or sometimes where it may simply be "timber" (*Iliad* 15. 410), albeit ship's timber (for which oak and spruce were preferred). In at least twelve places δρῦς/δρυός probably meant "oak" (Cunliffe 1963, p. 99), and the word often occurs as a symbol for something quintessentially strong and lofty ("lofty-crested"). The two words usually are glossed as "oak" by such authoritative—and indeed formidable—lexicographers and translators as Cunliffe and Murray.

---

[33] The word "Druid" itself is not connected with the *dorw-* reflexes, according to most authorities. Other Old Irish forms in this set include *dair, daro/darach, daur, daro, darai* (Eric Hamp, personal communication).

Most interesting are the *loci classici* where δρῦς is juxtaposed with other tree names. Twice in the *Iliad* it is found together with a word for pine (πεύκας; 11. 494, and 23. 328), in a way that suggests that the two taxa are to be read as coordinate, as on the same level of contrast (Conklin 1962). In two identical passages δρῦς co-occurs with the names of the poplar, ἀχερωΐς, and of "tall pine", πίτυς, once in the thirteenth book of the *Iliad* (389–93) and later in the same work, after the mortal combat between Patroclus and Sarpedon (16. 482):

> And he fell as an oak (δρῦς) falls, or a poplar, or a tall pine, that among the mountains shipwrights fell with whetted axes to be a ship's timber; even so before his horses and chariots he lay outstretched, moaning aloud and clutching the bloody dust.

This formulaic passage is not only intensely poetic, but delicately ambiguous. On the one hand, since the Greek "or . . . or" could also mean "either . . . or," an accurate translation would be "as a tree falls, either a poplar or a tall pine." On the other hand, it can be argued that δρῦς is to be read as coordinate with the words for "poplar" and "tall pine," and that the surely intended poetic impact is greater with a vivid "oak" as against the indefinite "tree" followed by a pedantic "either . . . or." And as I have already pointed out, δρῦς does mean "oak" in many other Homeric loci. On these grounds, the archaic passage from the battle scene, and the "oak" meaning of δρῦς, hark back to the pre-Homeric centuries—somewhere between the early Greek dialects and the late PIE.

The Greek *dorw-* reflexes show definite religious connections, though not as strongly as Celtic. The forms, *Dindrúme*, "Zeus grove," and Δρυ(ϝ)άς, "wood nymph," appear to be paralleled by the Latin *nymphis percernibus* (from PIE *$perk^w$-, "oak"). Greek δρῦς has been related to two words for snake, and these forms may reflect earlier religious practices. The Greek forms suggest that the early Greeks believed in oak sprites or spirits.

Let us now evaluate the relatively complex evidence from Greek and Celtic in favor of the "oak" gloss. First, the rich Greek and Celtic evidence carries well back into the "Proto-" period of each stock. Second, these two stocks share no important isoglosses, are noncontiguous, and have been so for as far back as the good evidence will take us—speculations about

Celtic-Dorian minglings on the banks of the Danube notwithstanding. By Meillet's requirement of phonologically regular correspondences between forms in at least two noncontiguous stocks, one would have to posit an "oak" meaning for PIE *dorw-. Third, the Homeric Greek and early Celtic evidence for an oak denotation is neatly and systematically concatenated with the evidence in these same stocks for an oak-Druid type of cult, which was a salient component in PIE culture, as I think I demonstrated above under *perkʷ-. Fourth, it is true that the various moral, legal, and psychological notions of "strength, firmness," and even "loyalty and truth" *could* possibly have developed from "tree-wood" ("wooden-headed," and so forth). But I think Osthoff was closer to nature and regular semantic change when he derived these meanings from "oak," in particular the species of oak which is hardest and which was dominant in the PIE homeland area—that is, the brown or English oak (*Quercus robur*). Fifth, the uniquely wide distribution and the rich formal differentiation of the reflexes may be a vestige of the important role of the oak in the lives of the PIE. Last, on more general grounds it seems probable that the primitive, arboreally oriented PIE distinguished several species of oak by distinct morphs, and that *ayg-, *perkʷ- and *dorw- served in this way. As the oak and mixed-oak forests were reduced and contracted, and as the speakers of the PIE dialects migrated into their new homelands—two simultaneous processes during the third and second millennia—the denotations of the *dorw- reflexes shifted to "wood, tree, hardness," and yet other referents; this would hold especially for the shift to "fir, tar, pinewood" and the like in the Baltic and North Germanic dialects, since the speakers are thought to have migrated into northern coniferous zones during the centuries when the oaks were receding. It is also quite possible that even in PIE times the main name for the oak—a short of *Urbaum*—was occasionally or dialectally applied to "tree" in general. Within pre-Homeric Greek δρῦς and δρυός could denote either "oak" or "tree" with disambiguation through social or literary context. By Classical Greek times the meaning had narrowed to the original PIE "tree." In more recent centuries the identical process has been documented in Germanic, where *eik* shifted from "oak" to "tree" in Icelandic—oaks being virtually absent in that country.

146

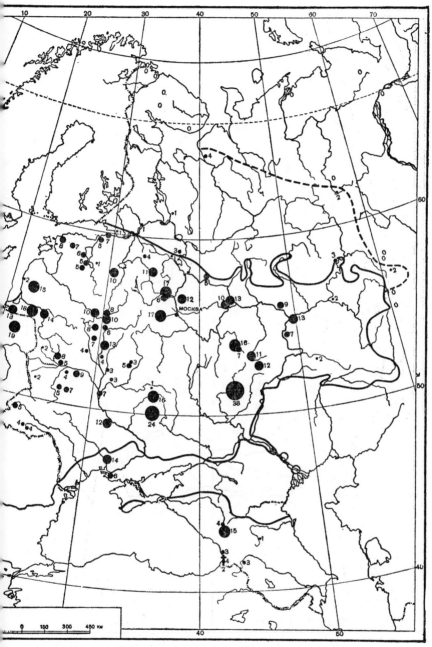

MAP 18. Distribution of *Quercus robur* and the Caucasian oaks in the middle Holocene (from Nejshtadt).

147

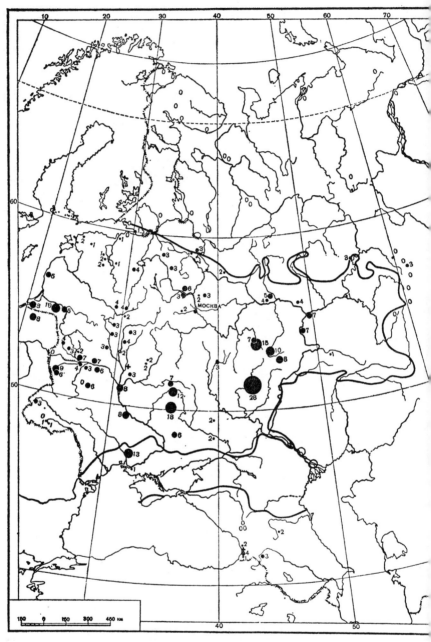

MAP 19. Distribution of *Quercus robur* and the Caucasian oaks in the late Holocene (from Nejshtadt).

148

On the basis of all these interconnected considerations I have concluded that the alternative "oak" hypothesis is as cogent as its more usually accepted rival.

19. *Miscellanica Arborea*

Having completed the relatively detailed analysis of the cases where a combination of the philological and botanical evidence supports the positing of a PIE tree, let us now briefly tabulate a score of additional cases where the linguistic evidence does not warrant positing a prototerm but may merit further study. I shall present the miscellanica in the alphabetical order of the referent in English:

1. acorn—Gothic *akran,* "acorn," Old Norse *akarn,* "fruit of wild trees, mast" (including acorns); Armenian *achern,* "to grow" (Lidén 1905–6, p. 503), or *achem*
2. alder (1)—Modern German (dialectal) *ludere/lutter,* "dwarf birch, mountain alder" (*Erle*); Greek *klēthrā, klēdra,* "sticky alder" (Frisk 1954, 1: 872)
3. alder (2)—Old Indic *varaṇa,* "tree (in general)"; Armenian *geran* (from **wer-nna*), "beam"; Albanian *verɛ* (from **werna,* "white poplar"); Celtic *werna,* as in Middle Irish *fern,* Welsh *gwern*
4. alder (3)—Armenian *lasteni,* "alder" (or elder?); Slavic, *lozá,* "branch, withy"; Lithuanian *lazda,* "hazel bush, stick, post"; Irish *lestar,* "barrel"
5. birch—Latin *betula,* "birch"; Welsh *bedwen,* Breton *bezvenu,* both "birch"; Albanian *bléteze* (meaning?)
6. cedar—Greek *κέδρος* and Lithuanian *kadagỹs,* both "cedar," but "die Ahnlichkeit beschränkt sich auf die erste Silbe" (Frisk 1954, 1: 808)
7. chestnut—Armenian *kaskeni,* "Kästenbaum" (Hübschmann); Old Norse *kask* (meaning?); Greek *κάστανος,* "chestnut" ("wohl Kleinasiatisch"; Frisk)
8. elder (1)—Armenian *geran,* "beam"; Albanian *verrɛ,* "white poplar"
9. elder (2)—Slavic *buz/boz/baz,* "elder," from *buzg,* from *busk,* from *sbuk* (Machek 1950); Gallic *skobiē,* "elder," and Dacian *seba,* "elder tree"; Hittite *shampukki,* "a caserole dish" (*ein Topfgericht*), the more limited meaning of which

149

as a cooked food made of elderberries is far from established (see J. Friedrich)

10. fig—Latin *ficus*, Greek σῦκον ~ ῖῦκον, Armenian *t'uz*, Burushaski *pfak*

11. fir—Latin *abies* and Greek ἄβιν, both "fir"; Illyrian and Scythian place names such as Abai, Abikē

12. hazel—Albanian *lethī*, *laithī*, "hazelbush"; Lithuanian *lazdá*, "hazelclump," Old Prussian *laxde*, "spearshaft"; Serbian *lijèska*, "hazelbush," Polish *laska*, "stick"

13. juniper—Latin *juniperus*; Middle Irish *aín*, "reed"; Old Norse *ēnir*, "juniper"

14. mountain ash—Latin *sorbus*; Old High German *sperboum*, "mountain ash"; Slavic *berkъ*, *Sorbus torminalis*, and various other Slavic terms denoting the *Atlas-*, *Mehl-*, *Else-*, *Maul-*, and *Sperberbaum*, and going back to an earlier **ber-/bre-*. On the other hand, Latin *sorbus* may be a cognate of the members of a distinct East Slavic set (e.g., Russian *sorobalín*, "blackberry") and a Baltic set (e.g., Lithuanian *serbentà*, "red current, black rhododendron"), although these are generally derived from a PIE root for "red." Some of these forms may go back to a PIE **sor-dho-s*, which referred to some bush or tree that bore red or black berries.

15. mulberry tree—Latin *morum*, Greek μόρον, Burushaski *biranč* (Basque *martšuka*)

16. oak (1)—Latin *ilex*, "holm oak"; the second element in Greek αἰγίλοψ, "oak with edible acorns"

17. oak (2)—Old Prussian *karige*, "mountain ash"; Proto-Germanic *karkús*, "grove, priest, idol" (Old High German *haru(gari)*, Old English *hearg*, "sacred grove, idol"); Indic, contemporary Punjabi *kars*, *karś*, *karšu*, the names for various kinds of oak (*ilex*, *dilatata*, *semicarpifolia*, mentioned in Hoops, also *hari-dru* in the Satapatha Brāhmana (13. 8.1.16) is the name of a tree, *Pinus deodora* (MacDonell and Keith 1958, 2: 499); there is also a similar Basque form that may indicate an ancient borrowing.

18. oak (3)—Indic *dhanuh*, "bow," *dhanvana*, "fruit tree"; Proto-Germanic **danwō*, with one eleventh-century gloss of "oak," but generally "pine" in Old High German (the Germanic form, with a metonymical transfer to "tannin"

Miscellanica Arborea

passed into French and eventually into some Slavic languages); Slavic *dǫbъ*, "oak" (Machek 1950, p. 153).

19. pear—Latin *pirum*, Greek ἄπιον, Burushaski *phéšo*
20. pine, cedar—Armenian *mair*, "pine, fir, cedar"; Latvian *mītra*, "boxtree"; Old Slavic *smrěchъ*, "juniper," *smřcha*, "cedar"
21. poplar—Greek ἄγνος "willow-like tree, chaste tree"; Slavic *jagnędъ*, "black poplar"
22. tamarisk—Latin tamarix, Burushaski *hərmuk*

The above forms are cited more or less as they were found in a variety of places, have not been carefully rechecked against the linguistic, philological, and botanical sources, and hence probably contain factual errors of various kinds.

4 Conclusions

Tree names are paradoxical. On the one hand, they are basic in a psychological and individual developmental sense—semantic primitives, if you will. On the other hand, tree names, because of their referents, are sensitive to ecological change or the migration of the speech community into a new region. The conclusions that follow deal first with the inventory of tree names and their apparent status as semantic primitives. Second come two sets of implicitly cultural conclusions: the more probable uses of the trees by the Proto-Indo-Europeans; and the implications of the arboreal evidence for theories of early tribal groupings and the relation of the speech communities to the natural environment.

Radical Concepts

The conjunctive approach has led to improving the definitions of the botanical referents of the PIE tree names from some relatively vague words in modern European dialects—often reflecting guesses by the urban Indo-Europeanist in his library —to relatively precise glosses such as might characterize the nomenclature and, implicitly, the perceptions of a primitive and partly forest-dwelling people. Below, using English terms as ready labels, are presented the eighteen tree units and the reconstructed PIE term or terms, and then, in botanist's Latin, the genera and the forty-one species that were probably known and discriminated by the PIE; as already explained earlier, these hypotheses about species are mainly extrapolations from relatively recent facts of distribution, diversification, and so forth. The exact reasons for positing the species and prototerms have been set forth in detail above under the etymologies, which the reader is urged to consult if he has questions. Obviously, no one early dialect had terms for all these species, since some of the latter were areally limited or in complementary ecological zones. And as is emphasized below, the tree names inferred *are not of equal status*, and fall into four groups: (1) nine very strong terms for the birch, the *wyt*-willow, the alder, the *wŷǵ*-elm, the ash, the beech, the acorn, and two oak terms, **perkʷ-* and **dorw-*; (2) a second group that is weaker or less widely accepted but still may be included in the "stronger set" (the *pwḱ-* conifer term, the *sVlyk*-willow, the aspen, the *klen*-maple, and the *tVḱso*-yew); (3) a third group of relatively weaker or areally limited terms, such as the two nut (tree) terms (**ar-*, **knw-*); (4) a final group of notably weak terms such as the juniper-cedar (**el-w-n-*) and the first oak word (**ayg-*). Let us now turn to the eighteen arboreal units.

1. The birch, early PIE **bherHǵo-*, denoting *Betulus*, probably *pendula* but possibly also *pubescens* and *humilis*.

2. The Scotch pine, early PIE **pytw-*, **pw/yK-*, denoting *Pinus sylvestris* (and perhaps, in certain areas, other species of pine, and the silver fir (*Abies alba*) and the common or European spruce (*Picea excelsa*)).

3. The junipers and cedars, possibly a late PIE **el-w-n-* denoting various species of *Juniperus* and *Cedrus*.

4. The aspens and poplars, northern or late PIE **osp-*, denoting *Populus*, mainly *tremula*, but possibly *nigra*, *alba*, and *canescens*.

5. The willows, early PIE **wyt-*, and **sVlyk-*, and perhaps **wrb-*, denoting *Salix*, probably including *alba* and *vitellina*, and probably involving some dichotomy between the osiers as against the tree willows.

6. The apples, northern **ăbVl-* and southern **maHlo-*, involving a dichotomy between wild and cultivated species or varieties of *Malum*.

7. The maples, PIE **klen-* and late PIE **akVrno-*, denoting species of *Acer*, probably including *campestris* and *platanoides*, and maybe *pseudoplatanoides*; both of the posited terms may go back to an early PIE **kL-n-*.

8. The alders, PIE **alyso-*, denoting *Alnus*, and possibly adapted to four regionally limited species: *barbata*, *incana*, *viridis*, and *glutinosa*.

9. The hazels, western **kos(V)lo-*, denoting *Corylus*, mainly *avellana*, and probably other species such as *colurna* and *maxima*.

10. The nut (tree)s, PIE **ar-* and western **knw-*, the latter

probably associated with the likewise western **kos(V)lo-*, and
used for the hazel (nut), whereas the former was presumably
used in the east for various kinds of nut (tree), including the
walnut (*Juglans regia*) and the chestnut (*Castanea sativa*).

11. The elms, PIE **wy̆ǵ-* and western (or western-cum-
Slavic) **Vlmo-*, denoting *Ulmus*, and probably involving some
subgeneric differentiation between *montana, laevis, campestris,*
and even other species; the contrasting terms in Germanic probably entailed some perceived difference between two classes
of elm.

12. The lindens, PIE **lenTā-*, **lēipā-* (both doubtful); the
genus *Tilia* was ubiquitous physically and probably important
technologically; it probably included early forms of *cordata,
platyphyllos,* and possibly *tormentosa* and *dasystyla.*

13. The ashes, PIE **os-*, denoting *Fraxinus excelsa* and
probably some combination of *F. ornus, F. oxycarpa,* and
Sorbus aucuparia.

14. The hornbeam, PIE *grōbh-*, denoting *Carpinus betulus*
and possibly *C. orientalis* and *caucasica.*

15. The beeches, PIE **bhāǵo-*, denoting *Fagus*, probably
sylvatica Linnaeus and *orientalis,* and possibly *sylvatica atropurpurea.*

16. The cherries, the speculative and problematical early
PIE **K(e)rn-* may have denoted the cornel cherry (*Cornus mas*),
the bird cherry (*Prunus padus*), and possibly other species of
Prunus (the sour, cultivated, and *mahaleb* species).

17. The yews, PIE **tV́kso-* and early PIE **eywo-* denoted
Taxus baccata.

18. The oaks, PIE **ayg-*, **dorw-*, and **perkʷ-*, denoted
Quercus in some sense, and may have been distributed among
the three main species: *petraea, sessiliflora,* and *robur;* it is
just as probable that **dorw-* originally meant "tree"; it is possible that other tree names (**gʷelH-* and **grōbh-*) were originally
applied to particular species of oak.

In the many cases above where two or more botanical species
may well have corresponded to a smaller number of proto-
terms, I would assume that the PIE speakers differentiated
the trees by compounds or modifier-modified constructions.

These conclusions depart markedly from any precedent.
Schrader, in the last century, limited the number of tree names

to three—the birch, the pine, and the willow—in part because he was arguing for a homeland on the steppe, where the natives supposedly know few trees. But Hirt, in his critique of Schrader's homeland theory, admitted only six names (1892, pp. 476–93). Meillet admits five (1937, p. 397), and, in various places, exemplifies his well-known caution by monitory notes: "the names of trees, in part ancient, are not for the most part clear: v. *fagus, quercus, fraxinus*, etc.," or (speaking of *alnus*), "the details of the word differ from one group to another, as [in the case of] the majority of the names of trees" (Ernout and Meillet 1951, 1: 41). Rigorous theoretical discussions of PIE seldom take account of more than the beech, the birch, and the oak. Against this background the present study, which argues for eighteen units, thirty names, and forty-one species, must seem unorthodox or even radical.

My painstaking review of the evidence on the PIE tree names has uncovered only three units that are probably or at least cogently connected etymologically with a verbal root. Two of the names for the willow, **wyt-* and **wrb-*, may well be connected with a root for "bend, twist," although even here the direction of derivation has not been established. A root for "slippery, sticky," and a second for "mild, soft," may be connected with PIE terms for the "linden." **Perk^w-*, or at least many reflexes in the *perk^w-* set, may derive from a root for "to strike." Otherwise, a number of possibilities have been posited at some time by some reputable scholar: (1) a root for "yellow" (*el-) may underlie the alder term; (2) the second term for "willow" (**sVlyk-*) may be etymologically connected with a second root for "yellow," or with another for "grass," or yet another for "meadow"—but all these conjectures are unlikely; (3) a root for "white" is often linked with the birch name; (4) the root for "hornbeam" may be similarly linked with a root for "to cut, carve"; (5) one of the maple terms has been linked with a root for "sharp." But all of these seven hypotheses are unpromising or untenable, and all but the "birch-light" connection have been widely rejected—with good reason. I have concluded that the great majority of PIE tree names were not deverbative nouns, but unanalyzable nominal roots, and that for their reconstruction the most relevant branches of linguistics are phonology and semantics.

155

There are other reasons for assuming that the PIE tree names were mostly unanalyzable roots. In two quite typical, contemporary, and noncontiguous Indo-European languages, English and Russian, most major tree names consist of or are derived from minimal radical elements: for example, cherry, fir, birch, and oak, and *vishnja, ël', buk*, and *dub*. In the Tarascan Indian language of Mexico (the only non-Indo-European language I know well), most native trees are named by distinct roots, as illustrated by *k'ú-ni, uṛí-ku, uṛú-si*, and *aká-mba* (each of these names includes a nominal suffix). From the point of view of a Tarascan or PIE huntsman or woodcutter, the main types of trees correspond roughly to what, in botanical terms, are genera, such as the ash, aspen, and birch. When a basic term refers to a species, or even a variety, as for the Scotch pine and the European beech, it is because that species or variety is the only representative of the genus in the area; in this sense, **bhāg̣os* and **py/wK-* are also generic names. Less frequently, distinct morphemes exist for two or even more subgeneric categories—as has been postulated for at least some dialects of PIE with the maple, and perhaps the oak; several species of oak are labeled by distinct roots in Tarascan, but the majority of tree names serve for genera.

Basic tree names are on a par with "mother, run, good, yellow, sun, son," and so forth, and with the names for the first five digits, or most primary kinship terms, in most languages. The semantic primitiveness of basic tree names may be a very general linguistic phenomenon, obscured or forgotten because so few philologists think of trees in these terms.[1] Recent ethno-

---

[1] I would attach considerable interest to the shape of the nominal roots as reconstructed, and their relation to root theory. The PIE forms as I have discussed them are scattered through most of the nominal classes: (1) athematic stems such as **os-*; (2) sonant stems such as the nasal **klen-*, the liquid **ăbVl-* and perhaps **ar-*, and the *w*-stem **dorw-*; (3) consonant stems, including *b*-stems such as *grōbh-*, *t*-stems such as **wyt-*, and velar stems such as **wy̆g̣-*. Most striking is the number of *o*-stems, including two masculine *o*-stems (**kosVlo-* and **akVrno-*), and at least seven feminine *o*-stems (**alyso-*, **bherHg̣o-*, **bhāg̣o*, **eywo-*, **Vlmo-*, **maHlo-*, and **tVkso*).

I have tried to specify the grammatical gender whenever the case was strong in Meillet's terms, or when there appeared to be some scholarly concensus—there is a copious literature of controversy and specula-

156

scientific research comparing the folk taxonomies of a wide
variety of languages has shown that generic-level groupings of
organisms tend strongly to be labeled by linguistically unitary or
unproductive composite terms, whereas species—as in Lin-

tion on this subject. Grimm, Specht, and Meillet, for example, argued
that the PIE perceived and classified trees as part of an animate set
which, according to Specht, also included other plants, stones, minerals,
body parts, sicknesses, and animal products (1943, p. 357). A second sequence of scholars, including Brugmann and Lehmann, tried to resolve
the entire issue on formal grounds. I regard these discussions as fascinating but consider the conclusions untenable in the sense that the data do
not allow a strong decision between the opposed hypotheses. Speculations
about the grammatical gender of PIE tree names are of course connected
with the facts of such gender in contemporary IE languages, where they
are often divided about equally between masculine and feminine.

Grammatical gender is connotatively connected with lexical gender in
Indo-European, and ultimately with trees as symbols in cultural and
psychological systems. Sigmund Freud and subsequent psychoanalysts
have always and invariably interpreted trees as unambiguous masculinity symbols, thereby, among other things, identifying themselves and
their patients as persons with urban mentalities for whom trees and not
types of trees are the semantic primitives. Actually, I think it can be
shown that at least in the more northern Indo-European stocks, such as
Russian and English, there is considerable internal differentiation, of
which I can only give some intuitive and impressionistic intimations here.
For example, the oak and the hornbeam are probably masculine lexically
(although both are grammatically feminine in German). The cherry seems
lexically feminine; in English this is manifested through such connotations as the cherry fruit as hymen, and Housman's "Loveliest of trees,
the cherry now . . ."—which is certainly not about a male image. But again
the German *Kirschbaum* is of course masculine (the tendency in German
and probably other Germanic languages to label trees by *-baum* compounds singularly distinguishes its arboreal gender system and is probably another source of Freudian masculinity symbolism). Other trees
are less marked, and this is often so in cases where the grammatical gender varies from language to language or stock to stock—as with the
apple, alder, hazel, elm, and yew. Sometimes there is drastic conflict, as
with the fir, which is grammatically and culturally masculine in German,
but feminine in Russian (and hence the subject of Roman Jakobson's be-
loved anecdote about translating from German into Russian a lyric of
Heine that concerns a romance between a pine and a palm). Finally, a
number of trees are feminine grammatically, lexically, and culturally
(and, I would suppose, in the psychic systems of individual speakers).
These trees are the willow, the aspen or poplar, and the linden. Above all
the birch (*berëza, die Birke*) figures as a symbol not only of femininity,
but of young, virginal femininity. In English, again, this can only be
manifested through connotation ("its virginal whiteness"), through

naean botany—are labeled by binomial expressions consisting of the generic name plus a single attributivizing expression. Such sets of generic names tend to totally partition the respective section of the environment. These and other recent conclusions regarding "the priority of the concept of genus" (Berlin 1969, p. 34) appear to accord with the independently attained findings of the present exploration of a prehistoric nomenclature.

Cultural Conclusions

Uses and Functions of the Trees

The etymologies presented above make scattered mention of the numerous uses and functions of trees among the PIE. These cultural conclusions are necessarily based on diverse evidence—as when a tree name also denotes a spear, or when two or more ancient texts congruently describe a ritual usage, or again, when the clinching material evidence has been excavated from an archaeological site. And diversity of evidence implies diversity in the validity of the conclusions. In summarizing these cultural conclusions below, however, I have not differentiated sharply between relative certainties and mere hypotheses, since wherever possible this has been detailed in the etymologies; to the archaeologist and cultural historian even a hypothesis—when seriously entertained by several Indo-Europeanists—is helpful in creating the mosaic of prehistory.

The uses and functions of the eighteen trees fall into four categories: foods, tools, miscellaneous, and religious.

Ten trees yielded food to these early men, to their domesticated animals, and to the wild game they hunted. Fruit came from the wild apple, and the wild and cornel cherries. Nuts were obtained, often in prodigal quantities, from the beech, the oak, the hazel, the hornbeam, and, in and around the Caucasus, the

---

lexical association (the birch as a young girl), and substitution ("she" rather than "he"). But the three levels of meaning—grammatical, lexical, and cultural—are all congruously feminine in the Germanic, Baltic, and Slavic languages, and the grammatical gender is also feminine in the more eastern Iranian, and even in late Vedic Sanskrit; the birch as a female symbol probably carries back without break to the Proto-Indo-Europeans of five thousand years ago.

walnut and the chestnut; nuts and apples are mentioned, often together, in early texts such as Tacitus. The shoots and leaves of the elm, ash, and linden, in that order of importance, were cropped for fodder, as has been shown in the brilliant archaeological-ethnological study by Troels-Smith. Last, the aspens and poplars yielded seeds, buds, bark, and twigs for the nurture of wild and domesticated stock, and for man in times of dearth.

Nine trees served for tools and weapons. The versatile oak probably was used for spears and boats, and possibly for bows. The ash and perhaps the hornbeam were worked into spears, wagon parts, and other implements requiring durable wood. The yew and the elm surely served for bows, and the juniper-cedar for ships and oars, as is reported in Homer. Willow osiers and shoots were woven and plaited, possibly into baskets and fences; more archaeological evidence on wattle-and-daub construction could substantiate these hypotheses. The Scotch pine and later the spruce and the fir were sources of resin, tar, and similar products; the conifer names, for example, are variously reflected with these meanings in five stocks. Finally, interesting but doubtful etymologies suggest that the hazel was used for light spears, the willow for wagon felloes, and the aspen for sacred instruments.

Five trees figured in PIE religion. The birch and linden may have been revered, or even sacrificed to in sacred groves; the comparative evidence from Finno-Ugric seems relevant here. The beech was sacred, and its bark may have been used to inscribe religious symbols. The yew played a role in both legal and religious ritual, as is evidenced, for example, in the ethnology of medieval Europe and by a potential cognate in Hittite. Last, and most significant, many lines of evidence show that the oak was worshiped in the form of sacred trees and groves, taboos against injuring the tree, and a symbolic linkage with four other cultural symbols: fire, lightning, the sky, and the high god. In sum, every tree probably had a function.

Implications for Groupings of the Speech Community: Counts and Sets

On the basis of their attestation in the daughter stocks, the tree names fall into three sets. The first set includes names and formulas that for various reasons may hark back to early or pre-PIE. The second comprises names that are weak on linguistic or semantic grounds or both. The third consists of fourteen tree names that are strong in terms of the linguistic, semantic, and external systems discussed in the introduction. It should go without saying that counts and quantity-based sets must be used with caution, and that the numbers, reflexes, and protoforms cited below can be evaluated only within the context of the etymological-botanical studies of the preceding chapter. Let us review the three sets in order, and then draw some synthetic conclusions.

The Archaic Set. Since the first set is based on distinct criteria, it is obviously going to overlap in part with the second and third sets. And in fact this first set *is* drawn from the second and third and consists of tree names that because of their form (e.g., providing important evidence for the laryngeals), or the number, spread, or geographical discontinuity of the attesting stocks (e.g., reaching from Indic to Baltic), or similar considerations, are to be assigned to the early or pre-PIE period (the fifth or early fourth millennium). This archaic first group includes the following:

1. **Dorw-* constitutes a special case because of the uniquely high number of supporting stocks (all twelve), the richness of the attesting, alternate forms, and the extraordinary variety in their denotation. **Dorw-* probably meant oak, or tree, or both, with the exact referent determined by the speech situation. On the other hand, it may also have been limited to a single species: the English oak (*Quercus robur*).

2. All the tree names of the strongly supported third set, which will be discussed below; notably ancient are the names for the birch (**bherHǵo-*), the ash (**os-*), one of the oak names (**perkʷ-*), one of the elm names (**wy̆ǵ-*), and possibly one of the willow names (**wyt-*).

3. Two names that also occur in the second and third sets are highly speculative:

a. An ancient word for the maple, **kL-n-*, reflected in the PIE strong term, **klen-*, and the weak term, **akVrno-*;

b. A word for the yew, **eywo-*, shows an array of more or less corresponding terms in eight stocks (in four of which the meaning is more or less "yew"), and also appears to have an Anatolian reflex in Hittite *eyan*, a ritually significant evergreen tree.

160

The Weak Set. The myrtle, laurel, and plane tree are not included at all in these counts because they are attested neither linguistically nor botanically; similarly, the larch and elder lack linguistic reflexes, are comparatively weak, and are geographically peripheral in their pollen remains. Otherwise, the second set consists of sixteen weak cases.

In the first subset of weak cases, there is good botanical evidence, but the relatively good linguistic evidence is limited to two or three stocks: a conifer term (*pytw-), one of the oak forms (*ayg-), one of the apple words (*maHlo-), the second maple word (*akVrno-), the second nut (tree) word (*ar-), and the third willow word (*wrb-). A particularly interesting subset of this subset comprises the terms reflected only in the three western stocks: the hazel word (*kos(V)lo-), the western nut term (*knw-), and one of the elm terms (*Vlmo-, if we discount the Slavic cognate).

In the second subset of weak cases, the tree name is attested both botanically and linguistically, but the latter is doubtful in some special way: for example, the *eywo*-yew, although allegedly reflected in seven or even eight stocks, presents so many phonological and semantic difficulties as to render the

TABLE 4

THE WEAKER NAMES

	Gr.	Celt.	It.	Gk.	Slav.	Balt.	Alb.	Arm.	Ana.	Ind.	Ir.	Toch.
1. *el-w-n-			+	+	?			+				
2. *pytw-			+	+			+			?		
3. *wrb-			+	?	+	+						
4. *ăbVl-	+	+	+		+	+						
5. *maHlo-			+	+			?		+			?
6. *akVrno-	+		+	+						?		
7. *kos(V)lo-	+	+	+		?	?						
8. *knw-	+	+	+									
9. *ar-				+	+	?	+					
10. *Vlmo-	+	+	+		?							
11. *lēipā-		?			+	+						
12. *lenTā-	+		?	?	+	+	+					
13. *ayg-	+		+	+								
14. *grōbh-			?	?	+	?	?					
15. *K(e)r-n-			+	+	?	?	?					
16. *eywo-	+	+	?	?	+	+		?	+			

161

name itself questionable; second, the hornbeam name and the first apple name are reflected in five stocks, but in each case four of the stocks may involve borrowing, from Slavic and Celtic respectively; third, the juniper-cedar is attested in three or possibly more stocks but raises troublesome and partly unsolvable questions of both form and meaning; fourth, both of the posited linden terms (**lēipā-*, **lenTā-*) involve serious irregularities, so that the second of them has to be listed as "weak," although apparently supported by three or four "strong" cognates; and finally, many scholars have advanced numerous arguments for rejecting the cherry term.

The stocks supporting the weak tree names are ordered fairly gradually into a series that runs from an extremely high Italic (10-3) to an Iranian zero (within the parentheses here and below, the first number denotes the relatively unambiguous cognates, whereas the one after the dash refers to the more moot or unlikely ones). In order of strength, the stocks are:

1. Italic (10–3)	7. Albanian (3–3)
2. Slavic (8–3)	8. Anatolian (2)
3. Germanic (8)	9. Armenian (1–1)
4. Greek (7–4)	10. Indic (–2)
5. Baltic (5–5)	11. Tocharian (–1)
6. Celtic (5–1)	12. Iranian (0)

The number of stocks definitely supporting each tree name ranges from two, as for **lēipā-* and **K(e)r-n-*, to four or five, as for **ăbVl-* and **eywo-*. The great majority are supported by three fairly good cognates.

The Strong Set. A third and final group, that of the strong cases, includes fourteen tree names (referring to ten arboreal units) that are reflected in four to nine stocks, at least two of which are noncontiguous: birch (**bherHǵo-*), pine (**py/wK-*), aspen-poplar (**osp-*), willow (**wyt-*, and perhaps **sVlyk-*), alder (**alyso-*), maple (**klen-*), elm (**wyǵ-*), ash (**os-*), acorn (**gʷelH-*), beech (**bhāǵo-*), one of the yew forms (**tVk̂so-*), and two strong terms that may have denoted oak (**perkʷ-* and **dorw-*). I have included the second oak name (**perkʷ-*), although many of the cognates in the nine stocks have been challenged or, in some cases, widely rejected. **Dorw-*, more or less supported by all stocks, is obviously a strong case, and has

162

TABLE 5

Cognates for the Strong Set of Names in the Strong Set of Stocks

	Slavic (Russian)	Germanic	Italic (Latin)	Greek	Baltic (Lithuanian)	Celtic
*bherHǵo-	berëza	MG *Birke*	*fraxinus*		béržas	
*pw/yK-	pëklo	OHG *fiuhta*	*pix, picea*	πεύκη	pušìs	(MI) *ochtach*
*osp-	osína	OE *æspe*			āpušė	
*sVlyk-	vetlá	OHG *salaha*	*salix*	ἑλίκη		(OI) *sail*
*wyt-		MG *Weide*	*vītis*	ϝῑτέᾱ	vytìs	(I) *fëith*
*alyso-	ol'khá	OE *alor*	*alnus*	ʼΟλιζών(?)	ēlksnis	(Proto-Celtic) *alisa*
*klen-	klën	ON *hlynr*		κλυό-(?)	klēvas	(W) *kelyn*
*wyĭǧ-	vjaz	LG *wīke*			vìnkšna	
*os-	jásen'	OE *æsc*	*ornus*	ὀξύη	úosis	(W) *onn-en*
*gʷelH-	zhëlud'		*glans*	βάλανος	gìlė	
*bhāǧo-	bu/ozъ	ON *bōk*	*fāgus*	φηγός		*bāgos (?)
*tVkso-	tis		*taxus*	τόξον		
*perkʷw-	(OR) Perun?	OHG *fereh-eih*	*quercus*		Perkúnas	*Hercynia*
*doru-	dérevo	OE *tree*	*dūrus*		dervà	(OI) *daur*

been tabulated on the chart of the strong set but is not included in the counts below.

What conclusions may be drawn from the thirteen remaining strong cases? Let us compare the stocks and see how many strong and weak cognates they contain that support the thirteen strong tree names (the names to the right indicate those not supported by the stock):

1. Slavic (12)	*sVlyk-
2. Germanic (11)	*gʷelH-, *tVḱso-
3. Baltic (10)	*sVlyk-, *bhāǵo-, *tVḱso-
4. Italic (10)	*osp-, *wyǵ-, *klen-
5. Greek (7–2)	*bherHǵo-, *osp-, *wyǵ-, *perkʷ-
6. Celtic (6–2)	*bherHǵo-, *osp-, *wyǵ-, *tVḱso-, gʷelH-
7. Indic (4–1)	
8. Iranian (4)	
9. Albanian (3–2)	
10. Armenian (2–1)	
11. Anatolian (1–1)	
12. Tocharian (0)	

As with the weak tree names, the degree of support runs in a fairly ordered series from an extremely high Slavic (twelve) and Germanic (eleven), to a practically negligible Anatolian (one) and Tocharian (zero). The total number of stocks supporting a tree name with good cognates ranges from eight (*wyt-, *os-), to seven (*perkʷ-), to six (*bherHǵo- *pw/yK-), to five (*wyǵ-, *gʷelH-, but the majority are definitely supported by four only (*osp-, *sVlyk-, *klen-, *bh āǵo-, *tVḱso-, *alyso-).

General Discussion

The foregoing etymologies and counts have led to substantive conclusions regarding the relative degree of affinity and discreteness between the early dialects—the interstock questions that are now of particular interest to students of early Indo-European dialects (Hoenigswald 1966, p. 2). But they also have led to conclusions about the probable interrelation of individual stocks and of sets of stocks to the natural environment. Both the dialectological and the ecological conclusions bear on the perennially fascinating question of the PIE homeland. Both cast a new and constructive light on the value of semantics and semantic change as a potential source for dialectal sub-groupings through the comparative method. Both have emerged, either alone or together, in the six specific conclusions to be discussed below.

It is crucial at the outset that one point be noted by the professional Indo-Europeanist. The fourteen stronger names are enough by themselves to establish the same six specific dialecto-logical conclusions—the divergent shifts of referent in Greek, the semantic innovations shared by Greek and Albanian, the relative weakness of Indic, Iranian, Albanian, Armenian, Anatolian, and Tocharian, the relative affinity of Slavic to PIE (with Germanic a close second), the various affinities between the western stocks, between the northern stocks, and between the classical languages, and finally, the special status of four stocks as a sort of core or nucleus for the inference of the arboreal system: Italic, Germanic, Baltic, and Slavic.

First, Greek is strong in both sets, with seven good cognates and four poor ones for the weaker set, and two-thirds support for the strong names. If we admit five moot cases, then two-thirds of the PIE tree names (twenty-one/thirty) are reflected in form in Greek. If we do *not* admit these moot cases—and we probably should not do so—then the degree of support is still over 50 percent. In sharp contrast to this preservation of form, almost half of the sixteen certain reflexes have shifted their denotation, usually to another tree. Some examples of this are the shifting of ash to spear and beech, of beech and perhaps hornbeam to oak, and perhaps of "tree" to oak, and of one yew word to bow and of another to service or bird cherry tree. These shifts, as well as other indications of terminological instability, presumably reflect the workings of powerful ecological or cultural forces.

My second conclusion differs from the major conclusions to follow in that it involves a relation between one of the six major stocks, Greek, and one of the six minor stocks, Albanian. In terms of purely numerical indices, or in terms of shared retentions, the relation of Albanian to Greek resembles that to Italic or Slavic. But the relation of Albanian to Greek is quite distinctive in terms of shared innovations, where the significant parallelism may involve up to ten tree names. Both stocks may have adopted the same southern apple term, Greek directly, Albanian through Latin from the same autochthonous source; both of the stocks in question share the fixed secondary apple meaning of "cheek." In at least two cases, Albanian and Greek display common shifts of referent: (1) PIE *$bh\bar{a}\hat{g}os$, "beech," shows up as Greek φᾱγός and (the admittedly problematical) Albanian *bungɛ*, both meaning "oak"; and (2) PIE *os-, "ash", shows up as Proto-Albanian *osk-, which went to *ah*, "beech," and as Proto-Greek, *$oskes$, which went to Homeric ὀξύη , "ash, spear," and Classical ὀξύα, "beech." The losses shared by these two stocks include one of the oak words (*$perk^{w}$-), and three western names—the *knw*-nut, the *Vlmo*-elm, and the hazel, and three distinctly northern names—the aspen, the birch, and probably the *klen*-maple. Other shifts and shared losses in arboreal denotation have been suggested, but seem to involve Albanian data that is questionable enough to render the comparisons of little worth: e.g., the *shkozë*-hornbeam. My second main conclusion, then, is that we are left with one shared borrowing, two shared shifts, and seven shared losses between these two contiguous stocks.

Coordinate losses of terms and shifts of referents within one relatively uniform semantic set such as the arboreal one would appear to be a semantic analogue of the shared innovation in phonology, which is still regarded as the most valid criterion for early dialect groupings (Hamp 1966; Hoenigswald 1966)— granted that shared loss is the weakest form of innovation. The number of semantic losses and shifts shared by Greek and Albanian could reflect some ancient (late PIE) congruity or affinity in the semantic or cultural structure. One trouble with this interpretation is that the early Albanians were probably closer to the Italics and Slavs than to the Greeks. The shared innovations could just as well reflect the parallel responses of two similar ethnoarboreal systems to similar conditions, such as the absence of the birch. Perhaps the arboreal nomenclature of many other IE stocks—in place of Albanian—would have shifted in the same way.

Third, of all the stocks, Slavic is the closest to my reconstructed PIE arboreal system. Slavic ranks first in the stronger set of tree names (twelve out of thirteen), and ranks second, after Italic, in its support of the weaker set, with eight strong and three weak cognates out of sixteen. On the basis of the dyadic associations involving the thirteen stronger names only, to be discussed below, the six main stocks can be ordered on the basis of the number of such associations they form with *any* stock, as follows: Slavic forms forty-five such dyads; Germanic forms forty-one; Baltic forms thirty-seven; Italic and Greek both form thirty-five; and Celtic forms thirty-four. Clearly, Slavic is central in terms of this parameter.

All three divisions of Slavic—Eastern, Western, and Southern —show several reflexes of at least one term in each of the eighteen PIE tree categories; in fact, a sample of six modern languages, including Russian, Ukrainian, Czech, Polish, Serbocroatian, and Slovenian, shows 100 percent support of at least one term of all eighteen units. This degree of support hardly drops when one adds Bulgarian and Slovak (in these counts I am including the Slavic reflexes of *$K(e)rn$- and *$Vlmo$-). Of the total of thirty tree names, twenty-three are reflected in Slavic, and most of them with great regularity in many languages. Several tree names are supported by over a dozen Slavic languages. The attestation is particularly strong in the Slavic reflexes of the PIE birch (e.g., Ukrainian *beréza*), apple (*jábluko*), maple (*klyj*), nut (*orích*), yew-willow (*ýva*), ash (*jásen*), alder (*víl'cha*), and elm (*vjaz*). Slavic (e.g., Ukrainian) is also remarkably strong on names with otherwise weak or limited support, such as the aspen-poplars (*osýna*), the juniper-cedars (*jalovéć*), the hornbeam (*hrab*), and the linden (*lýpa*). To a greater degree than any other stock, the Slavic reflexes also denote the same physical type of tree that one would posit for PIE.

The widely ramifying and comparatively regular reflexes in Slavic suggest that the speakers of the Common Slavic period lived in an ecological (i.e., arboreal) zone similar or identical to that of the PIE, and that, since the Common Slavic period, the speakers of the various Slavic dialects have for the most part continued to occupy such an area. It has been largely in historic times that the Slavs have expanded into parts of the Balkans, northern Russia, Siberia, and so forth. The Baltic and Italic stocks do not provide as much evidence on as many trees in as many languages, and the close rival, Germanic,

Conclusions

supports three fewer tree names; and two other names specifically lack support in the English and North Germanic areas because the genera in question were probably lacking until recent historic times (see table 7). Yet, despite the arguments marshaled here, I would be the first to insist that the arboreal evidence cannot be used in *isolation* to construe a conclusive argument for a PIE homeland in the Ukraine or the Cossack steppe.

Fourth, six stocks provide a support for the two sets of tree names that is relatively scattered and fragmentary—with the exception that several of them retained reflexes of the apple words, and, of course, all six retained reflexes of **dorw-*. Not

TABLE 6

SOME SLAVIC COGNATES

Tree	Russian	Serbocroatian	Polish
birch	*berëza*	*brëza*	*brzoza*
conifer	*pëklo*	*pàkao*	*piekło*
juniper	*jálovets*	*jéla* (?)	*jałowiec*
aspen	*osína*	*jàsíka*	*osa, osina*
willow	*vìt'*	*vìti*	*wić*
willow	*vérba*	*vŕba*	*wierzba*
apple	*jábloko*	*jàbuka*	*jabłko*
maple	*klën*	*klën*	*klon*
alder	*ol'khá*	*jóha, jóva*	*olcha, olsza*
nut	*orékh*	*òrah*	*orzech*
elm	*ílem*		*ilem*
elm	*vjaz*	*vêz*	*wiąz*
linden	*lut*		
linden	*lípa*	*lìpa*	*lipa*
ash	*jásen'*	*jàsên*	*jasień*
hornbeam	*grab*	*gràb*	*grab*
beech	*buziná*	*bûs*	*bez*
cherry	*cherëmukha*		*trzemcha*
yew	*íva*	*ìva*	*iwa*
yew	*tis*	*tìs*	*cis*
acorn	*zhëlud'*	*zhëlud*	*żołądź*
oak	*Perúnъ*	*Perun*	(Polabian) Peräunedån
oak/tree	*dérevo*	*drìjevo*	*drzewo*

SOURCE: Vasmer

168

TABLE 7

SOME GERMANIC COGNATES

Tree	Old English	Old Norse	Old High German
birch	*berc/birce*	*bjǫrk*	*birka*
conifer			*fiuhta*
aspen	*æspe*	*askr*	*aspa*
willow	*welig*	*sélja*	*salaha*
willow	*wīthig*	*viþir*	*wīda*
apple	*æppel*	*epli*	*apful*
maple	*hlyn*	*hlynr*	*līn-boum*
maple			*ahorn*
alder	*alor*	*ǫlr*	*elira*
hazel	*hæsl*	*hasl*	*hasal(a)*
nut	*hnutu*	*hnot*	*(h)nuz*
elm	*ulmtrēow*	*almr*	*ēlm(o)*
elm	*wīce* (?)		(Lg) *wīke*
linden	*līthe*	*lind*	*linta*
ash	*æsc*	*askr*	*ask*
beech	*bōk*	*bōk*	*buohha*
yew	*īw*	*ȳr*	*īwa*
oak	*āk*	*eik*	*eih*
oak	*furh*	*fura*	*fereh- ∼ foraha*
oak/tree	*trēo*	*tre*	

SOURCE: Kluge

counting this latter term, Albanian, Armenian, and Indic each provide a total of three or four relatively good cognates, and one to five weak ones, but are generally weak in both sets. Iranian, though of medium strength in the strong set (four out of thirteen) falls away sharply in the weak set to zero. For the combined strong and weak sets, Tocharian yields only one moot cognate, and Anatolian provides only three, none of which have been generally accepted (although I personally would accept *maḫlash* and *eyan*). These paucities in the six stocks presumably reflect combinations of substratum influence (e.g., Anatolian, Indic), or of linguistic acculturation (e.g., Armenian), or of movement into a radically different environment (Indic, Tocharian), or the lateness of the evidence (Albanian), or the paucity of any sort of evidence for tree names (Tocharian). The semantic shifts in the six stocks generally followed independent paths. Despite these restrictions, however, and with the egregious exception of Tocharian, the weakly supporting stocks on the southern and eastern marches often help greatly in determining the Indo-Europeanness of a name, particularly where, as with the aspen, birch, and willow, the far-flung reflexes correspond well with each other phonologically.

Fifth, in both the stronger and the weaker sets we find a singularly high degree of both phonological and semantic correspondence between these main stocks: Slavic, Germanic, Italic, Baltic, and a bit lower, Celtic, and Greek. I will discuss further on the close ties between Baltic, Slavic, and Germanic, and the way Germanic links the western stocks with Baltic-Slavic, while Italic links them with Greek and is itself particularly close to Baltic-Slavic. Otherwise, all the six stocks form from six to eight dyadic pairs with one another. But within the six main stocks, four have come to constitute a sort of platform

Sl. Ger. Bal. It. Gr. Celt. Ind. Iran. Alb. Arm. Ana. Toch.

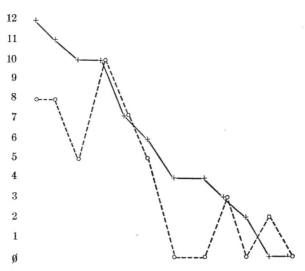

CHART 4. The weak and strong sets. The graph represents both the weak and strong tree names and the weak and strong linguistic stocks. The left-to-right ordering is dictated by the relative strength of the strong names. The weak cognates of tree names are not reckoned above ($-n = \emptyset$). The *dorw-* cognates are not reckoned. +———+ for the strong names, ○———○ for the weak names.

for reconstructing the PIE arboreal nomenclature, and, in fact, cognates for almost all the fourteen strong tree names can be found in the limited sample of four languages within the first four of these stocks: Classical Latin, and Modern Lithuanian, English, and Russian (a number of other Germanic or Slavic languages could be substituted here). English still has reflexes for fourteen of the eighteen PIE units, and Russian and several other Slavic languages still have reflexes for all eighteen. These four stocks provide the core evidence in a way that somewhat resembles the function of Vedic, Avestan, and Homeric Greek within the verbal system as presented by Meillet (1937; chapter 5), with the important distinction that in the former case the primacy has emerged as a result of the sort of relatively simple induction that largely typifies the present study. In sum, the notion of a set of four core stocks or six, if we include Celtic and Greek), is most significant for problems of dialectology and early migration. A comprehensive statistical analysis of the sort of fact discussed in this chapter would doubtless lead to other conclusions, significant for PIE dialectology, as would the rigorous semantic analysis of other domains or fields.[2] The overall evidence for the cognates for the twelve stocks in both the strong and weak sets is stated in chart 4.

The last conclusion—really a set of conclusions—involves strong dyadic relations within the six strong stocks, and just as strong tryadic relations involving transitive relations between three dyads. To begin with, all the correspondences listed are shared by three or more stocks, but there is great variation in the way any two stocks do or do not support the same tree names, with a range from twenty to eight shared correspondences. Second, if we want to state the degree of arboreal cohesion between the stocks, we calculate the total number of dyads, which is fifteen, by the formula $x = 6 (5)/2$, which comes from the general formula $x = n(n - 1)/2$. The number of cog-

[2] For a far more complex procedure involving a statistical approach to the problem of Indo-European subgroupings, see Kroeber 1960, and Kroeber and Chrétien 1937 (and the references in these articles to work by Czekanowski, Ross, and Ellegård). Kroeber's seventy four units were phonological and morphological, and one wonders how the inferred affinities would change if he added comensurate data from lexical semantics and syntax.

TABLE 8
Dyadic Cohesions

Stock	16 Weak	13 Strong
Germanic-Celtic	5	8
Germanic-Italic	8	7
Germanic-Greek	4	7
Germanic-Slavic	5	10
Germanic-Baltic	4	9
Celtic-Italic	5	7
Celtic-Greek	1	7
Celtic-Slavic	4	7
Celtic-Baltic	4	6
Italic-Greek	9	7
Italic-Slavic	8	8
Italic-Baltic	7	6
Greek-Slavic	5	8
Greek-Baltic	6	6
Slavic-Baltic	10	10

nates shared by any one dyad in the strong and weak sets is
then tabulated, as in table 8. It then becomes possible to state
in a relatively explicit manner the way in which the evidence
for tree names supports various affinities between stocks
(and, implicitly, between such stocks and the natural environment). Among the numerous generalizations which could so
be drawn, the following seem relatively significant.

First, two dyadic associations. The association between the
two "classical languages," Latin and Greek, is very high
(sixteen), and is rivaled only by Italic and Slavic. It is exceeded
only by Slavic and Baltic, which share the most cognates within
both the stronger and the weaker sets, for a total of twenty.
Within the weak set, Slavic and Baltic variously support the
same ten tree names out of a total of twelve supported in any
way by either (i.e., 9–3 for Slavic, and 5–5 for Baltic); the
glaring exception is constituted by the Slavic cognates for
Vlmo- (Russian *ílem*, etc.), and they are moot. Within the
strong set, both stocks support the same eight tree names,
although Slavic also supports the beech, the *sVlyk*-willow,
and the *tVk̑so*-yew. On the combined counts for the two sets,
then, Baltic and Slavic are appreciably closer to each other
than either is to any other stock.

172

The second main conclusion to be drawn from these cohesions would appear to involve combinations of exceptional dyads into several tryads. At one extreme, that of low assocation in both sets, Celtic, Baltic, and Greek are all significantly distant from each other in terms of this parameter—as is congruous with their geographical separation. Germanic-Greek and Celtic-Slavic are also relatively low. At the other extreme, that of strongly linked tryads, the combined counts involving both strong and weak names show that Italic, Germanic, and Slavic, are all relatively close (fifteen, sixteen, and fifteen, respectively). But on the basis of the much more valid cognates of the strong set alone, Germanic is as close to Slavic (ten), and nearly as close to Baltic (nine), as either of the latter is to each other. These three "northern stocks" jointly support six names (although never exclusively)—notably the birch, the aspen, and the northern apple terms. In sum, the analysis of dyadic associations between the stocks yields two strong tryads: Italic-Germanic-Slavic and Germanic-Slavic-Baltic.

There is also a special affinity between the members of the familiar western trio of Italic, Celtic, and Germanic. These three stocks support the same five tree names out of a total of fifteen weak tree names supported in any way by either. Three or four of these five are shared *exclusively* by these three stocks, whereas if one takes any three stocks at random, one finds that *none* share an exclusive tryad—the (expectable) exceptions being Baltic and Slavic with Germanic, and with Italic (both two shared tryads). In other words, the cohesion between the western stocks is more meaningful because of the number of stocks, and of cognates—three in each case. The western stocks also generally agree within the strong set of cognates: among the total of thirteen (not counting *dorw-), only Celtic lacks the birch and only Italic the *klen*-maple, although both Celtic and Italic lack the *wyǵ*-elm, and Celtic and Germanic together lack the *tV̇kso*-yew. In sum, the three western stocks rank with Italic-Germanic-Slavic, and Germanic-Slavic-Baltic. In terms of these types of tryads, Germanic is central.

The various strong cohesions involving Italic, Germanic, Slavic, and Baltic in the north-central area and Celtic, Italic, and Germanic in the west support the case for the affinity between these stocks that has already been made on other grounds by other scholars—with the exception that Italic is not usually linked with Slavic! I would add the evidence of these shared retentions to the phonological and morphological evidence already adduced (e.g., by Porzig); such shared retentions within clearly marked semantic sets, like shared phonological retentions, are a valuable if widely underrated criterion for dialectology (Watkins 1966, p. 30).

Bibliography

Linguistic Works

Abaev, V. I. 1958. *Istoriko-Etimologicheskij Slovar' Osetinskogo Jazyka*. Vol. 1, A–K. Moscow and Leningrad: Izdatel'stvo Akademii Nauk SSSR.

Balchikonis, J. 1941. *Lietuviu kalbos žodynas*, 1. Vilnius.

Bartholomae, Christian. 1904. *Altiranisches Wörterbuch*. Strassburg.

———. 1918. Zur Buchenfrage. Eine sprachgeschichtliche Untersuchung. *Sitzungsbericht der Heidelberger Akademie der Wissenschaften*. 1 Abhandlung (20 pages).

Bazell, C. E. 1949. The problem of the morpheme. In *Readings in linguistics, II*, ed. Eric Hamp et al. Chicago: Univ. of Chicago Press.

———. 1952. The correspondence fallacy in structural linguistics. In *Readings in linguistics, II*, ed. Eric Hamp et al. Chicago: Univ. of Chicago Press.

Bender, Harold H. 1922. *The home of the Indo-Europeans*. Princeton: Princeton Univ. Press.

Benveniste, Emile. 1935. *Origines de la formation des noms en indo-européen*. Paris: Adrien-Maisonneuve.

———. 1937. *Noms d'armes orientaux en grec*. 1. *tókson*. Comp. Emile Boisacq. *Annuaire de l'Institute de Philologie et d'Histoire Orientales et Slaves* 5: 37–41. Brussels.

———. 1949. Noms d'animaux en indo-européen. *Bulletin de la Société de linguistique de Paris* 45: 74–103 (especially part 1: Le nom du porc).

———. 1954. Problèmes sémantiques de la reconstruction. *Word* 10: 251–64.

175

————. 1955. Homophones radicales en indo-européen. *Bulletin de la Société de linguistique de Paris* 51: 14–29.

Berger, Hermann. 1956. *Mittelmeerische Kulturpflanzen aus dem Burushaski. Münchener Studien zur Sprachwissenschaft.* 9: 4–34 (27–34 on the apple). Munich: J. Kitzinger.

Berlin, Brent. 1969. Evidence for the concept of genus in folk science. Unpublished.

Berlin, Brent; Breedlove, Dennis E.; and Ravin, Peter H. 1968. Covert categories and folk taxonomies. *American Anthropologist* 70, no. 2: 290–300.

Berneker, Erich. 1908–13. *Slavisches etymologisches Wörterbuch.* Heidelberg: Carl Winter.

Birnbaum, Henrik. 1966. The dialects of Common Slavic. In *Ancient Indo-European dialects*, ed. Henrik Birnbaum and Jaan Puhvel., pp. 153–99. Berkeley and Los Angeles: Univ. of California Press.

Birnbaum, Henrik, and Puhvel, Jaan. 1966. *Ancient Indo-European dialects.* Proceedings of the Conference on Indo-European Linguistics held at the University of California, Los Angeles, April 25–27, 1963. Berkeley and Los Angeles: Univ. of California Press.

Bloomfield, Leonard. 1933. *Language.* New York: Henry Holt.

Blumenthal, Albrecht von. 1934. *Die Iguvinischen Taffeln. Text. Übersetzung. Untersuchung.* Stuttgart: W. Kohlhammer.

Böhtlingk, Otto, and Roth, Rudolph. 1855–75. *Sanskrit-Wörterbuch.* Vols. 1–7. St. Petersburg: Kaiserlichen Akademie der Wissenschaften.

Boisacq, Emile. 1938. *Dictionnaire étymologique de la langue grecque.* Heidelberg: Carl Winter.

Brugmann, Karl. 1902–3. *Kurze Vergleichende grammatik der indogermanischen Sprachen. Number 2. Lehre von den Wortformen und ihrem Gebrauch.* Strassburg: K. J. Trübner.

Brunnhofer, H. 1901. Worterklärungen zum Rigveda. *Beiträge zur Kunde der indogermanischen Sprachen.* 26: 101–9.

Buck, Carl D. 1933. *A comparative grammar of Greek and Latin.* Chicago: Univ. of Chicago Press.

176

———. 1949. *A dictionary of selected synonyms in the principal Indo-European languages: A contribution to the history of ideas.* Chicago: Univ. of Chicago Press.

Bulmer, Ralph. 1967. Why is the cassowary not a bird? A problem of zoological taxonomy among the Karam of the New Guinea highlands. *Man* 2: 1–25.

Caesar, Gaius Julius. 1963. De bello Gallico. Classic Interlinear Translations. New York: David McKay.

Calder, George. 1917. *Auraicept Na N-Eces. The scholar's primer* (texts of the Ogham tract). Edinburgh: John Grant.

Chantraine, P. 1933. *La formation des noms en grec ancien.* Collection linguistique publiée par la Société de linguistique de Paris: Honoré Champion.

———. 1968. *Dictionaire étymologique de la langue grecque.* Paris: Klincksieck.

Chao, Yuen Ren. 1934. The non-uniqueness of phonemic solutions of phonetic systems. *Bulletin of the Institute of History and Philology, Academia Sinica.* 4, part 4: 363–97.

Conklin, Harold. 1962. Lexicographical treatment of folk taxonomies. In *Problems in lexicography*, ed. Fred W. Householder and Sol Saporta. Bloomington: Indiana University Research Center in Anthropology, Folklore, and Linguistics. Publication 21.

Corominas, J. 1955. New information on Hispano-Celtic from the Spanish etymological dictionary. *Zeitschrift für keltische Etymologie*, pp. 30–58.

Cowgill, Warren. 1960. Gothic *iddja* and Old English *ēode. Language* 36: 483–501.

———. 1965. Evidence in Greek. In *Evidence for laryngeals*, ed. Werner Winter. The Hague: Mouton.

Cunliffe, Richard J. 1963. *A lexicon of the Homeric dialect.* Norman: Univ. of Oklahoma Press.

Cuny, A. 1916. Notes grecques et latines. *Mémoires de la Société de linguistique de Paris*, pp. 193–214.

Diels, Paul. 1932. *Altkirchenslavische Grammatik.* Part 1. *Grammatik.* Heidelberg: Carl Winter.

Ehelolf, Hans. 1933. Heth. milit = "Honig." *Orientalistische Literaturzeitung*, pp. 1–7.

————. 1938. *Keilschriftkunden aus Bogasköi*. Vol. 29. Berlin.

Eilers, Wilhelm, and Mayrhofer, Manfred. 1962. Kurdisch *būz* und die indogermanische "Buchen"—Sippe. *Mitteilungen der anthropologischen Gesellschaft in Wien* 92: 61–92.

Ernout, A., and Meillet, A. 1951. *Dictionnaire étymologique de la langue latine*. Vols. 1–3. 3d ed. Paris: Klincksieck.

Evans, D. Ellis. 1967. *Gaulish personal names*. New York: Oxford Univ. Press.

Falk, H. S., and Torp, A. 1910. *Norwegisch-Dänisches etymologisches Wörterbuch*. Vols. 1–2. Heidelberg: Carl Winter.

Feist, Sigmund. 1913. *Kultur, Ausbreitung, und Herkunft der Indogermanen*. Berlin.

————. 1939. *Vergleichendes Wörterbuch der gotischen Sprache. Mit Einschluss des Krimgotischen und sonstigen zerstreuten Überreste des Gotischen*. Leiden: E. J. Brill.

Fraenkel, Ernst. 1913. Graeca-Latina. *Glotta*, pp. 22–49.

————. 1962. *Lithauisches etymologisches Wörterbuch*. Heidelberg: Carl Winter.

Friedrich, Johannes. 1952. *Hethitisches Wörterbuch*. Heidelberg· Carl Winter.

Friedrich, Paul. 1966. Proto-Indo-European kinship. *Ethnology* 5: 1–36.

————. 1967. Review of *Ancient Indo-European dialects*, ed. Henrik Birnbaum and Jaan Puhvel. *American Anthropologist* 69: 409–11.

————. 1969. Proto-Indo-European trees. In *Proto-Indo-European and the Proto-Indo-Europeans*, ed. George Cardona and Henry Hoenigswald. Philadelphia: Univ. of Pennsylvania Press. *In press*.

Frisk, Hjalmar. 1954, 1965. *Griechisches etymologisches Wörterbuch*. Heidelberg: Carl Winter.

Georgakas, D. 1941. Beiträge zur Deutung als slavisch Erklärter Ortsnamen. *Byzantinische Zeitschrift*, pp. 351–81.

Georgiev, V. 1947. Ho spēks, un cas de déglutination. *Word* 3: 77–79.

Gołab, Zbigniew. 1967. The traces of vr̥ddhi in Slavic. In *To Honor Roman Jakobson* 1: 760–70. The Hague: Mouton.

Goodenough, Ward H. 1956. Componential analysis and the study of meaning. *Language* 32: 195–216.

Grégoire, H.; Goossens, R.; and Mathieu, M. 1949. Asklèpios, Apollen, Smintheus et Rudra: Études sur le dieu à la taupe et le dieu au rat dans la Grèce et dans l'Inde. Academie Royale de Belgique. Classe des Lettres. *Mémoires* 45: 127–73.

Griffith, R. T. H. 1897. *The hymns of the Rig Veda*. Benares.

Hall, J. R. C., and Merritt, H. D. 1960. *A concise Anglo-Saxon dictionary*. Cambridge: Cambridge Univ. Press.

Hamp, Eric. 1964. Urslavisch čeršja. *Zeitschrift für slavische Philologie*. Vol. 31, no. 2: 298–300.

————. 1966. The position of Albanian. In *Ancient Indo-European dialects*, ed. Henrik Birnbaum and Jaan Puhvel, pp. 97–123. Berkeley and Los Angeles: Univ. of California Press.

————. 1969. Albanian *bredh* and the Indo-European birch. Unpublished.

Hehn, Victor. 1894. *Kulturpflanzen und Haustieren in ihrem Übergang aus Asien nach Griechenland und Italien sowie in das übrige Europa*. Berlin: Gebrüder Bornträger.

Hirt, Herman. 1892. Die Urheimat der indogermanen. *Indogermanische Forschungen* 1: 464–85.

Hoenigswald, Henry. 1950. The principal step in comparative grammar. *Language* 26: 357–64.

————. 1965. Indo-Iranian evidence. In *Evidence for laryngeals*, ed. W. Winter, pp. 93–100. The Hague: Mouton.

————. 1966. Criteria for the subgrouping of languages. In *Ancient Indo-European dialects*, ed. H. Birnbaum and J. Puhvel, p. 1–13. Berkeley and Los Angeles: Univ. of California Press.

Hofmann, J. B. 1950. *Etymologisches Wörterbuch der griechischen Sprache*. Munich.

Holder, Alfred. 1961. *Alt-Celtischer Sprachschatz*. Vols. 1–3. Graz: Akademische Verlagsanstalt.

Homer. 1960. *The Iliad*. 2 vols. Trans. A. T. Murray. Loeb Classical Library. Cambridge: Harvard Univ. Press.

————. 1960. *The Odyssey*. 2 vols. Trans. A. T. Murray. Loeb Classical Library. Cambridge: Harvard Univ. Press.

Hoops, Johannes. 1905. *Waldbäume und Kulturpflanzen im germanischen Altertum*. Strassburg: Karl J. Trübner.

Hubert, Henri. 1932. *Les Celts depuis l'époque de la Tène et la civilization celtique*. Paris: La Renaissance du Livre.

Hübschmann, Henrich. 1897. *Armenische Grammatik: 1. Armenische Etymologie. Leipzig*.

Ivanov, V. V. 1958. K etimologii baltijskogo i slavjanskogo nazvanij boga groma. *Voprosy Slavjanskogo Jazykoznanija* 3: 101–12.

Jakobson, Roman, and Halle, Morris. 1952. *Fundamentals of language*. The Hague: Mouton.

Janert, K. L. 1963–64. Zur Wort- und Kulturgeschichte von Sanskrit sphyá- (Pali phiya). *Zeitschrift für vergleichende Sprachforschung* 79: 89–111.

Jaskiewicz, Walter C. 1952. Mythology: Jan Łasicki's Samogitian gods: A study in Lithuanian. *Studi Baltici* (9 n.s.-1): 65–106. Florence.

Jokl, Norbert. 1923. *Linguistisch-kulturhistorische Untersuchungen aus dem Bereiche des Albanischen*. Berlin and Leipzig: Walter de Gruyter.

————. 1929. Zur Vorgeschichte des Albanesischen und der Albaner. In *Wörter und Sachen*, pp. 63–91. Heidelberg: Carl Winter.

Kluge, Friedrich. 1963. *Etymologisches Wörterbuch der deutschen Sprache* (Mitzka-Schirm revision). Berlin: Walter Gruyter.

Kretschmer, Paul. 1921. Der Götterbeiname Grabovius auf den Tafeln von Iguvium. In *Festschrift Adalbert Bezzenberger*. Göttingen: Vandenhoeck and Ruprecht.

————. 1927. Makedon: álidza. *Glotta*, pp. 305–6. Göttingen: Vandenhoeck and Ruprecht.

Kroeber, Alfred L. 1960. Statistics, Indo-European, and taxonomy. *Language* 36: 1–22.

Kroeber, Alfred L., and Chrétien, C. D. 1937. Quantitative classification of Indo-European languages. *Language* 13: 83–103.

180

Krogmann, Willi. 1955, 1957. Das Buchenargument. *Zeitschrift für vergleichende Sprachforschung* 72: 1–29; 73: 1–25.

Kuiper, F. B. J. 1954. Two Rigvedic loanwords: Sprachgeschichte und Wortbedeutung. In *Festschrift Albert Debrunner*, pp. 241–50. Bern: Franke Verlag.

Kuryłowicz, Jerzy. 1927. "ə indo-européen et ḫ hittite. In *Symbolae grammaticae in honorem Ioannis Rozwadowski* 1: 95–104. Krakow.

———. 1935. *Études indoeuropéennes*. Vol. 1, Krakow.

Lambertz, Max. 1954. *Lehrgang des Albanesischen*. Berlin: Deutscher Verlag der Wissenschaften.

Lane, George S. 1967. The beech argument: A re-evaluation of the linguistic evidence. *Zeitschrift für vergleichende Sprachforschung* 81. no 3/4: 198–212.

Lehmann, Winfred P. 1953. *Proto-Indo-European phonology*. Austin: Univ. of Texas Press.

Lejeune, Michel. 1955. Celtiberica. *Acta Salamanticensa. Filosofía y Letras*. Vol. 7, no. 4. Universidad de Salamanca.

Lewis, Henry, and Pedersen, Holgar. 1961. *A concise comparative Celtic grammar*. Göttingen: Vandenhoeck and Ruprecht.

Liddell and Scott. 1961. *A Greek-English lexicon*. Revised and augmented by H. S. Jones. Oxford: Clarendon Press.

———. 1963. *A Greek-English lexicon* Abridged ed. Oxford: Clarendon Press.

Lidén, E. 1905–6. Baumnamen und Verwandtes. *Indogermanische Forschungen* 18: 485–509.

Lyons, John. 1968. *Introduction to Theoretical linguistics*. Cambridge: Cambridge Univ. Press.

Macdonell, A. A., and Keith, A. B. 1958. *Vedic index of names and subjects*. London: John Murray.

Machek, Vaclav. 1950. Quelques noms slavs de plantes. *Lingua Poznaniensis*, pp. 145–61. Poznañ.

Malkiel, Yakov. 1954. The place of etymology in linguistic research. *Bulletin of Hispanic Studies* 31: 78–90.

Mann, Stuart. 1941. Indo-European semi-vowels in Albanian. *Language* 17: 12–24.

Bibliography

Marchant, J. R. V., and Charles, Joseph F. 1955. *Cassell's Latin dictionary*. London: Cassell.

Mayrhofer, Manfred. 1956. *Kurzgefasstes etymologisches Wörterbuch des Altindischen*. Vols. 1–2. Heidelberg: Carl Winter.

Meillet, Antoine. 1902–5. *Études sur l'étymologie et le vocabulaire du vieux slave*. Paris: Bibliotèque de l'école des hautes études, no. 139.

———. 1923. Les formes nominales en Slave. *Revue des études slaves*, 3: 193–204.

———. 1926. Le vocabulaire slave et le voc. indo-iranien. *Revue des études slaves* 6: 164–74.

———. 1937. *Introduction à l'étude comparative des langues indo-européennes*. 1964 reprinting by the Alabama Linguistic and Philological Series, no. 3. University: Univ. of Alabama Press.

Meyer, A. 1951. Zwei Inselnamen in der Adria. *Zeitschrift für vergleichende Sprachforschung*, pp. 76–106.

Meyer, Gustav. 1891. *Etymologisches Wörterbuch der albanesischen Sprache*. Strassburg: Karl Trubner.

Meyer, Gustav. 1891. Etymologisches: Makedonisch χλινότροχος *Indogermanische Forschungen* 1: 319–29.

Mikkola, J. J. 1894. *Berührungen zwischen den westfinnischen und den slavischen Sprachen*. Vol. 1. *Slavische Lehnwörter in den westfinnischen Sprachen*. Helsinki.

Morgenstierne, George. 1947. Metathesis of liquids in Dardic. *Særtrykk Fra Festskrift til Professor Olaf Bloch*, pp. 145–54. Oslo.

———. 1956. *Indo-Iranian frontier languages*. Vol. 3. *Pashai language*. Oslo.

———. 1954. The Waigili language. *Norsk Tidsskrift for Sprogvidenskap*. 17: 146–324.

Moszyński, K. 1957. *Pierwotny zasiąg jezyka prasłowiańskiego*. Wrocław.

Múgica, Plácido Berrondo. 1965. *Diccionario Castellano-Vasco*. Bilbao.

Nehring, A. 1954. Die Problematik der Indogermanenforschung. *Wiener Beiträge* 4: 211.

Niedermann, Max. 1902. Notes d'étymologie latine. In *Mélanges linguistiques offerts à Antoine Meillet*, pp. 97–111. Paris: Klincksieck.

Osthoff, Hermann. 1901. *Etymologische Parerga.* Leipzig: S. Hirzel.

———. 1905. Zwei Artikel zum Ablaut der a:u-basen. 1. Zur Geschichte des Buchennames. *Beiträge zur Kunde der indogermanischen Sprachen* 29.

Otten, Heinrich. 1958. *Hethitische Totenrituale.* Deutsche Akademie der Wissenschaften zu Berlin. Institut für Orientforschung. Berlin: Akademie Verlag.

Pallottino, M. 1955. *The Etruscans.* Harmondsworth: Penguin.

Pedersen, Holger. 1909. *Vergleichende Grammatik der keltischen Sprachen.* Göttingen: Vandenhoeck and Ruprecht.

Persson, P. 1912. *Beiträge zur indogermanischen Wortforschung.* 2 vols. Uppsala and Leipzig.

Pike, Kenneth L. 1968. *Language in relation to a unified theory of the structure of human behavior.* The Hague: Mouton.

Pokorny, Julius. 1959. *Indogermanisches etymologisches Wörterbuch.* Bern and Munich: Francke Verlag.

Polomé, Edgar G. 1966. The position of Illyrian and Venedic. In *Ancient Indo-European dialects*, ed. Henrik Birnbaum and Jaan Puhvel. pp. 59–77. Berkeley and Los Angeles: Univ. of California Press.

Porzig, Walter. 1954. *Die Gliederung des indogermanischen Sprachgebiets.* Heidelberg: Carl Winter.

Preobrazhensky, A. G. 1951. *Etymological dictionary of the Russian language.* New York: Columbia Univ. Press.

Pritchard, James B., ed. 1955. *Ancient Near Eastern texts.* Princeton: Princeton Univ. Press.

Sapir, Edward. 1923. *Language.* New York: Holt.

———. 1936. Internal linguistic evidence suggestive of the northern origin of the Navaho. *Language* 38: 224–35.

———. 1951. Time perspective in aboriginal American culture: A study in method. In *Selected writings of Edward Sapir*, ed. David G. Mandelbaum, pp. 389–463. Berkeley and Los Angeles: Univ. of California Press.

Bibliography

Schrader, Otto. 1917–29. *Reallexicon der indogermanischen Altertumskunde: Grundzüge einer Kultur- und Völkergeschichte Alteuropas.* Berlin: Walter de Gruyter.

Senn, Alfred. 1966. *Handbuch der lithauischen Sprache.* Vol. 1. *Grammatik.* Heidelberg.

Shaw, R. B. 1876. On the Ghalchah language (Wakhi and Sarikoli). *Journal of the Asiatic Society of Bengal* 45: 139–278.

Solmsen, Felix. 1901. *Untersuchungen zur griechischen Laut- und Verslehre.* Strassburg: Karl J. Trubner.

Solta, G. R. 1960. *Die Stellung des Armenischen im Kreise der indogermanischen Sprachen.* Vienna: Mechitharistenbuchdruckerie.

Specht, Franz. 1943. *Der Ursprung der indogermanischen Deklination.* Göttingen: Vandenhoeck and Ruprecht.

Sreznevsky, I. I. 1958. *Materialy dlja Slovarja Drevnerusskogo Jazyka.* 3 vols. Moscow.

Stern, Gustav. 1931. *Meaning and change of meaning.* Bloomington: Indiana Univ. Press.

Stokes, Whitley. 1895. Hibernica. 8. The glosses on the Bucolics. *Zeitschrift für vergleichende Sprachwissenschaft,* pp. 62–86.

Sturtevant, E. H. 1928. Original *h* in Hittite and the mediopassive in *r. Language* 4: 159–70.

———. 1931. Changes of quantity caused by Indo-Hittite *h. Language* 7: 115–24.

Szemerényi, Oswald. 1952. The development of the Indo-European mediae aspiratae in Latin and Italic. *Archivum Linguisticum.* Vol. 4, Fasc. 1: 27–54.

———. 1960. Etyma latina I. 2. Fraxinus-farnus-alnus-ornus. *Glotta* 3/4: 225–32.

———. 1962. Principles of etymological research in the Indo-European languages. *Innsbrucker Beiträge zur Kulturwissenschaft* 15: 175–212.

Tagliavini, Carlo. 1937. *L'Albanese di Dalmazia.* Firenze: L. S. Olschki.

Thieme, Paul. 1953. Die Heimat der indogermanischen Gemeinsprache. In *Abhandlungen der geistes- und socialwissenschaft-*

lichen Klasse. Akademie der Wissenschaften und Literatur, pp. 535–610. Wiesbaden.

―――. 1964. The comparative method for reconstruction in linguistics. In *Language in culture and society,* ed. D. Hymes, pp. 584–98. New York: Harper and Row.

Turner, R. L. 1965. *Comparative dictionary of the Indo-Aryan languages.* London: Oxford Univ. Press.

Vasmer, Max. 1950–58. *Russisches etymologisches Wörterbuch.* 3 vols. Heidelberg: Carl Winter.

Ventris, Michael, and Chadwick, John. 1959. *Documents in Mycenaean Greek.* Cambridge: Univ. of Cambridge Press.

Vries, Jan de. 1961. *Altnordisches etymologisches Wörterbuch.* Leiden: E. J. Brill.

Wackernagel, Jakob. 1896–1957. *Altindische Grammatik.* (published at wide intervals, sometimes with co-authors) Göttingen: Vanderhoeck and Ruprecht.

Walde, A., and Hofmann, J. B. 1938. *Lateinisches etymologisches Wörterbuch.* 2 vols. Heidelberg: Carl Winter.

Watkins, Calvert. 1966. Italo-Celtic revisited. In *Ancient Indo-European dialects,* ed. H. Birnbaum and J. Puhvel, pp. 29–50. Berkeley and Los Angeles: Univ. of California Press.

Winter, Werner, ed. 1965. *Evidence for laryngeals.* The Hague: Mouton.

Wissmann, W. 1952. Der Name der Buche. *Vorträge und Schriften der Deutschen Akademie der Wissenschaften,* 50. Berlin.

Botanical and Anthropological Works

Butzer, Karl W. 1964. *Environment and archeology.* Chicago: Aldine.

Childe, V. Gordon. 1958. *The Dawn of European civilization.* New York.

Collingwood, G. H. 1947. *Knowing your trees.* The American Forestry Association.

Cook, Arthur B. 1940. *Zeus: A study in ancient religion.* 3 vols. Cambridge.

Bibliography

Firbas, Franz. 1949. *Spät- und nacheiszeitliche Waldgeschichte Mitteleuropas nördlich der Alpen.* Vol. 1. Jena.

Frazer, George. 1911. *The golden bough.* 12 vols. London: Macmillan.

Frenzel, Burkhardt. 1960. Die Vegetations- und Landschaftszonen Nord-Eurasiens während der letzten Eiszeit und während der postglazialen Wärmezeit. In *Abhandlungen der Akademie der Wissenschaften und Literatur. Mathematisch-naturwissenschaftliche Klasse,* no. 13 (1959): 935–1099, and no. 6 (1960): 289–453. Mainz.

———. 1967. Climate change in the Atlantic/Sub-Boreal transition on the Northern Hemisphere: Botanical evidence. In *Proceedings of the Internal Symposium on World Climate from 8,000 to 0 B.C.,* pp. 99–123. Royal Meteorological Society.

Gimbutas, Marija. 1956. *The prehistory of eastern Europe.* Part 1. Cambridge.

———. 1960. From the Neolithic to the Iron Age in the region between the Vistula and the Middle Dnieper rivers: A survey. *International Journal of Slavic Linguistics and Poetics* 3: 1–12.

———. 1963. The Indo-Europeans: Archeological problems. *American Anthropologist* 65: 815–37 (translated and updated as Die Indoeuropaer: Archeologische Probleme, p. 538–71 in *Die Urheimat der Indogermanen.* Darmstadt: Wissenschaftliche Buchgesellschaft).

———. 1963. The Indo-Europeans: Archeological problems. *American Anthropologist* 65: 815–37 (translated and updated as *Die Indoeuropäer*).

———. 1966. The relative chronology of neolithic and chalcolithic cultures in eastern Europe north of the Balkan peninsula and the Black Sea. In *Chronologies in Old World archaeology,* pp. 459–502. Chicago: Univ. of Chicago Press.

———. 1966. Proto-Indo-European culture archeologically reconstructed. Paper presented at the Third International Congress of Indo-Europeanists, 23–25 May 1966.

———. 1967. Ancient Slavic religion: A synopsis. In *To honor Roman Jakobson* 1: 738–60. The Hague: Mouton.

Godwin, F. R. S. 1966. Introductory address. In *Proceedings of the International Symposium on World Climate, 8,000 to 0 B.C.*, pp. 3–14. Royal Meteorological Society.

Harlow, William H. 1957. *Trees of the eastern and central United States and Canada.* New York: Dover.

Hemberg, E. 1918. Bokens *(Fagus silvatica* L.*)* invandering till Skandinavein och dess spridningsbiologi. *Skogvardsforenings Tidskrift* (as cited in Lane, Krogmann).

Holmberg, Uno (= Uno Harva). 1927. *Finno-Ugric, Siberian mythology.* Archeological Institute of America. Boston: Marshall Jones Company.

Komarov, N. L., gen. ed. 1934. *Flora SSSR.* Leningrad: Izdatel stvo Akademii. Nauk.

Kubitzki, K., and Munnich, K. O. 1960. Neue C-14 Datierungen zur nacheiszeitlichen Waldgeschichte Nortwestdeutchlands. *Berichte der deutschen botanischen Gesellschaft* 73: 137–46.

Langer, Susanne K. 1951. *Philosophy in a new key.* New York: The New American Library (Mentor).

Lemmon, Robert S. 1952. *The best loved trees of America.* Garden City: The American Garden Guild and Doubleday and Company.

Lindemann, R. L. 1942. A trophic-dynamic concept of ecology. *Ecology* 23: 399–418.

Lorimer, H. L. 1950. *Homer and the monuments.* London.

Meusel, H. 1943. *Vergleichende Arealkunde.* 2 vols. Berlin.

Nejshtadt, M. J. 1957. *Isotorija lesov i paleografija SSSR v Golotsene.* Moscow.

Sebeok, Thomas, and Ingemann, Frances J. 1956. *Studies in Cheremis: The supernatural.* Viking Fund Publications in Anthropology, vol. 22. New York: Wenner-Gren Foundation for Anthropological Research.

Siebert, Frank. 1967. *Contribution to anthropology: Linguistics I (Algonquian).* Foreword by A. D. DuBlois. National Museum of Canada, bulletin no. 214. Anthropology series 78. Ottawa.

Snodgrass, Anthony. 1964. Early Greek armour and weapons. Edinburgh Univ. Press.

Straka, Herbert. 1960. Spät- und postglaziale Vegetationsgeschichte des Rheinlandes auf Grund pollenanalytischer Untersuchungen. *Berichte der deutschen botanischen Gessellschaft* 73: 307–18.

Szafer, W. 1935. The significance of isopollen lines for the investigation of the geographical distribution of trees in the postglacial period. *Bulletin de l'Academie polonaise des sciences et des lettres. Classe des sciences mathematiques et naturelles.* Serie B: *Sciences Naturelles*, 1.

———. 1954. Stratygrafia plejstozenu w Polsce na podstawie florystycznej (with English summary). *Rosznik polskiego towarzystwa geologisznego.* 22: 1–99. Krakow.

Tansley, A. G. 1935. The use and abuse of vegetational concepts and terms. *Ecology* 16: 284–307.

Thienemann, A. 1918. Lebensgemeinschaft und Lebensraum. *Naturw. Wochenschrift.* N.F. 17: 282–90, 297–303.

Troels-Smith, J. 1960. Ivy, mistletoe and elm. Climate indicators—fodder plants. *Banmarks Geol. Undersoegelse.* Series 4, vol. 4, no. 4.

Vermeule, Emily. 1964. *Greece in the Bronze Age.* Chicago: Univ. of Chicago Press.

Walter, Heinrich. 1954. *Grundlagen der Pflanzenverbreitung. Arealkunde. Einfuhrung in die Phytologie.* Vol. 3, part 2. Stuttgart.

Wasson, R. Gordon. 1968. *Soma: Divine mushroom of immortality.* With a section by W. D. O'Flaherty. Ethnomycological studies no. 1. New York: Harcourt, Brace, and World; The Hague: Mouton.

Waterbolk, H. T. 1968. Food production in prehistoric Europe. *Science* 192: 1093–1102.

Woodbury, Angus M. 1954. *Principles of general ecology.* Toronto: Blakiston.